No Option But Sabotage

PREFACE

It was spring 2024, and I was driving east from Eugene, Oregon, into the Willamette National Forest. The towering green Douglas firs, cedars, and pine trees hugged the road for much of the drive, climbing up the hills, and along the rushing water of the streams, rivers, and creeks that spidered out along the landscape. The view was breathtaking. But there were pockets along the drive where instead of the lush green foliage, I could see charred earth and stands of trees that looked like clumps of burnt match sticks. Further north from the road, these pockets would become huge, demarcated lines, with the verdant green giving way to hillsides of grayish-brown death—areas where wildfires in 2020 and again in 2023 had engulfed parts of western Oregon. The 2020 Oregon wildfires in particular were among the most destructive in the state's history. They killed eleven people, torched 5,000 homes, and covered more than 1.2 million acres, much of it over Labor Day Weekend.[1]

The people and vehicles traveling on the road with me included a mix of hikers, campers, boaters, and large flatbed trucks hauling timber, or wood products. Logging remains a major economic industry in this part of Oregon.[2]

My destination was the Fall Creek Trailhead #1, about 30 miles south and east of Eugene. I was headed there on the suggestion of "Nicole" (not her real name), an environmental movement activist and lawyer who spent much of her time defending other activists and leftist protesters. She said that if I wanted to see "where it all happened" I had to see the old-growth forests of Fall Creek.[3]

CONTENTS

Preface viii
Acknowledgments xi
List of Named Interviewees xiii

1. What Makes a Movement Radical?   1

2. Birth of a Radical Movement and Schisms   22

3. Punk, Animal Rights, and the Movement   43

4. Kaczynski's Shadow and the Rise of the Earth Liberation Front   60

5. Repression and Operation Backfire   86

6. From the Ashes of Backfire to the Pipelines, Forests, and Roads   102

7. From Ecofascists to Raw Milk   135

8. Soup and Disruption   154

9. Rise Again?   166

Methods Appendix   187
Bibliography   197
Notes   208
Index   249

To my wife and two little guys—kind, curious, brave, and always love.

OXFORD
UNIVERSITY PRESS

Oxford University Press is a department of the University of Oxford.
It furthers the University's objective of excellence in research, scholarship,
and education by publishing worldwide. Oxford is a registered trade mark of
Oxford University Press in the UK and in certain other countries.

Published in the United States of America by Oxford University Press
198 Madison Avenue, New York, NY 10016, United States of America.

© Thomas Zeitzoff 2026

All rights reserved. No part of this publication may be reproduced, stored in a retrieval system,
transmitted, used for text and data mining, or used for training artificial intelligence, in any form or
by any means, without the prior permission in writing of Oxford University Press, or as expressly
permitted by law, by license or under terms agreed with the appropriate reprographics rights
organization. Inquiries concerning reproduction outside the scope of the above should be sent
to the Rights Department, Oxford University Press, at the address above.

You must not circulate this work in any other form
and you must impose this same condition on any acquirer.

CIP data is on file at the Library of Congress

ISBN 9780197796849

DOI: 10.1093/oso/9780197796849.001.0001

Printed by Sheridan Books, Inc., United States of America

The manufacturer's authorized representative in the EU for product safety is
Oxford University Press España S.A. of Parque Empresarial San Fernando de Henares,
Avenida de Castilla, 2 – 28830 Madrid (www.oup.es/en or product.safety@oup.com).
OUP España S.A. also acts as importer into Spain of products made by the manufacturer.

No Option But Sabotage

THE RADICAL
ENVIRONMENTAL MOVEMENT
AND THE CLIMATE CRISIS

Thomas Zeitzoff

When I arrived at the Fall Creek Trailhead #1, I could see why it was such a special place. Myriad species of ferns and towering green trees, some more than 200 feet tall and 7 feet wide, sloped down into the rush of the pale green waters. Birds could be heard above the din of the creek. But as I tried to get further along the trail road to enter deeper into the Fall Creek area, I saw cones and a large sign blocking the road. Much of the surrounding area was closed due to the 2023 fires.[4] Fall Creek was not just a breathtakingly beautiful spot to go for a hike, but also the site where environmental activists engaged in one of the longest tree-sits to prevent the cutting of old-growth forest. For more than five years, from spring of 1998 to November of 2003, activists set up a makeshift village with canvas and ropes nearly 200 feet in the air to protest the 90-plus acres being put up for sale by the U.S. Forest Service.[5] And in 1996, two separate federal ranger stations were burned in arson attacks within Willamette National Forest. These attacks were some of the first carried out by the leaderless Earth Liberation Front (ELF).

The old-growth forests and rugged beauty of the Willamette National Forest serves as a microcosm for the trajectory of the broader radical environmental movement. It's been the site of fights between loggers and activists, and the center of several forest defense campaigns involving road blockades, tree-sits, and sabotage by the ELF. And the forest is now facing a growing threat from wildfires supercharged by climate change.[6]

This was my first time in the Pacific Northwest. I had traveled there to meet with current and former environmental activists to answer the two questions that are at the core of this book.

First, what had happened to the radical environmental movement? After 9/11, groups like the ELF and other radical environmentalists were considered the number-one domestic terror threat in the United States.[7] But by the end of the decade, they ceased their activity of arson and property destruction. I wanted to know why.

Second, given the threat from climate change, where was the radical environmental movement going? Would record-setting temperatures, wildfires, and increasing carbon emissions from fossil fuels lead activists to turn once again to more radical tactics?[8]

This trip to the Pacific Northwest was part of my search for answers. In this book, I'll draw on my time there, as well as interviews with other activists and experts, to trace what happened to the radical environmental movement and to explore what the future may hold.

***

There's one point I want to flag going forward. Given the sensitive nature of many of the interviews for this book—including discussion of illegal actions, the fact that many of the people I interviewed had spent time in prison or faced legal threats, and my wish to make respondents feel comfortable—all names have been changed. Some specific locations and dates have also been anonymized. For example, "St. Louis, Missouri" might appear as a "city in the Midwest" and "July 2004" might be described as "the early 2000s."

ACKNOWLEDGMENTS

Writing a book is never easy. Trying to write an accessible but rigorous book about a movement in which activists have carried out sabotage, served time in prison, and are rightfully suspicious of outsiders was challenging. But it was made easier by the many people who supported me along the way.

To all the people—activists, experts, law enforcement officers, and journalists—who shared their stories and perspectives with me, and whose voices make up much of this book, all I can say is thank you. This book wouldn't have been possible without your willingness to spare your time and discuss your opinions and experiences. So again, thank you.

I am incredibly indebted to my academic colleagues and friends who provided support and feedback on various stages of this project. These include seminar participants at the American Political Science Association annual meeting, as well as seminar participants at American University; Brown University; the University of California, Berkeley; the University of Haifa; and the University of Western Ontario.

I am also grateful to Tricia Bacon, Hannah Baron, Bruce Bueno de Mesquita, Sarah Colbourn, Omar Garcia-Ponce, Anna Getmansky, Joshua Gubler, Alison Jacknowitz, Tyler Jost, Joshua Kertzer, Rose McDermott, Leslie Pickering, Cynthia Miller-Idriss, Brendan Nyhan, Tolga Sinmazdemir, Chagai Weiss, Lauren Young, and Joseph Young for their support, helpful comments, and suggestions.

This book was vastly improved and sharpened thanks to the insightful comments and suggestions of Joseph Brown, Shana Gadarian, Jennifer Hadden, Scott Parkin, and Keith Woodhouse, who participated in my book conference in February 2025. They deconstructed the book and helped me rebuild it in a better and more accessible way.

To Eric Lupfer, my literary agent, thank you so much for shaping and guiding the initial rough idea of a pitch that I came to you with. Thank you so much to David McBride, Angela Chnapko, Emily Benitez, Swetha Kodimari, and Betty Pessagno, the anonymous peer reviewers, and the team at Oxford University Press for their sharp eyes and help in shepherding this manuscript along.

Bethany Leap, Divya Ramjee, Alexandria Samson, Diana Wallens, and Grace Gold provided fantastic research assistance, particularly on the dataset of more than 1,300 eco direct actions that helped inform one of the core puzzles of this book—what happened to the radical environmental movement?

To my parents, Maggie and Peter, and my brother, David, thank you so much for your love, for stoking my intellectual curiosity, and for offering feedback on earlier versions of the book.

To my wife, Jocelyn, thank you and I love you. You read early drafts of this book, heard me speak out loud too many of its passages while watching our TV shows, and embraced my newfound love of hiking and wolf shirts. To my two little guys, Donovan and Miller, part of writing this book was wanting to understand what kind of world you are growing up in. I love you both so much.

Finally, to all the activists, environmental and climate scientists, and policymakers fighting to make the world better in the face of the dramatic risks posed by climate change—thank you.

LIST OF NAMED INTERVIEWEES

Aaron – Climate activist and strategist
Adam – Anarcho-primitivist philosopher and activist
Alicia – Climate justice and anti-capitalist organizer
Bernard – Ecological activist and member of Earth First!
Blake – Activist, filmmaker, publicized actions for Earth Liberation Front
Brandon – Anti-repression organizer
Brett – Activist involved with animal rights, anti-globalization, and climate movements
Cameron – Veteran, climate organizer, and activist
Caroline – Climate justice and environmental organizer
Cedric – Earth First! organizer and activist
Chana – Animal rights and environmental activist
Charles – Academic who studies radical movements
Dan – Anti-pipeline activist
Dylan – Academic, activist, and social ecologist
Faith – Climate justice activist
Gary – Animal liberation activist and spokesperson
Gavin – Primal anarchist activist
Grace – Climate activist and organizer
Grant – Movement activist and scholar
Helen – Off-grid homesteader
Isaac – Core member of Earth First!
Jack – Longtime law enforcement officer
Jesse – Activist, publicized actions for Earth Liberation Front

Jim – Conservation activist, Earth First!
Ken – Activist, former editor of *Earth First! Journal*
Kevin – Union organizer and Earth First!
Leila – Youth climate activist
Luann- Longtime environmental activist
Luke – Animal rights activist and former prisoner
Marianne – Ecoactivist and Earth First!
Mark – Core member of Earth First!
Max – Activist and antifascist academic
Molly – Raw milk enthusiast
Nathan – Former direct action activist
Nicole – Movement lawyer and activist
Nick – Far-right researcher
Parker – Forest defender
Reed – Activist and information security specialist
Rick – Longtime law enforcement officer
Richard – Academic, activist, and environmental ethicist
Robert – Animal liberation activist, former prisoner, and historian of the movement
Ross – Animal rights activist and former prisoner
Ryder – Raw milk dairy farmer
Sadie – Direct action and anti-pipeline activist
Sam – Climate justice activist
Seth – Academic and environmental historian
Stacey – Anarchist and environmental activist
Stephen – Animal Liberation Front activist and former prisoner
Sue – Raw milk dairy farmer
Ted – Animal rights and environmental activist
Tim – Direct action organizer in the climate movement
Violet – Anti-pipeline activist and prison supporter

I

What Makes a Movement Radical?

I WAS STANDING OUTSIDE OF a shipping port a short drive from Seattle. It was a cool and sunny afternoon in late spring 2024, and there were stacks upon stacks of logs at the port's loading dock, and a small armada of boats was tucked neatly away in the adjacent harbor. Cameron had picked the port given its history as a place where environmental activists and antiwar activists had clashed with police and industry (as noted in the preface, names of those quoted in the book are pseudonyms). Cameron was in his late thirties; he was wearing a hat and a darkly colored sweatshirt and had some stubble. He also had a ragged but adorable Pomeranian with him. But it was his sweatshirt and not his dog that caught my attention. The sweatshirt said, "Prevent Abortions Get a Vasectomy," and had a picture of a pair of scissors. As we shook hands, I said to Cameron: "nice sweatshirt, very subtle" and he laughed. Cameron began showing me around his hometown, pointing out different places where he had clashed with right-wing activists back in 2020, during the Black Lives Matter protest and in the lead-up to the 2020 presidential election. While we were chatting, an older lady yelled out from a passing SUV, "Awesome sweatshirt, man . . . less abortions, I love it!" Cameron yelled back, "thanks for the love, but I don't think you got the message!" He then said to me that he was going to get a sweatshirt that said, "Abortion Forever"—just so people wouldn't be confused where he stood.

I was introduced to Cameron through a mutual activist friend. Cameron and I chatted and Zoomed a few times, and we even met up in the early spring of 2024 when he was in Washington, D.C.[1] I had plans to travel to the Pacific Northwest that May, and Cameron was just a short drive from Seattle, so we agreed to meet up. It was always interesting talking to him because he had a dark but wicked sense of humor. He was also one of the few people outside of academia who enjoyed reading dense academic books on political violence.

Cameron had a circuitous journey into activism. He had grown up in the Pacific Northwest, or Cascadia, the bioregion designation that he and some other left-leaning activists preferred to call it. As a teenager, he devoured every action and war film he could find, from *Independence Day* to *Saving Private Ryan*. Cameron told me that he wanted to serve his country and have a purpose. Then 9/11 happened, and he volunteered to join the U.S. Army. He joined a special operations unit, and he later deployed to Afghanistan. But he ultimately became jaded with the war and with U.S. foreign policy in general. As Cameron said, "I became very disillusioned with what I thought we were supposed to do versus what we were actually doing" in Afghanistan. He decided he wanted out of the military, but he knew that he could be recalled and deployed. This was 2007 and the height of the Iraqi insurgency against U.S. forces. Cameron was able to fight off his call-up to the army, and he became an antiwar activist. Through his coursework in college and his growing antiwar activism, he also grew to see the connections between his antiwar stance and looming social and environmental catastrophe. Cameron then started participating in environmental direct actions like blocking oil ships and tankers into ports.

Cameron and I continued to a dimly lit dive bar. It was the kind of place that plays Johnny Cash and the Stones, and where it's unclear if it's 3:00 p.m. or 3:00 a.m. We'd been chatting for a bit when I mentioned his sweatshirt and the interaction with the lady in the car. He told me he had been thinking for a long time about what it meant to have kids. And why people, especially in the movement, would have them.

He pointedly looked at me and said, "Look I'm not critiquing, but I am curious. You have two young kids." I said, "Yeah, I have two young kids, and it's a ton of work, money, worry, getting sick, my back feeling like someone took a sledgehammer to it sometimes. But I love it, man."

Cameron responded, "Yeah, I wanted kids so bad, but then I thought about it. I have a lot of friends with kids. I like kids. I was just at a wedding for two people active in the movement last week, and it was amazing. More than 100 people dancing, even a banner drop, like we were doing some kind of radical direct action."

Cameron laughed and then continued: "And kids, tons of kids. But everyone I know who has kids, they drop out of the movement. They stop being active. They have excuses: 'my kid is sick, they have a school thing, etc.' and it makes sense. But for me, from a selfish perspective I can't do that. Yeah, I wanted kids, but I'm at peace with my choice and that's also why I got a vasectomy. When they [right-wingers] are shooting protesters, and trans people are in camps, who do you think all my friends with kids are going to come to?" He let the last question hang in the air for a second.

To Cameron, having kids was a luxury that he felt he couldn't afford. The stakes were too high. The climate crisis was accelerating, Republican states were passing more laws targeting activists, and the looming specter of a potential second Trump term in 2024 hung like a shadow (more on this later). The setting for our conversation mattered, too. The Pacific Northwest—with its history of logging, radical environmental activism, and punk ethos—had been a crucial incubator for activists in the 1990s and early 2000s. It still resonated with current activists like Cameron.

Cameron wasn't the first person to ask me about my decision to have kids. I had a Zoom call scheduled with Chana, a self-described troublemaker and animal rights activist in February 2022.[2] I remember saying to my wife that I knew this was going to be an interesting interview just from Chana's email. Right below her email signature she had phrases such as "Go Vegan," "Protect Water, Earth, and Animals," and "Eating Animals Causes Pandemics." She was Zooming in from her farm on a tropical island. Chana had a wicked sense of humor and was equal parts Zen Buddhist and quick-witted New Yorker. She grew up in New York

City in the 1980s and joined the group People for the Ethical Treatment of Animals (PETA) as a high schooler. Throughout the 1980s, while in college, she started getting more into animal rights activism.

Chana had also come under the spell of Judi Bari, a charismatic environmental leader in the 1980s and 1990s whose goal was to bring labor and environmental activists together. Chana participated in the Headwaters Campaign, a multi-year protest that began in the 1980s to protect old-growth redwood forest in northern California.[3] It included the 1990 Redwood Summer, a coordinated campaign of protests, civil disobedience, and sabotage under the auspices of the most influential radical environmental group at the time, Earth First!, which was led by Judi Bari. But a mysterious car bomb in March of 1990 critically injured Bari and brought additional law enforcement and media attention to the campaign.[4] I'll talk more about Bari in the next chapter.

Chana was also part of a group of activists who engaged in sabotage, tree-sits, and lockdowns—chaining themselves to equipment and to Pacific Lumber (the major logging company) office buildings to halt logging. Chana told me about how meaningful participating in the lockdown at Pacific Lumber was to her, using words like "sacred" to describe how she felt. But she also told me how scary it was to be confronted by the police and the chainsaws of lumberjacks. And she spoke of how awful and traumatic being pepper sprayed was—saying it "fucks with your psyche."

Yet it wasn't just Chana's stories of life as an activist that caught my attention. Rather, it was an offhand comment she made. I had yawned a bit toward the end of our call, and I profusely apologized to her. I said I wasn't bored by our conversation at all. I just had been up late with my three-and-a-half-year-old son, who woke up in the middle of the night coughing. Chana laughed, and said, "oh, so you're a breeder." I thought I misheard her, and she assured me that, no, she was playfully mocking my wife's and my decision to have kids. She said it was just a silly thing she and other activists called those who chose to procreate. But then she told me that that she had intentionally chosen not to have kids. She said, "I believe humans are the most invasive species on the planet. We are the only species that pollute their own water, soil, and food. Mother Nature tends to step in when things like that happen."

In a not-so-subtle way, she was implying that climate change and the COVID-19 pandemic (as her email signature pointed to) were natural consequences of our disregard for the planet as a species.

Chana's anti-procreation views reflected her belief that humans had abused the natural world through environmental degradation and overpopulation. This was an outlook she shared with many of her activist friends from this era. She saw population concerns as central to the radical environmental movement's core beliefs.

This focus on population, and what it meant for the planet, was not a bizarre sideshow to the radical environmental movement. Rather, as we will see, concerns about overpopulation, and later, climate change, brought urgency to the movement, driving activists to embrace tree-sits, civil disobedience, and even sabotage and property destruction. For most activists, the goal was not destruction for its own sake. Instead, these actions emerged from a deep commitment to conserving nature and wilderness, stopping pollution, and later cutting carbon to prevent environmental collapse. The ethos was one of self-defense. It is an ethos that guides activists as they ask themselves today: what should we do? And what are we willing to risk to save the planet from climate change?

***

I got interested in the radical environmental movement following a question from an undergrad student in my class in the spring of 2019: "Professor, why don't we see more violence associated with the environmental movement [in the U.S.]?" It had been nearly fifty years since the first Earth Day celebration in 1970 and the birth of the modern environmental movement. And nearly forty years since the group Earth First! emerged in 1980 promoting publicity stunts, blockades, and sabotage tactics to defend the environment. Inspired by Earth First!, more radical actors like the ELF carried out a series of arson and bombing attacks in the 1990s and early 2000s. The aggressive evolution, and the inability of the authorities to find many of the perpetrators, led the FBI to label "ecoterrorism" the major domestic terror threat after 9/11. Yet by the end of the decade, the radical environmental movement had largely gone silent. This silence was puzzling because it coincided with increasing alarm about climate change.

Every semester in my class we talk about Ted Kaczynski, the Unabomber. And every semester I notice more and more students nodding along in agreement with his antitechnology and pro-wilderness manifesto—at least the parts that didn't involve killing people and bringing down industrial civilization. Like their peers, many of my students are greatly worried about climate change, and several have participated in climate protests and marches.[5] But climate marches, or even the random defacing of a popular painting,[6] are a far cry from Kaczynski, the ELF, or the sabotage of Earth First! So, where are the radical actions to match the worry of climate activists and environmentalists? I didn't have a satisfactory answer to my student's question, and it gnawed at me, so I posted it to Twitter.

In response to my tweet, one of my colleagues messaged me and asked if I was familiar with the "Green Scare." I wasn't, so I started doing some digging around. I watched Marshall Curry's 2011 documentary *If a Tree Falls: The Story of the Earth Liberation Front* (ELF) about the rise and fall of the ELF, the leaderless radical environmental group that engaged in arson and sabotage, largely in the Pacific Northwest, from the mid 1990s to 2010. I read Will Potter's *Green Is the New Red: An Insider's Account of a Social Movement Under Siege* about the government's investigation and repression of the radical environmental movement.[7] Yet I came away from this initial research with more questions than answers. It struck me as bizarre that in the post-9/11 period the FBI had labeled ecoterrorism the number one domestic terror threat. How did property destruction and vandalism that didn't kill anyone qualify as terrorism in the first place? Why were groups like the ELF, with their sabotage tactics, considered even more dangerous than white supremacist groups or right-wing militias that had actually killed people?

But what really nagged at me was why, by 2009, the radical environmental movement largely ceased using its most radical tactics. The shift away from more radical tactics seemed at odds with the growing urgency of climate change. In 2017 David Wallace-Wells published an article called "The Uninhabitable Earth" in *New York Magazine*.[8] The article painted a worst-case scenario of drastic warming, famine, wildfires, war, ocean acidification, economic and social and mass extinctions. It was the most-read piece in the magazine's history. By 2024, these worst-case scenarios that Wallace-Wells described seemed unlikely. But in the words of a 2023 report by the United Nations Intergovernmental Panel on Climate Change, "potential catastrophe" awaited the planet if we did not limit warming to less than 1.5 degrees Celsius from pre–Industrial Revolution levels.[9] Yet, by June 2024 scientists declared that we had breached the mark, recording twelve straight months of average temperatures above 1.5 degree Celsius.[10] Climate scientist and critic of the idea of "climate doom"[11] Michael Mann argued in his 2023 book *Our Fragile Moment* that the world has the power to avoid climate catastrophe, but only if we act quickly and smartly.[12]

The effects of climate change are not just an idea behind academic debates between climate scientists, but real and tangible. For instance, in 2020, one of the worst wildfire seasons on record torched more than 4 million acres, blotting out the sun and making the air unbreathable throughout much of northern California.[13] Closer to home, I vividly remember July 2023 in suburban Washington, D.C. with my wife and two small children. The sky was a hazy gray and the sun a small, distant orange sphere. It looked apocalyptic, and I remember our nearly five-year-old asking, "Daddy why is the sun so dark?" But it wasn't just the haze and the gloom; we had some of the worst air quality in the world,[14] and we were supposed to limit our time outside. This was all caused by the unprecedented drought and heat in Canada that led to one of the worst wildfire seasons in Canadian history, with its smoke choking much of the eastern United States.[15]

My experience wasn't isolated. In 2023, nine in ten Americans said they had been affected by extreme weather such as heat waves, hurricanes, tornadoes, and major flooding.[16] And in 2023 a Pew Research Center study found that a majority of Americans (54%) viewed climate change as a major threat, up 10 percentage points since 2010.[17] Shouldn't the increased anxiety about climate change translate into greater political action?[18] But this increase masks large partisan divisions. This same 2023 Pew study showed that 78% of Democrats called it a serious issue compared to only 23% of Republicans.

Given the seriousness of the climate threat, the relative quiet of the radical environmental movement in the United States is puzzling. It's even more puzzling given that climate activists in other wealthy countries have raised the intensity of their tactics—deflating more than a thousand SUV tires (U.K.),[19] blocking oil terminals (U.K.) and coal mines (Germany), disrupting airports (Germany),[20] and even fighting street battles with police (France).[21] There's also a long history of Indigenous land defenders in the Global South who have faced violent threats from developers and agribusiness, particularly in Colombia and Brazil.[22]

Origins: Earth First!, Population, and Tensions

Concerns about overpopulation, pollution, and preservation of the wilderness drove the rise of the U.S. environmental movement in the late 1960s and early 1970s. While mainstream activists pressured local, state, and federal governments into creating new environmental regulations and protections,[23] a more radical current simmered beneath the surface.

We began this chapter talking about population and procreation for a reason. There's an ugly history to this concern of population and overpopulation, and the history of the American environmental movement is filled with racist, far-right ideas and people. "These immigrants, Jews, and foreigners who adopt the language of the native American [White man], they wear his clothes, they steal his name and they are beginning to take his women … but they seldom adopt his religion or understand his ideals and while he [the White man] is being elbowed out of his own home the American looks calmly abroad and urges on others the suicidal ethics which are exterminating his own race." This idea—that Whites are committing racial suicide and are ceding Western countries to foreigners, Jews, and non-Whites—would be at home at a number of present-day rallies for far-right, White nationalist parties.

But these aren't the words of the modern, racist, far-right. Rather, this passage comes from Madison Grant's *The Passing of the Great Race*.[24] Grant's book influenced much of the racial and Nordic supremacy in Adolf Hitler's *Mein Kampf*.[25] Hitler thought so highly of the book that he even wrote Grant a gushing letter to tell him that "the book (*The Passing of The Great Race*) is my bible."[26] Grant's racist manifesto is still influential. It's an inspiration for the modern-day Great Replacement conspiracy theory, a racist idea that elites, and Jewish elites in particular, are trying to increase the non-White population in Western countries to dilute the power of the White race. We will talk more about this in Chapter 7, in which we discuss ecofascism.

Grant wasn't just a racist polemicist dressed up as an academic. He was also an important environmentalist. He was one of the founders of the American conservation movement, he helped save the American bison and the California redwoods, and he pushed for the creation of several national parks.[27] In the early 1900s, Grant rubbed elbows with Teddy Roosevelt and other prominent American conservationists; race science was a core belief that united these early conservationists.[28] For Grant and other early American conservationists, maintaining America's pristine wilderness went hand in hand with maintaining the purity of America's racial stock, particularly that of Northern Europeans.[29]

Decades later, Paul Ehrlich's 1968 bestseller *The Population Bomb* brought a new twist on the population debate.[30] Ehrlich framed overpopulation as an environmental threat. He talked about walking through the "stinking hot night in Delhi" and being frightened by the screams, people defecating, urinating, and the "mob" atmosphere. He even compared it to hell. Ehrlich's thesis is straightforward. He argued it's a mathematical fact that there are too many people in the world, and there is not enough food and resources. While not as explicitly racist as Grant and earlier conservationists, critics claim that Ehrlich's book engaged in racist fearmongering.[31] For example, the book focused on overpopulation in places like Delhi, India, and the Global South, where non-White people reside, rather than say New York City (~8 million), which had more than twice the population of Delhi (~3 million), but a majority White population in 1970.

One of the major ideas that came from Ehrlich's book was the "population question." It's such an innocuous-sounding question. But it divided the radical environmental movement from the beginning (more on this in Chapter 2). The population question is also used by present-day far-right White nationalists to justify attacks against on non-Whites under the banner of ecofascism (more on this in Chapter 7). At a fundamental level, the population question refers to whether environmentalists should advocate for reducing the Earth's population. Ehrlich thought they should, and he'd go on to be a prominent advocate of the zero population growth (ZPG) movement. To Ehrlich and his supporters, it was a simple equation: more people consuming more resources, killing more species, and burning more fossil fuels means more environmental degradation. Zero Population Growthers like Ehrlich believed countries should use voluntary birth control methods and limit immigration to achieve a demographic equilibrium in which the birth rate of a country is equal to the death rate.

Ehrlich's book was incredibly influential, particularly among conservationists. It came in the wake of Rachel Carson's 1962 *Silent Spring*, which detailed the horrors of chemicals and pollution, particularly pesticides.[32] Two other major events also symbolized the growing threat to the environment: the Santa Barbara Oil Spill of 1969, which dumped 3 million gallons of oil into the coastal waters, killing scores of wildlife, and a fire in the heavily polluted Cuyahoga River in Cleveland, also in 1969.[33] An emerging environmental consciousness that population and pollution were killing the Earth would lead to the first Earth Day in 1970.

In the 1970s, new activists and ideas started to influence the environmental movement. The "New Left" that emerged from the 1960s civil rights struggles and anti-Vietnam protests was initially skeptical of ecological causes.[34] They viewed reducing poverty, ending racism, and subduing imperialism as the main goals, and they saw environmental degradation as a side effect of these core issues, or, even worse, a distraction. But this mindset began to change around the time of the first Earth Day. Activists like Keith Lampe and those affiliated with new groups like Ecology Action, founded in the Bay Area, sought to connect environmental causes with the main social issues of the day: imperialism, racism, and sexism.[35] These new activists brought the dramatic flair of street pranks and disruption of other New Left groups like those led by Abbie Hoffman and the Yippies to the environmental movement.[36]

Nature lovers, outdoors survivalists, and hunters had long had a tense relationship with development, especially in the American West.[37] Frustrated by government inaction, some took matters into their own hands. They sabotaged bulldozers, pulled up survey stakes, and occasionally used arson to defend what they saw as the last bastion of the pristine wilderness in the United States.

From this wellspring of discontent, a group of fed-up environmental activists formed Earth First!. With a motto of "No compromise in defense of Mother Earth!," Earth First! combined a deep reverence for nature and a willingness to engage in civil disobedience and sabotage to protect wilderness.[38] The radical environmental movement had arrived.

Defining the Radical Environmental Movement

What do we mean by "the radical environmental movement"? Radical movements are born out of a frustration with compromise and inaction, and a belief that without increased pressure nothing will change. The radical environmental movement is no different. It emerged from increasing frustration among activists in the 1970s with mainstream environmental groups like the Sierra Club, which they felt were too accommodating and not doing enough to preserve wilderness. This frustration culminated in the third mention of EF!'s 1980 founding so far.

As we will see, Earth First!'s stated goal of ecodefense reflected three features that continue to shape the radical environmental movement today.

First, the radical environmental movement is made up of individuals united by a belief that environmental harm demands resistance. For early activists associated with Earth First!, this belief was rooted in ecocentrism. This quasi-religious conviction that nature was sacred and was worth protecting for its own sake was the guiding philosophy.[39] Later activists, including those aligned with green anarchism and the more recent climate justice movement, viewed environmental destruction as one symptom of broader social ills caused by political oppression, capitalism, or racism.[40] But no matter their ideological differences, all radical environmentalists feel that threats to the environment demand direct action.

Second, the radical environmental movement isn't defined by membership lists or formal organizations. Groups like Earth First! reject traditional hierarchies and instead favor decentralized networks. These networks thrived in activist hubs like Eugene, Oregon, and in subcultures like punk rock, which served as pipelines to radical environmentalism and helped nurture activists.

The third defining feature of the radical environmental movement is its tactical repertoire. Radical activists embrace direct action, including civil disobedience and, notably, sabotage, to defend against threats to the environment. This direct action model was shaped by radical environmental activists' explicit rejection of mainstream nongovernmental organization (NGO) ideas of incremental change.[41] This wasn't just a difference in tactics. Rather, the schism between the radical and mainstream environmental movements reflected a fundamentally different worldview. For early radicals, the threat to wilderness was existential. The idea of working through the policy process, what some derisively called "gradualism," was at best a failed strategy and at worst capitulation.[42] This commitment to confrontation continues to this day to set radicals apart from more mainstream activists.

While ideologies have evolved, targets have shifted, and tactics have changed, three core ideas continue to define the radical environmental movement: (1) a belief that environmental destruction is a profound moral harm, (2) a commitment to leaderless organizing and subcultures that sustain activist communities, and (3) a willingness to use sabotage in defense of the environment.

***

Approaching the Movement

I've always been fascinated with why people participate in political violence. But up until this project, most of my research had taken me to places outside the United States. For my dissertation, I studied responses to terrorism and ethnic riots in Israel and Palestine. I later explored the effects of exposure to wartime violence on political attitudes of people in Georgia, Turkey, and Ukraine. In Mexico I tried to understand why exposure to narco-violence leads some people to support punitive punishment and lynching.

But researching the radical environmental movement was different. And in many ways, it's been harder. While there are above-ground ecoactivists who engage in civil disobedience and block traffic or chain themselves to oil platforms, others choose to engage in clandestine action. People in the movement are incredibly suspicious of outsiders and those who want to talk to people in their ranks. As we'll see, this suspicion is a strategic response to government infiltration and repression. A further complication is that many of the actions carried out by individuals in the movement involved sabotage that never made it into mainstream newspapers. And if that weren't enough, many activists in the movement eschew hierarchy, favor leaderless tactics, and don't always agree on the motives for a given act of sabotage.

Because the radical environmental movement is loosely organized and sometimes uses clandestine tactics, I cast a wide net to try to truly understand it.[43] I started by researching how the pace of actions and tactics had changed across time. Even defining what constitutes a radical environmental action is tricky. Yet the thread that connects the backwoods sabotage of the early Earth Firsters! to the anarchists of the Pacific Northwest, and to the pipeline protests of Appalachia is the idea of "direct action."

Direct action is something different from peaceful protests and holding signs. Tim, a direct action organizer in the climate movement, told me, "When I train activists, I talk about direct action as a philosophy; it's about taking matters into our own hands. It's a philosophy that can cover anything from monkeywrenching to civil disobedience."[44] And it's this willingness to put your body and your safety on the line that separates ordinary activism from radical activism. So direct action encompasses everything from disruptive civil disobedience (e.g., tree-sits, blockades, or locking oneself to a gate or piece of machinery), to vandalism, animal releases, or even more violent actions like arsons and bombings. It's also a contentious strategy designed to disrupt, and it's one that falls outside of conventional political actions like voting or lobbying.[45]

Getting information about these direct actions was not straightforward. There have been previous efforts focused on cataloguing violent or sabotage attacks by environmental and animal rights groups—so-called ecoterrorist attacks.[46] But no one had put together a complete list of civil disobedience tactics like tree-sits and chaining oneself to an object or equipment to prevent its use ("lockdowns") that were crucial to the movement. A further complication was that many of the illegal actions carried out by activists were done clandestinely. I began working with my research assistants to track down news articles from local newspapers, communiques from radical environmental websites, and old pdfs of zines and journals, and I even hand-compiled lists from activists I interviewed. For example, Robert, an animal liberation activist who had spent several years in prison, had compiled a 130-page list of claimed actions carried out by the Animal Liberation Front (ALF) over forty years of actions.[47] He generously emailed me a pdf copy of the list of ALF actions and told me, "I hope you do something worthwhile with it."

A core part of my research was interviewing activists in the movement. Many activists I wanted to speak with had carried out illegal actions. Some had faced criminal charges, several spent time in prison, and a few were under active investigation. Many were active or got involved just after a period of intense investigation and repression by federal, state, and local law enforcement in the early 2000s, the period known as the Green Scare. As a result, many activists have adopted a norm of security culture: (1) don't talk about sabotage actions that have happened, especially not to anybody who wasn't directly involved, (2) communicate on encrypted platforms or applications (like Signal), and (3) be suspicious and skeptical of outsiders wanting to talk to you. This meant it was initially tricky to find activists willing to open up about the movement. I started by focusing on people who I knew were more public-facing activists—spokespeople, those with public personas, or those who had given interviews on their past in the movement. I also targeted people I labeled as "academic-activists" who had participated in actions, but also done research on the radical environmental movement. These two groups were crucial as they vouched for me and connected me with activists who were maybe hesitant to talk at first.

I ended up interviewing more than 110 activists, researchers, academic experts, journalists, and law enforcement personnel who were familiar with the past and current iterations of the radical environmental movement. I also took steps to minimize the risks to those I interviewed.[48] The majority of interviews were done with activists (65%). As noted earlier, all names of the interviewees in this book are pseudonyms. I've also generalized dates (e.g., citing fall instead of October, early 1990s instead of 1991) and locations (e.g., city near Seattle vs. Tacoma). I avoided asking activists direct questions about their actions. Rather, I tried to understand their thoughts about different strategies, such as mass civil disobedience versus clandestine actions, or how repression has changed the way they engage in activism.

WHAT MAKES A MOVEMENT RADICAL   15

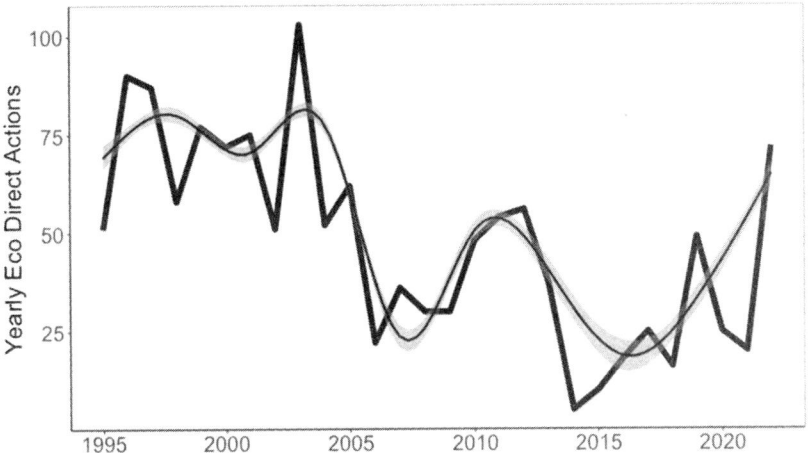

FIGURE 1.1 Yearly counts of eco direct actions (1995–2022). The shaded curve shows a smoothed line that highlights the overall trend in the data.

In every interview, I asked two questions: (1) why did the radical environmental movement collapse in the early 2000s, and (2) what does the future of radical actions look like? For activists, I also asked about their pathway into environmental activism. As we will see later in this book, the era in which each of the activists became involved—whether they started off as disheartened conservationists, animal rights activists, vegan punk rockers, anarchists, or Black Lives Matter activists—provides important clues that will help us understand the past, present, and future of the movement. These pathways and subcultures bring their own set of rules, moral codes, and, crucially, attitudes toward tactics.

I documented over 1,331 direct actions in the United States between 1995 and 2022. This timeframe starts with the final Unabomber attack in 1995 and the emergence of the Earth Liberation Front, and it extends through the rise of the youth climate justice movement in the early 2010s. Figure 1.1 shows the overall trend in direct actions during this period. Direct actions increased in the late 1990s, peaking in 2003 with over 100 incidents. After that, activity dropped sharply starting in 2004, reaching its lowest point in 2014 with just two recorded events. This decline closely aligns with the onset of what activists refer to as the

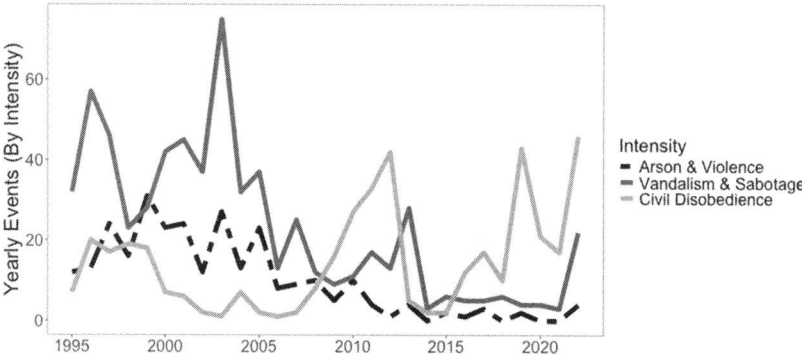

FIGURE 1.2 Yearly counts of eco direct actions (1995–2022). Data disaggregated by tactic intensity.

"Green Scare," a period marked by intensified government repression targeting radical environmental activists.[49]

However, the data also reveal a notable increase in direct actions starting around 2015, a trend that hasn't been fully captured in previous studies. Figure 1.2 breaks down these direct actions into three categories:

1. Civil disobedience—including lockdowns, tree-sits, and blockades.
2. Vandalism and sabotage—including property destruction, graffiti, and animal releases.
3. Violence and arson—including bombings, shootings, and arson.

As Figure 1.2 shows, violence, arson, and sabotage peaked in 2003 before dropping dramatically and remaining relatively low from 2010 onward. In contrast, the increase in direct actions since 2013 has been driven largely by a rise in civil disobedience, with some recent growth in vandalism and sabotage as well. This uptick in civil disobedience is significant, especially as we consider the potential future trajectory of the movement.

The data also reveal important patterns within the movement. Throughout the late 1990s and early 2000s, activists increasingly turned to sabotage and arson as part of their repertoire. But the number of these more radical actions eventually declined. Civil disobedience also became less common, before reemerging in the early 2010s. What the data do not tell us, however, are the answers to our critical questions: Why did the movement embrace radical tactics in the late 1990s and early 2000s? Why did it collapse in the mid-2000s? And perhaps most important, given the growing threat of climate change, are we on the brink of a resurgence in more radical tactics?

Three Eras

This book focuses on the U.S. radical environmental movement from 1980 through 2025. While activists throughout this period share some common traits, such as a belief in the value of nature, a preference for nonhierarchical organizing, and a willingness to engage in civil disobedience and property destruction, there are key differences in ideology, tactics, and targets. For this reason, it's helpful to divide the movement into three rough eras.

The Earth First! Era (1980–1995). The first era is the Earth First! era, lasting from 1980 to 1995. This period was dominated by Earth First!, a group founded on the principles of ecocentrism—the belief that nature has intrinsic value beyond human interests and was worth protecting. Some early Earth First!ers even rejected industrial civilization itself. As Earth First! grew, internal divisions emerged. Deep ecologists, who believed wilderness protection should remain the group's sole focus, clashed with social ecologists and anarchists, who saw environmental problems as inseparable from social issues. Civil disobedience: tree-sits, forest blockades, and spiking trees with metal spikes to prevent logging (though this practice was later abandoned) were the tactics of this era. Sabotage, also known within the movement as monkeywrenching, was also common.[50]

The Earth Liberation Front Era (1995–2008). The second era, lasting from 1995 to 2008, was dominated by the ELF's actions. Emerging from the anarchist wing of Earth First!, the ELF embraced green anarchism and the concept of total liberation—the idea that environmental, human, and animal oppression are fundamentally linked. The ELF was known for its clandestine structure. Activists operated in autonomous cells and carried out acts of economic sabotage, vandalism, and property destruction through arson. The ELF's use of arson represented marked escalation from Earth First!'s small-scale sabotage.[51]

The Climate Justice Era (2008–Present). The third and current era, the Climate Justice Era, began in 2008. Groups like Mountain Justice, the Valve Turners, Extinction Rebellion, and Just Stop Oil have shaped this period. Unlike earlier groups, Climate Justice activists explicitly connect the climate crisis to capitalism, racism, Indigenous land struggles, and inequality, framing environmental protection as part of a broader fight for social justice. For many activists in this period, social concerns are as important as the environmental ones. This era's tactics are defined by mass mobilization. Large-scale protests, road and pipeline blockades, protest theater, and strategic disruption have become common. While sabotage continues to occur, civil disobedience is the dominant tactic.[52]

The Questions

Two key questions first drew me to the radical environmental movement, and they run throughout the book.

First, what happened to the radical environmental movement during the ELF era (1995–2008)? Why did activists turn toward sabotage and property destruction, actions that led the FBI to declare the movement the number-one domestic terror threat after 9/11? And by the end of the decade, 2010, why had this once prominent movement seemingly gone silent? What happened?

Second, given the escalating threat from climate change, why haven't we seen a resurgence of sabotage and property destruction to match the urgency of the moment? What's behind the calculus of present-day activists? Is sabotage considered ineffective? Are state repression and surveillance too powerful? Or is a resurgence coming?

These questions are not just central to understanding the radical environmental movement. They are also at the heart of my own field of study, political violence.

Why do people and social movements challenge the status quo? When do grievances become powerful enough to mobilize people to a cause?[53] How do social networks and subcultures nurture these grievances and shape emerging movements?[54] Political opportunity also matters. When does a decline in repression, division among elites, or shifts in public opinion create fertile ground for a movement to grow?[55]

The question of repression is crucial. How do governments respond to radical movements with surveillance, informants, and prosecutions? Why does repression sometimes destroy a movement, while at other times, it backfires, and it makes the movement even stronger?[56]

Finally, how should movements organize, and which tactics should they choose? Should activists seek to build a broad-based movement? Or is a small cadre, a vanguard, more effective at disruption and inflicting costs upon targets? Relatedly, are radical tactics like property destruction and violence always counterproductive? Or can they push the public toward greater support for movement demands?[57]

Yet one more question sits at the heart of this book and the radical environmental movement itself: how far should activists go to protect the planet? Activists have wrestled with this question for decades. This book traces how radical environmentalism surged, collapsed, and may rise again in an era of climate crisis and renewed repression. It shows how subcultures, state crackdowns, and shifting activist networks shaped the movement, and how those same forces may shape activists going forward.

Throughout the book, we will hear from both activists and experts. Their stories and reflections offer insight into the movement's past, present, and future. From founding members of the original Earth First! to green anarchists active in the Pacific Northwest, to current climate justice activists, these voices show a movement that is still wrestling with the title of this book: Is there no option but sabotage?

***

The argument in this book rests on three core ideas.

First, subcultures and recruitment networks are crucial. Earth First! emerged from a conservation ethos centered on protecting nature for nature's sake. Early Earth First!ers revered wild spaces and embraced civil disobedience and sabotage to defend them. But as the movement evolved through the 1980s and 1990s, new activists drawn from punk, anarchist, and animal rights subcultures reshaped its ideology.

These new activists challenged Earth First!'s ecocentric focus. They argued that environmental destruction was part of a broader system of oppression linked to capitalism, racism, and inequality.

Out of this anarchist- and punk-infused scene emerged the ELF, a clandestine network of autonomous cells. Unlike the older Earth First!ers, the ELF activists escalated tactics with property destruction and arson.

Second, state repression drastically reshaped the movement. As ELF actions escalated, the government responded aggressively. They branded the ELF activists as "ecoterrorists" and launched an intense crackdown after 9/11 that sympathetic activists call the Green Scare. The government's use of informants, grand jury subpoenas, and stiff prison sentences devastated the movement. Key ELF members were arrested, while others—even those uninvolved in the ELF arsons—faced intimidation and surveillance. This wave of repression crushed the Pacific Northwest's radical environmental scene and signaled to future activists that sabotage would carry severe costs.

Following the repression of the ELF and other activists in the mid-2000s, the Climate Justice Era emerged—and this brings us to the present day. The Climate Justice Era has been characterized by fights to limit carbon and by pipeline struggles rooted in Indigenous solidarity. The activists are also different. Fewer activists come from punk rock or animal rights, and more come from youth-focused climate movements. Activists in this era see climate change as an interlinked problem that needs to be addressed, like racism, Indigenous rights, and inequality. Concerns over climate change are fused with ideas of antiracism and anticapitalism. As a result of the different pathways into activism and past repression, there's less clandestine sabotage and more mass protest and disruptive actions.

Third, the effects of climate change are driving increased urgency. The year 2024 was the hottest year on record, breaking the record set in 2023. Meanwhile, the reelection of Donald Trump in 2024 threatened to reverse decades of environmental progress. The second Trump administration has promised to dismantle key environmental protections, such as the Clean Air Act and the Clean Water Act, and to open up logging in old-growth forests.[58] At the same time, new laws have criminalized or increased penalties for civil disobedience, a core tactic of the climate justice activists.[59] The state's surveillance capabilities have also expanded. Tools like cell phone tracking, facial recognition, and AI-powered search have given authorities unprecedented power to track and target activists.[60]

As climate threats intensify and traditional protest tactics face mounting repression, activists are being forced to decide what risks they're willing to take. The title of this book, *No Option But Sabotage*, is not a statement; it's an open question and one that activists themselves are debating and considering.

This book follows the radical environmental movement's evolution across three distinct eras: the Earth First! Era (1980–1995), the ELF Era (1995–2008), and the current Climate Justice Era (2008–present).

In Chapter 2 we'll discuss the rise of Earth First! and the internal divisions that emerged as the movement struggled to reconcile competing ideological visions over whether activists should focus solely on wilderness. In Chapter 3, we'll explore the important but often overlooked influence of animal liberation activists and punk music in shaping the radical environmental movement.

Chapter 4 explores how the Unabomber's ideas echoed themes that influenced the ELF's emergence in the Pacific Northwest and its use of property destruction and arson. In Chapter 5 we'll detail the period known as the Green Scare and examine the effects of the government's aggressive post-9/11 crackdown on radical environmentalists.

In Chapter 6 we will explore the rise of the climate justice movement, which emerged in the aftermath of the ELF's decline. We'll shift our focus in Chapter 7 to discuss ecofascism and other right-wing environmental currents, like the raw milk movement. We'll show how these movements co-opt traditional environmental concerns about population and pollution through a right-wing lens.

The recent wave of disruptive tactics from climate justice activists is the focus of Chapter 8. We'll see how activists have adopted creative and confrontational tactics designed to capture public attention, such as road blockades and symbolic vandalism. Finally, Chapter 9 returns to one of the book's central questions. What does the future of radical environmental activism look like? In the face of increased climate urgency and intensified repression, will activists once again view sabotage as necessary?

2

Birth of a Radical Movement and Schisms

I WAS THRILLED WHEN ISAAC agreed to talk with me.[1] He was one of the original core members of Earth First!, and so I was very curious to hear his thoughts on its formation and early years. My first question to Isaac was a soft opening question, one designed to put him at ease: "What was it like to be a part of Earth First! at the beginning?" It had the opposite effect. Isaac stopped our conversation right there. He said it was very important to distinguish that he was a core part of the "original Earth First!" and its fierce willingness to defend wilderness. He took great pride in this. But Isaac also wanted to make it clear to me that he had nothing to do with the more left-leaning, anarchist elements that he said later infiltrated Earth First!.

As we'll see, Isaac's journey from wilderness advocate and Earth First! founder to someone alienated from his own group reflects the movement's origins and the divisions that later emerged.

***

Sometimes books capture a cultural moment. And sometimes books influence that moment. Edward Abbey's 1975 novel, *The Monkey Wrench Gang*, accomplished both. It tapped into the nascent ecodefense movement and inspired the formation of Earth First!.[2] In the book, a ragtag cast of characters become frustrated as developers encroach on wild spaces in the American Southwest. They then embark on a campaign of sabotage of empty trains and bulldozers. Given the popularity of the book in environmental circles, the term *monkeywrenching* became a common way to describe sabotage in defense of the environment.

Earth First! was founded in 1980 by Dave Foreman, Ron Kezar, Bart Koehler, Mike Roselle, and Howie Wolke. The group was a mix of veterans from the mainstream conservation movement (Foreman, Koehler, and Wolke), a leftist activist (Roselle), and a former U.S. Park Service Ranger (Kezar).[3] The group's ethos, "No compromise in defense of Mother Earth!," hinted at their strategy. Earth First! and its supporters would do whatever it took—including sabotage—to defend wilderness. One of their first big actions was a banner drop at the 710-foot-high Glen Canyon Dam in Arizona. The Earth First!ers unfurled a giant black sheet of plastic down the face of the dam so that it looked as if the dam had a crack in it. This was a publicity stunt, but it was also designed to give homage to Abbey's book, as the cracking of Glen Canyon Dam was a central part of *The Monkey Wrench Gang*. Abbey himself was at the dam when the banner was unfurled.[4]

Yet, the formation of Earth First! was not just fan fiction coming to life. It was a response to the real grievances and frustrations of many activists with the mainstream environmental movement. In the 1970s, the U.S. Forest Service undertook Roadless Area Review and Evaluations (RARE II). This review was launched to decide which parts of the United States would remain roadless and thus wilderness, and which parts would be allowed to be developed.[5] At the time Foreman was working with the Wilderness Society, a mainstream conservation lobbying group. Foreman and others were aghast at the RARE II recommendations. What was galling to Foreman and others who would go on to form the core of Earth First! was the acquiescence of mainstream groups like the Wilderness Society and Sierra Club to what they viewed as unacceptable levels of development. In January 1979, the release of the RARE II recommendations with its minimal area of protected wilderness was the final straw.[6] Foreman and others felt that the mainstream movement wasn't taking strong enough action to protect wilderness. And thus in 1980 Earth First! was born.

Isaac's journey into Earth First! reflected a pathway that many of the original core members of the group traveled. He grew up moving around the country often, and he ended up going to college in New England in the early 1970s. Isaac interned his freshman year in the U.S. Forest Service but quickly became disillusioned. He derisively described the main duties of his job as getting coffee for senior rangers and protecting clear cuts for the lumber and timber industry. The disgust that Isaac felt toward U.S. Forest Rangers would become mainstream within Earth First!, where rangers were contemptuously referred to as "Freddies."[7]

Isaac's jaundiced view of mainstream activism was crucial to pushing him into Earth First! After college, in the mid-1970s, he headed out to the Mountain West to work with the Sierra Club. In Wyoming he met activists affiliated with Friends of the Earth, an organization that was formed in 1969 by disaffected Sierra Club members, including the former president of the Sierra Club, David Brower, who were opposed to nuclear power.[8] As Isaac recounted, it was while he was in Wyoming that he began to see how biased the U.S. Forest Service was toward the lumber industry. He also became jaded with mainstream groups like the Sierra Club. He began monitoring logging sites and mapping roadless areas for wilderness designation in northwest Wyoming with little more than money for food and beer. It was in this capacity that he became friends with Dave Foreman and Bart Koehler.

While recounting his friendship with Foreman and Koehler, Isaac talked to me about monkeywrenching as both a tactic and a philosophy. In the early 1980s, he started carrying out his own monkeywrenching actions—pulling up survey stakes, pouring sugar in bulldozers—for which he eventually faced prison time. Other Earth First!ers were accused of spiking trees in the Willamette National Forest.[9] Tree spiking is putting a metal or other kind of spike or rod into a tree; after loggers have taken the tree to a sawmill, the spike in it can damage the saw or even the person operating the sawmill. Given the possibility of injuring timber workers, tree spiking was and remains a controversial tactic within the movement, and we will discuss it in more detail in future chapters.[10]

Isaac stopped me when I asked him about tactics. He told me, "Yes, I engaged in monkeywrenching." And he said that yes, *Earth First! Journal* published communiques and a list of monkeywrenching and sabotage actions. But to Isaac monkeywrenching wasn't the core part of Earth First! the way the media and others made it out to be. Rather,

Earth First! was an umbrella movement of activists who vigorously defended wilderness because they didn't believe human lives were intrinsically worth more than animals or plants. They were ecocentrists. And it was this ecocentrism that formed the core of Earth First!. Monkeywrenching would become another important part of the movement. As Isaac told me, "We [original Earth First!ers] had an official position that we wouldn't [as representatives of Earth First!] participate in monkeywrenching [under the Earth First! name]. But we wouldn't condemn [others who did it] as long as it was nonviolent."

It's important to point out that even though there were big personalities in the early Earth First!—like Roselle and Foreman—there wasn't any real hierarchy. Early Earth First!ers and readers of *Earth First Journal* were not part of a formal organization, with members paying dues. Rather, it was a loose social group of people who connected with the idea that mainstream environmental groups weren't doing enough to protect wilderness.[11] Decisions were made by consensus, and while some leaders such as Foreman, or later Judi Bari, carried greater weight, the group generally encouraged individuals and small groups to set up their own campaigns and tree-sits.[12] This ability to take direct action without hierarchical leadership was a major draw for disaffected activists.

Another part of Earth First!'s appeal was its image, which stood in contrast to that of the Ivy-League, genteel ways of mainstream environmental groups. In the early days of Earth First!, Dave Foreman and his co-founders explicitly cultivated a cowboy counterculture image.[13] Like members of an outlaw motorcycle gang, they lived outside the rules, but rather than big bikes, motorcycle patches, and disdain for traffic laws, they adopted cowboy hats, Wrangler jeans, and support for monkeywrenching.

This outlaw image was precisely what drew Ken into Earth First!.[14] He grew up in New England as an avid lover of nature, but he became frustrated with mainstream environmental groups early in his high school years. In an unusual twist, he told me that it was his mother who helped radicalize him. She was a librarian who recognized his passion for environmental issues, so when he was in high school, she got him a subscription to *Earth First! Journal*. He devoured the articles, and he even went to see Dave Foreman and Bart Koehler speak in person.

At first, Ken was put off by the approach taken by Dave, Bart, and the other Earth First!ers. As Ken told me, "as a polite New Englander I was bothered [a] bit by their rough-and-tumble style and cowboy demeanor, especially when talking about mainstream groups [like the Sierra Club]."

But Ken read and did more research on his own, and he came around to the Earth First! viewpoint. He would eventually serve as an editor at the *Earth First! Journal* and come to see the utility of cultivating an outlaw image and monkeywrenching as a winning strategy. In his view, it helped the movement gain media attention, and without the media attention and the people who engaged in civil disobedience and monkeywrenching, they wouldn't have been able to protect wilderness from loggers and development. "Without Earth First! and other small groups [like us] who put our bodies on the line to protect the forests, we would have very little old growth forests left in the West."

Ken also viewed Earth First! as an asset to the more mainstream environmental movement. He paraphrased for me a quote from David Brower, former Sierra Club president and founder of Friends of the Earth. Ken told me, "As David Brower said, 'I needed to found Friends of the Earth to make the Sierra Club look moderate. And Dave Foreman and company needed to found Earth First! to make the rest of us look moderate.'"

***

Ecocentrism and monkeywrenching were defining issues in the early days of Earth First!. But so was the population question that we first touched on in Chapter 1. This question centered on whether you agreed with Paul Ehrlich and supporters of *The Population Bomb* that overpopulation was a core environmental threat—on par with pollution and wilderness destruction—and required urgent action. Or whether you disagreed, and you thought population growth was overblown. Or whether you really thought the population question was used to give cover to racists, xenophobes, and misanthropes.[15] This population question would become an important divide in the movement.

During my conversation with Isaac, a core early member of Earth First! whom we met at the beginning of this chapter, I asked him about the population question. In response, he grew animated, his voice changed, and he said, "I like that you asked me about this! Overpopulation is public enemy number one, the root cause of all environmental and social problems on planet Earth. Anybody who calls themselves an environmentalist or conservationist and doesn't talk about overpopulation is walking around with blinders."[16] Another revealing part of my interview with Isaac dealt with the critics of these overpopulation arguments. Some argued that since population growth was happening in the Global South, and many of those concerned about population were putting forth solutions for stopping population growth in the Global South, the whole question was racist. Isaac said, "And when I hear those accusations of 'racist,' it makes my blood boil. Why do you think we as a species are not reducing greenhouse emissions—it's a constantly growing population. It's one step forward with solar and wind farms [reducing emissions] that is completely negated by population growth [two steps backwards]."

Ken, the former editor of *Earth First! Journal*, also emphasized the importance of the population question.[17] He said that many environmental groups shied away from addressing it because they didn't want to be labeled as "racist." But he made his position on population very clear: "we have to address the population question to deal with the extinction [of species] and the climate issue. You can't have one without the other."

Up to this point, our conversation had been flowing freely. Yet, when I brought up the issue of immigration with Ken and questioned how many of those concerned about overpopulation had made alliances with hardcore anti-immigration groups, he became a bit guarded and gave an answer that any politician would be proud of. He obfuscated, while still making it clear which side of the divide he was on. "We have decided to not get into the immigration issue at all following Trump. He made that issue toxic. Dave Foreman said what he had to on this topic in his book *Man Swarm* (2011)."[18] Foreman, the Earth First! founder and deep ecologist, was obsessed with overpopulation, and his hardline stance opposing further immigrants won him plaudits from anti-immigration activists, but it also made him a pariah among many within the environmental movement.

Ken went on to tell me that "[i]mmigration should be part of the equation, and we are not arguing for or against immigration debates, but it needs to be said." It was clear from what Ken was and wasn't saying that he and many others like him from the early Earth First! days viewed immigration to the United States as an environmental problem, and greatly favored restricting it.

The idea that overpopulation leads to environmental degradation is not a settled ecological fact.[19] But it's not the real issue. The problem is that once you say that there are too many people, it can quickly slip into *too many of which people?* Many from the deep ecology wing were extremely concerned about overpopulation and made common cause with anti-immigration hardliners.

I remember vividly my conversation with Richard,[20] a self-described environmental ethicist and philosopher. He talked about getting involved in environmental fights in Georgia in the late 1970s and grappling with projected population growth. To Richard this was the main problem: all these projections and fights presupposed population growth. He began meeting with like-minded activists concerned with population growth. Richard argued that even though he knew was going to get "labeled a racist," immigration was the main source of population growth in the United States, and since "we've given up on the population [and the immigration] argument in the U.S., we have lost more green space."

One of the people Richard cited when we chatted was John Tanton, a person who would go on to found some of the most restrictive anti-immigration groups. Tanton was an ophthalmologist, philanthropist, former president of the nonprofit group Zero Population Growth, and an environmentalist.[21] As part of Planned Parenthood, the abortion rights group, and also the Sierra Club, Tanton unsuccessfully tried to push both groups into adopting platforms that would drastically reduce immigration into the United States.[22] Frustrated by his inability to push existing activist groups in his anti-immigrant direction, Tanton founded the Federation for American Immigration Reform (FAIR) and the Center for Immigration Studies (CIS). The innocuous names of these two groups would belie their virulent opposition to immigration, particularly non-White immigration into the United States. Tanton founded or played a key role in a total of thirteen different anti-immigrant groups and advocacy organizations. These groups and the advocates they produced would become known as the Tanton Network. This network even helped cultivate Stephen Miller, who would later become President Trump's political advisor, deputy chief of staff, and chief anti-immigrant hardliner.[23]

But Tanton didn't just favor restricting immigrants; he also sponsored several White nationalist publishing houses and journals. He even wrote the following in a letter in 1993: "I've come to the point of view that for European-American society and culture to persist requires a European-American majority, and a clear one at that."[24] His activism and views on race and immigration led the Southern Poverty Law Center (SPLC) to label him "the racist architect of the modern anti-immigrant movement."[25] We'll return to this racist, anti-immigration strain in Chapter 7, when we examine ecofascism—an ideology that draws in part on the ideas of Tanton and other anti-immigration deep ecologists.

When I mentioned some of these quotes from Tanton to Richard, he responded: "Tanton helped found a bunch of groups to address immigration—which I support—and I've never seen him as a sinister figure. I have heard him say a few comments, which don't sound good to me. But you can always question people's motives."

The formation of Earth First! galvanized activists around the idea of wilderness first. As mentioned earlier, it cultivated an outlaw image that took the Western cowboy archetype and added a fierce wilderness ethos to it. Earth First!ers were defined by both their opposition to mainstream tactics like those used by the Sierra Club and their willingness to engage in monkeywrenching, or light sabotage. But as we've seen, cracks in the group over issues like overpopulation and immigration were already forming.

***

Of all the interviews I conducted with former activists, one name elicited more polarized opinions than any other. Those who disliked him told me he was an "egomaniac,"[26] an "ecofascist,"[27] and a "racist, anti-immigrant misanthrope."[28] Others had mixed views: "an asshole, but he was right that leftist politics would cannibalize the movement."[29] His supporters told me he was a charismatic leader who created "a powerful place for nature and wilderness to be protected and fought for."³⁰

The man they were all talking about was Dave Foreman, one of the original founders of Earth First!. He was one of the most prominent population control advocates. His critics said that Foreman just hated humans as a species, and they pointed to comments he had made that appeared to cheer on the famine in Ethiopia in the 1980s: "Human suffering resulting from drought and famine in Ethiopia is tragic, yes, but the destruction there of other creatures and habitat is even more tragic."³¹

Foreman was also no leftist. He would often refer to himself as a "redneck for wilderness."³² But he was instrumental in creating Earth First! and its ethos of "No compromise in defense of Mother Earth." He even co-wrote a book on sabotage tactics for activists: *Ecodefense: A Field Guide to Monkeywrenching*, which would become a bible among radical environmentalists engaging in sabotage.³³

The cover of his memoir, "Confessions of an Eco-Warrior," shows a picture of Foreman with a full beard, penetrating eyes, fisherman's hat, and muscled forearms crossed, staring at the camera, wearing an Earth First! shirt; its logo combined a wrench representing the monkeywrench side of activism and a prehistoric hammer for the deep ecology.³⁴ Reading his memoir, you could see his appeal. Foreman was brash and funny. He justified monkeywrenching, calling it "a proud American tradition, existing happily in the shadows while decorous Americans bow before the brightly lit Great God Private Property." Foreman also said monkeywrenching was a necessary tactic to protect nature and wilderness from those things that would try to destroy it.³⁵ He also talked about his belief in deep ecology: "wilderness has value in and of itself," and said that human lives should not be privileged over the lives of other living things. And in a tongue-in-cheek plea to his followers, he urged them to both explore wilderness and to "piss on developers' graves."³⁶

Murray Bookchin could not have been more different from Foreman. Bookchin had a bushy mustache and was partial to cardigans, frumpy shirts, suspenders, and the occasional beret that gave him the look of a leftist intellectual—which he very much was. He grew up in New York City, the son of Jewish immigrants. As a teenager in the 1930s, Bookchin, like many other young leftists, was active in the youth Communist Party. But he eventually broke with the party over the Stalin–Hitler pact in 1939. After serving in the U.S. Army during World War II, Bookchin was active in labor organizing and eventually found his way to other dissident Marxist groups.

In the 1960s, Bookchin became an intellectual fixture in the burgeoning leftist counterculture movement.[37] He published a book critical of the use of pesticides, *Our Synthetic Environment*, under a pseudonym a few months before Rachel Carson's more famous *Silent Spring*.[38] In 1964 he connected the problems of capitalism to the problem of the environment, laying the groundwork for his "social ecology approach."[39] In doing so, Bookchin helped to bring together environmentalists and other leftists who were critical of the capitalist status quo.[40]

Bookchin taught at various universities, including the Alternative University in New York City, City University of New York: College of Staten Island, and, finally, Ramapo College. In 1974, he founded the Institute for Social Ecology. That would become his intellectual church, from which he spread the gospel of social ecology to the broader environmental movement. Bookchin and followers of his social ecology approach believed that social problems could not be separated from environmental problems. This viewpoint was in stark contrast to the beliefs of the deep ecologists and founders of Earth First!.

The rift in the radical wing of the environmental movement between Bookchin's social ecologists and Dave Foreman and the deep ecologists was a profound one. Like many intraparty fights, this was a particularly ugly one because it was happening inside the proverbial radical environmental tent. The pages of *Earth First! Journal* were filled with support for tree-sits, forest defense, and sabotage actions, but they also became the site of some nasty exchanges between supporters of Bookchin and Foreman. The quotes from Bookchin's obituary in *The New York Times* in 2006 gives some idea of the tenor of the debate. Gary Snyder, a poet and deep ecology supporter, made the following comment to *The Los Angeles Times* in 1989: "Although he (Bookchin) claims to be an anarchist, he writes like a Stalinist thug." Bookchin and his acolytes regularly referred to deep ecologists as "ecofascists" because of their advocacy for population reduction.[41]

Foreman and Bookchin eventually agreed to meet for a "dialogue" in New York City in 1989. What's interesting about the dialogue, which was eventually published as a book along with a pair of retrospective essays from the two, is how much Bookchin and Foreman agreed with one another. They both referred to themselves as "radical ecologists," believed the mainstream environmental organizations were largely ineffective (and many actively bad), favored wilderness designation to protect species and biodiversity, and also agreed that the current politics were broken. But Bookchin and Foreman also highlighted their differences. The book included retrospective essays published by each a year after their meeting. In the closing paragraphs of Foreman's retrospective essay, "Second Thoughts of an Eco Warrior," Foreman emphasized that the reason he left Earth First! was his discomfort with the "old" versus the "new guard" in Earth First!; Foreman identified with the old guard. He believed he was holding up the lineage of wilderness-first conservationists. He argued that the new guard of economic justice activists who came out of the 1960s leftist movements had corrupted Earth First!'s goals. Foreman viewed it as a hostile takeover of Earth First!, and he didn't feel comfortable being part of a broadly left-leaning movement that didn't focus solely on the environment.[42]

As Foreman's own words show, the deep ecology-versus–social ecology schism was not just about ideas, but also about the different kinds of people attracted to the movement. The old guard of wilderness, backwoods conservationists like Foreman and other founders of Earth First!, were being replaced by more urban, social justice activists who hailed from other left-wing movements. These different pathways into Earth First! and radical environmentalism in general would have an outsized impact on the movement going forward.

***

When I interviewed activists from this era there were small clues that hinted at allegiances. For example, I could often guess which side of the Bookchin–Foreman divide an activist fell on based on how they answered this question: "How would you describe your role in the movement?" The Foreman and deep ecology supporters tended to identify themselves as "conservationists." In contrast, Bookchin supporters and other social ecologists often referred to themselves as "environmental activists," "movement organizers," or "leftist activists."

Jim, an activist who ran in the same circles as Dave Foreman, made this exact point about the importance of his identity at the beginning of our conversation. When I asked him what his relationship to the environmental movement was like, Jim stopped me before our interview got going. He wanted to make sure I understood that he was a "conservationist activist," not an environmental activist, and that those distinctions were important to him. To Jim and others, it signified very different worldviews and pathways into the movement.

Jim had a salt-and-pepper beard and glasses, and he had a disarming, warm manner. He could have passed for a cool high school English teacher. Like Isaac and Ken, he grew up in New England in the 1970s. The second thing Jim told me after he emphasized his identity as a conservationist was that he was brought up as a "polite Yankee." He and others like him were culturally distant from the Pacific Northwest anarchist scene that would later come to dominate Earth First! and the Earth Liberation Front (ELF). He said he supported and had participated in monkeywrenching to stop unfettered destruction of the wilderness. But Jim also told me that the pointless vandalism and property destruction that would become part of the radical environmental repertoire was not his Earth First!.

He also spoke about Dave Foreman with an almost religious reverence. To Jim, Dave was a charismatic leader who embodied the philosophy of biocentrism. It was all about wilderness and about defending public lands from a spiritual perspective. Foreman and several others even cultivated a nature-centered spirituality, putting a pagan calendar in an early issue of *Earth First! Journal*.[43] But Foreman wasn't the only apostle of the movement who felt that they were part of a deeper, quasi-religious movement. Jim emphasized how the early versions of *Earth First! Journal*, with its nods to paganism and Mother Nature, were quasi-religious texts.[44] Earth First! married apocalyptic rhetoric about what was happening to animals and the environment with a message of hope and efficacy via ecodefense. Nature and wilderness needed to be protected, and to protect them was a spiritual calling.[45]

Jim said that Dave Foreman's "Earth First! tribe" was intoxicating, and he eagerly joined. He said it was "groovy" to be part of the defense of public lands and wilderness. The Earth First! he loved being part of was an activist movement that had the philosophical heft to back their civil disobedience and monkeywrenching, which he called "throwing a monkeywrench in the machine [of development]." Jim also smiled when he told me: "yeah, and there were cute girls, too."

As his point at the beginning of this chapter suggested, Isaac, one of the original core members of Earth First!, had a lot to say about what Earth First! later became.[46] He told me how, in the beginning, the fact that Earth First! was not a top-down organization was an asset. It meant that the organization was not beholden to leadership, there was a diversity of ideas, and no one person could be targeted by industry groups or the government to stop Earth First!. Yet, Isaac said that as Earth First! became a "cool radical organization," this loose structure backfired. He felt it changed seemingly over night. Suddenly "urban, leftist anarchist ideologues" and anti-hunting peace activists were flooding to Earth First!. And even worse to Isaac, they were all overly concerned with social justice activism—which in his opinion had "nothing to do with wilderness."

Isaac then recounted a vivid example of how the new Earth First! activists didn't understand the group's roots. He told me about a time when he and some of the other prominent Earth First!ers were invited on a daytime talk show to talk about radical environmental activism. The participants included Isaac, another core Earth First! member, and a new guy from the northern California wing. To Isaac, the new guy was a total stereotype of an urban, leftist activist. He had long hair, a long beard, and somewhat squinty eyes, and "looked like Charles Manson."

Before they went on the talk show, Isaac, his fellow core Earth First! member, and this new guy visited a media consultant in New York. During the meeting, the media consultant asked them about the meaning of one of the Earth First! symbols: a clenched green fist inside a circle. Before Isaac could respond, the new guy said: "the fist represents solidarity with the oppressed workers of the world." With this response Isaac lost it, and turned to the new guy and exclaimed: "That's bullshit! I designed the logo. It means militant defense of Mother Earth. Nothing more and nothing less."

Isaac told me that by the end of the 1980s the split within Earth First! between the old guard and the new leftist activists became a chasm.

At the annual meeting, known as Round River Rendezvous, there were people doing hippie energy circles. To him the whole vibe had shifted to something he didn't recognize. Isaac told me that both he and Dave Foreman were good buddies. They were hunters, and "Dave," he said, "was basically a Republican who liked wilderness." He added that Earth First! had evolved into a home for the counterculture, converting into something that Isaac and the other "old guard [of Earth First!] didn't recognize"—and didn't want any part of. So, he and several others eventually left.

***

Another major personality within the movement was Judi Bari, the Earth First! organizer in northern California mentioned in Chapter 1. Bari was decidedly not allied with the deep ecology wing. Instead, she was trying to forge alliances between radical environmental groups and organized labor.

To her supporters, Bari was a visionary. Kevin was one such Bari supporter.[47] He identified as a union guy with environmental sympathies and was active in Earth First! from the early 1990s to the mid-2000s. My interview with Kevin also started off a bit differently than those with the others. Before we even got into talking about his background, Kevin said he wanted me to understand something. He said the radical environmental movement that he was a part of was nonviolent and didn't advocate terrorism. Ted Kaczynski and the Unabomber weren't part of his movement. There was a subset who advocated "misanthropy and primitivism," but those weren't what he and Judi Bari supporters were about. They were only about stopping environmental destruction "in its tracks."

Kevin began working with the International Workers of the World (IWW) when he hooked up with Judi Bari. At that time, Bari was trying to form an alliance between environmentalists and timber workers, and Kevin helped with some of the promotional materials. While Bari and her supporters were trying to organize timber workers and environmentalists, they were also engaged in tree sitting and civil disobedience. Kevin argued that Bari played a key role in marshaling West Coast Earth First! groups toward her vision and a shifting their tactics. Bari and her followers publicly disavowed monkeywrenching and sabotage in favor of civil disobedience and an alliance with labor.⁴⁸

Kevin emphasized Bari's charisma and intelligence, and added that he loved her sharp tongue. He was a union guy, and Bari was arguing that one didn't need to make a choice between saving the trees or the logging jobs. It resonated with him, and he quickly became a convert.

Bari is also famous for being the victim of a pipe bomb attack in May 1990. The bomb exploded under her seat while she was driving, gravely wounding her. The authorities initially suspected that Bari and the other passenger in the car, activist Darryl Charney, had accidentally set off their own bomb. A jury later found the FBI and the Oakland Police Department guilty of violating Bari's and Charney's civil rights and awarded them $4.4 million in a 2002 federal lawsuit. Kevin wanted me to know that at his core he believed that the bomb was planted by someone with corporate interests who saw Bari's alliance with labor and timber as a threat. To this day, no one has been arrested for the bombing, and the identity of who planted the bomb remains a mystery.⁴⁹

***

Yet not all Earth First!ers were as enamored with Bari as Kevin was. Many of the early Earth First!ers found Bari to be a self-aggrandizer. Mark was one of these critics.⁵⁰ Mark was a core member of Earth First! at its founding. He had a long career in environmental activism and would go on to be a central member of other environmental groups, like the Rainforest Action Network (RAN). I had an inkling that Mark was going to be a fascinating person to talk with after the first time we connected. One of his fellow Earth First!ers put us in touch via email. Mark replied and said that he usually requested interviewers to "bring a good bottle of Scotch," but that he would make an exception this time. Like other early First!ers, Mark also told me that he preferred the term *conservationist* to *environmentalist*—since that was what he was about: conserving nature.

As a teenager in the late 1960s, Mark was involved in various leftist causes, including civil rights and protesting the Vietnam War. He got into activism in the mid-1970s, after being involved in fights in Wyoming over the logging and oil fields. He then hooked up with other conservationists, and they engaged in civil disobedience to try to halt the expansion of oil fields and save the old-growth forests. Mark was also against coyote hunts that were common back then. But one of the problems Mark and others soon encountered was that he and other conservationists were getting labeled as "hippy backpackers" from out of town, and that made it hard for them to recruit locals. So, he and his friends "started wearing cowboy boots to indigenize" themselves and recruit more followers. He also said that the cowboy boots helped them stand out and gave them a macho swagger, which he felt was necessary because they were always outnumbered by the loggers and oil workers.

Mark was a core member of Earth First!. And it is this background that also gave him his unique take on the role of monkeywrenching and sabotage. Mark told me he was under no illusions that this small group of environmentalists could use sabotage to stop oil and timber companies. Rather, the goal was "to raise a ruckus" and get media attention. There were some isolated forms of sabotage—such as pulling up survey stakes, jamming locks, and slashing tires of logging vehicles—happening side-by-side with the civil disobedience.

Mark told me that in these early days there were many more losses than wins. Clear cutting of forests continued, and so there was a need to rethink tactics. By the mid-1980s, many members of Earth First! turned toward the controversial tactic of tree spiking. Tree spiking was a militant tactic designed to prevent forests from being harvested for lumber. It also received widespread coverage in the media and attention from law enforcement.[51] Mark described that tree spiking was condemned by the large environmental groups, but ordinary environmental activists, by and large, loved it. They were finally fighting back against the timber companies. Yet, the news media began to cover these "timber wars" and accuse environmentalists of "going mad" when they carried out tree spikings.[52] In 1987, the practice gained national attention when a lumbermill worker in northern California, George Alexander, was badly injured. Alexander was operating a bandsaw when a large nail, believed to be a tree spike, shattered his saw blade, struck him in the face, and nearly killed him.[53] Earth First! activists were blamed, and public opinion strongly turned against tree spiking. Mark likewise advocated against the tactic.

In 1985, in the Willamette National Forest in Oregon, Earth First! held its first tree-sit to protect the old-growth Douglas Fir trees prized by loggers.[54] Mark emphasized that fallout from tree-spiking incidents solidified his belief that Earth First! needed to shift tactics and get the public on the side of the environmentalists. They needed less sabotage and more strategic civil disobedience. He and other members of Earth First! even conducted their own public opinion polls. Mark told me that their polling had found that at the beginning of their civil disobedience campaign only 5 percent of Oregonians believed there should be a moratorium on old-growth logging. But by the end of the 1980s that number had moved close to 25 percent, a win for the Earth First!ers in Mark's eyes.

Mark also had a more pressing reason to shift tactics. He realized that extreme tactics were alienating the public. Environmental activists were already unpopular in much of the Mountain and Pacific West. Loggers and business interests had carried out numerous threats and actual violence against activists.[55] And there had been death threats against Judi Bari in the lead up to the Redwood Summer in 1990. Even before the 1990 car bombing that injured her and Darryl Charney, Bari received death threats in the lead-up to Redwood Summer, the civil disobedience campaign to protect the California redwoods from logging.[56] So as Mark told me, they had to cool it with some of their more radical tactics for two reasons. First, activists needed the media's sympathetic treatment of their protests. And second, activists needed the police to at least nominally protect them because he and other activists "didn't want to get killed by the loggers" who vastly outnumbered them and were out for blood.

As Mark saw it, Bari's role in the Earth First! and radical environmental movement had been "mythologized." The bombing had lionized her, but it obscured that, at least to Mark, Bari wasn't very effective in organizing labor and timber interests. She wasn't willing to compromise enough on her hardline stance of a full moratorium on logging the redwoods to gain the backing of loggers. Furthermore, the IWW Local #1 that she organized was more of a fantasy than an effective organizing presence.

Mark also had a lot to say about Redwood Summer. He told me it was successful despite Bari's organizing shortcomings. "The thing is, there are enough people that really like redwoods. . . . it was successful [in spite of Bari]." Mark pointed to the thousand of activists who participated: between 3,000 and 5,000 were involved in Redwood Summer, based on some estimates.[57] They carried out actions such as chaining themselves to equipment (lockdowns), which led to hundreds of arrests and raised the salience of protecting the redwoods. It was a true mass mobilization.[58]

At the same time as Redwood Summer, there were public signs of a schism in Earth First! between two of its co-founders, Mike Roselle and Dave Foreman. Roselle had come from a more leftist, progressive background, whereas Foreman was first and foremost a conservationist. In his 1990 resignation letter, Foreman criticized the leftist direction that Earth First! had taken, believing it was filled with "yippies and hippies" and was too much of a counterculture movement.[59] As Roselle saw it, Foreman was giving fodder and comfort to the timber lobby and other enemies of Earth First!, who could say, "look at Earth First!, it's even too radical for its founder now."[60] Roselle called Foreman an "unrepentant right-wing thug."[61] He later apologized for his words but maintained that "[s]ome of the things that Dave said [such as saying that the HIV/AIDS was 'nature seeking its balance,'[62] or cheering on famines in Ethiopia] put us in a bad situation when we'd go out and work with other community groups."[63] Roselle added that even though Foreman has resigned from Earth First!, he was still one of its most recognizable figures. So the fact that Foreman had a "PR problem" meant that the whole radical environmental movement had a PR problem.[64]

***

In the early to mid-1990s Earth First! was at a crossroads. Foreman, its charismatic founder and leader, had left the group. Many of the old wilderness-first members followed Foreman and left as well. Bari was severely injured by the car bomb in 1990, and then was later diagnosed with cancer.[65] In many ways, the Bookchin social ecology wing had won out. Earth First! was no longer solely focused on wilderness. The social ecology critique that environmental problems were inherently human problems, and vice versa, were no longer controversial. It was against this backdrop that anarchist ideas began to take hold. The anarchists transformed both Earth First! and the radical environmental movement writ large.

Murray Bookchin and Judi Bari helped plan the leftist direction that the radical environmental movement would take. But it wasn't just the persuasiveness of their ideas. There was a confluence of factors that would tug the environmental movement into the anarchist direction.

***

It's not surprising that Earth First!'s rhetoric and actions might have attracted a more extreme element. Seth, an academic and environmental historian, has chronicled the rise of Earth First! and the radical environmental movement.[66] He also has an interesting perspective. Before becoming an academic, Seth grew up in the Bay Area and was a big hiker and backpacker. He ended up working for the U.S. Forest Service. While at his job there, Seth told me he was able to see different sides of the wilderness debate. To ranchers, loggers, conservatives, and right-wing militia folks, the U.S. Forest Service was run by "jackbooted thugs" who restricted grazing and hunting and did the dirty work of environmentalists. And to the environmentalists, the U.S. Forest Service, or "Freddie's," as they were derogatorily called by activists, were in the pocket of Big Timber. These constant fights over wilderness, and over who had a right to the land, were integral to shaping Seth's interest in environmental politics and history.

During our conversation, Seth made a particularly important point. Earth First! at its core was an antiestablishment movement. As he told me, "A lot of the Earth First! rhetoric was, 'conventional reform and political institutions have failed us.'" If that's the case, then activists "have to take things into our (their) own hands. And the only way to stop industrial civilization is to spike the trees." So, it's not surprising that other antisystem individuals, such as urban anarchists, were attracted to the movement.

Grant, as both a scholar and a former Earth First! activist, also had unique insights into these generational divides in the movement.[67] He grew up in the Pacific Northwest in the mid-1990s and was a self-described dreadlocked Earth First!er, a far cry from Dave Foreman's cowboy boots and hats. Grant said that he and others from his generation of Earth First! were all about getting rid of the "macho Dave

Foreman" energy. Their main interest was highlighting the intersection of ecological problems and social problems. As Grant told me, it "was a shift from deep ecology to anarchism." To Grant, the younger folks identified with anarchism, whereas the old guard was hostile to anarchism, antiracism, and antifascism—all the ideas that Grant and his fellow cohort of activists cherished.

But as Grant's described it, these tensions were a direct result of who was coming into Earth First! and other radical environmental groups. The movement was becoming "more urban and less wilderness focused." And these urban environmental activists came in with a different ethos. We'll hear more from Grant in the next chapter.

As Dave Foreman's resignation letter signaled, many of the old guard Earth First!ers were appalled at the leftist-anarchist direction the group was taking. Mark, one of the core founding members of Earth First! whom we got to know earlier in this chapter, was outraged by the infiltration of leftist anarchists into the movement. But it wasn't just the ideological differences that he had with the new anarchist bent: it was their tactics. Mark accused them of lacking "flexibility." He even jokingly told me that these new activists weren't really "green [environmentalists], they were red and black [the colors of anarchism and socialism]." He felt they had little or no allegiance to the environmental movement. In contrast to the outdoorsy wilderness types that defined the old Earth First!ers, Mark saw the new activists as left-wing types who weren't interested in the strategic pressure campaigns required by environmental activism. In his words, "they just wanted to fight the cops." Mark saw the more aggressive tactics coming into the movement as a huge mistake. The radical environmentalists lost their nonviolent, civil disobedient ethos, and they "forgot about Gandhi, Bayard Rustin, Fred Shuttlesworth [and others who preached non-violence][68]... instead their adherents decided to wear black and break windows. They lost the rules [for effective resistance campaigns]."

***

There are three important takeaways from this period of Earth First!. First, the radical environmental movement was grounded in a shared ethos. Wilderness and the environment were worth defending, and mainstream environmental groups weren't doing enough. In response, civil disobedience, and even sabotage, were seen as legitimate and necessary tactics.

Second, radical movements are not formed in a vacuum. They reflect the networks and subcultures that formed them. Earth First! was no different. In its early days, the core Earth First! members were disaffected conservationists with a deep reverence for nature. They cultivated a cowboy, roughneck, counterculture image exemplified by figures like Dave Foreman.

Third and finally, movements evolve. Factions emerge.[69] Sometimes a faction even overtakes the original group or movement.[70]

The split between the deep ecologists and social ecologists became a rupture. It ultimately led many of Earth First!'s founders to leave the group. But it's also not so surprising. Earth First! itself was a product of a breakaway faction and the perceived failings of the mainstream movement.

In the end, it was the social ecology wing that gained the upper hand. Their idea that the oppression of humans, animals, and the environment are all interconnected laid the foundation for green anarchism and total liberation. These new philosophies didn't merely justify direct action and sabotage; their adherents argued that such tactics were essential to confront systems of domination.[71]

The roots of this shift toward green anarchism also brought a new kind of activist into the movement. As we'll see in the next chapter, the animal rights movement and the straight-edge punk scene brought new people, new energy, and a new ethos into the radical environmental fold. Some of those activists would go on to form one of the most notorious factions: the Earth Liberation Front.

3

Punk, Animal Rights, and the Movement

"DO YOU HAVE ANY REGRETS or things you would do differently?" This question came from an undergraduate student in my class in February 2024. She asked the question to Robert, an animal rights activist, who had spent nearly two years in prison for engaging in vandalism and releasing animals from fur farms. That week in class we were discussing pathways into radical activism and the connections between the animal liberation movement and the punk rock scene. Given the topic, I asked Robert if he would Zoom into my class as a special guest, and he agreed. Activists associated with the animal liberation movement, and the leaderless Animal Liberation Front (ALF), had carried out vandalism, property destruction, and release of animals from testing laboratories and fur farms—the exact type of actions for which Robert was convicted. Given the topic, I thought it would be a valuable experience for my students to hear from Robert. I wanted them to try to understand how someone like Robert got into in activism and why he was willing to carry out actions that ultimately landed him in prison.[1]

Robert had dark brown hair and stubble and was wearing a baseball hat for a band associated with the vegan punk straight edge movement. Vegan straight edge is a subculture within the punk movement that developed in the 1980s and 1990s and preached veganism, along with abstinence from drugs and alcohol. Robert's Zoom background had posters and flyers from animal liberation zines and vegan punk bands.

Robert thought for a moment about the question from my student and responded. "Yeah, I have some regrets." He paused again. "I regret that I didn't do more. I should have freed more animals from slaughter and torture. I wish I realized that prison wasn't so bad, and it wasn't as scary as they make it out to be, and that the [prison] sentences aren't as long as they want us to believe." After we thanked Robert for Zooming into the class, several students expressed their surprise at Robert's candor, and in particular his response to the question about whether he had any regrets. His answer even surprised me a bit. Though it shouldn't have. I had gotten to know Robert well while researching this book. As discussed in Chapter 1, we had become close enough that he was willing to share his list of major ALF actions with me and my research assistants.

After Robert's Zoom call ended, one of my students remarked, "Yeah, he's pretty hardcore, isn't he?" This was an adjective I would use to describe Robert as well. His ethos was "hardcore," and it was also his pathway into activism.

***

If Earth First! had morphed into a bastion of the conservationists, survivalists, zero population growth advocates, and deep ecologists, we might be writing a very different history of the movement. But it didn't. The socially conscious and anarchist-inspired wing of the radical environmental movement became dominant. And many of these new ecoradicals had a shared background in the hardcore punk scene and animal rights activism.

Before I started conducting interviews for this book, I did some background reading. It was clear that there was some overlap between the radical animal and radical environmentalist movements, but they were largely treated as distinct.[2] The ELF was often framed as the next iteration of Earth First!, and while there was some crossover with the ALF, they were typically seen as separate.

Yet what I began to discover in interviews with activists from this period was that a fusion of punk and animal rights had injected something distinct into the movement.

Many of those who were drawn to the radical environmental movement in the late 1990s and early 2000s came up through the vegan straight edge hardcore scene and animal rights activism. They listened to bands like Earth Crisis, which preached the straight edge vegan lifestyle, and they read magazines like *No Compromise* and *Bite Back*, which covered or celebrated animal releases, arson, and vandalism of fur farms. Robert was no exception, telling me that the "vegan hardcore scene" on the West Coast, particularly the Pacific Northwest, was instrumental in his political awakening.[3]

The data from Chapter 1 backs this up. Between 1995 and 2022, there were 222 incidents involving the most extreme tactics: arson and bombings. The vast majority—199—occurred during the ELF era (1995–2008). Nearly half of those incidents (ninety-four) took place in just three states: California, Oregon, and Washington. Something was clearly brewing on the West Coast.

To tell Robert's story, and to understand the rise of the West Coast scene, we first have to cross the ocean to the U.K. The animal liberation movement emerged in the U.K. in the 1970s and 1980s, from the broader anti-cruelty and anti-hunting movement. In the 1960s, hunt sabotage organizations that used non-violent tactics to physically block and prevent hunts from being carried out became more common across the U.K.[4]

U.K. activist Ronnie Lee was a core figure in this burgeoning movement. After getting interested in animal rights activism, Lee became a vegan, and then in 1972 he joined up with his local Hunt Saboteurs Association. The group did exactly what the name implied: it used civil disobedience to disrupt hunts.[5] But Lee grew frustrated with the commitment to nonviolence and with what he deemed a lack of decisive action to protect animals. So Lee and his friends formed their own offshoot of the Hunt Saboteurs Association, and—in a nod to the early 19th- and 20th-century historical animal rights activist groups known as Bands of Mercy—they called it the "Band of Mercy."[6] With the Band of Mercy, Lee and his fellow activists took a more confrontational attitude toward protecting animals. They sabotaged hunt vehicles and committed arson, and they also started freeing animals in raids they termed "animal liberations."

Lee was eventually arrested in 1974 and served a year in prison for participating in a raid on an animal research lab. While in prison, he began thinking about the strategy and tactics of other animal rights activists and how they could be improved. When he was released in 1976, he founded the Animal Liberation Front (ALF).[7]

The ALF's goals were as follows:

1) "Liberate" animals from fur farms, factory farms, laboratories, or other places of abuse.
2) Use direct action or other means to inflict financial damage on those who harm or exploit animals.
3) Show the world the pain and suffering of animals.
4) Take all steps to minimize harm to humans and animals.
5) Allow anybody who is vegan or vegetarian and abides by these principles to claim an action under the ALF.[8]

There are a few things to take note of in the ALF principles. First, it urged militant direct action to save and rescue animals, and it advocated doing economic harm and damage to anyone hurting animals. It also established a litmus test for activism—you had to be vegan or vegetarian at the very least. If you couldn't refrain from eating meat, then you weren't a real ALF activist, and you had no business in their movement. Finally, there was no formal hierarchy, so anybody carrying out an action and adhering to the principles could claim it in ALF's name. This leaderless resistance model in which actions were carried out by anonymous activist cells and then claimed with communiques for a particular group would also become popular with other environmental groups like the ELF.

In 1975, just a year before the ALF was founded, the book *Animal Liberation* was published.[9] In the book Australian philosopher Peter Singer argued against speciesism, or the discrimination of beings because they belong to a different species. Singer also argued that animals deserved a life of dignity and reduced suffering, and that humans should avoid consuming animal products, embrace veganism, and limit experimentation on animals. Going forward, *Animal Liberation* would become a cornerstone text for animal liberation activists.

Meanwhile in the United States, in the late 1970s and early 1980s, activists began to carry out limited actions under the ALF banner. In 1984, one action in particular brought notoriety to the burgeoning U.S.-based ALF scene. Inspired by the ALF, activists broke into the University of Pennsylvania Head Injury Clinical Research Laboratory in Philadelphia. At the lab, the activists smashed equipment and seized more than 60 hours of footage of researchers who were using a machine to inflict massive head trauma on baboons as part of their study. The activists then turned the footage over to People for the Ethical Treatment of Animals (PETA), a mainstream animal rights group that produced a short documentary called *Unnecessary Fuss*.[10] The fallout from the documentary was immediate. The laboratory had its funding cut off, and it became the target of an investigation by the U.S. Department of Health and Human Services. It eventually closed. To animal liberation activists this was a huge victory.[11]

I vividly remember talking to Gary, an animal liberation activist who has served periodically as an aboveground spokesperson for clandestine animal liberation activist groups like the ALF.[12] Gary had dark glasses, graying hair, and a soft Texas twang. His first career had been as a surgeon, but his then-wife, who was "running with the animal rights crowd," got him interested in the animal rights struggle. As a doctor, the idea that animals could also feel pain, and thus shouldn't be made to suffer, resonated with Gary's Hippocratic oath. He became a vegan and started speaking out for animal liberation.

Part of why I mentioned Gary's voice is that his calm twang belied the intensity of his ideals. He told me that if we could get beyond spieciesism and recognize the ways that animals were suffering, there would be way more direct action—both legal and illegal. He mentioned anticolonial, antiracist, and anti-Apartheid struggles, and said, "you don't get results without illegal direct action and even violence. If you are serious about the struggle for animal liberation, then one strategy that has to be deployed is the use of force—[sometimes] by any means necessary." This willingness to use force, and even advocate violence, had gotten Gary into trouble before. He had been banned from entering countries because of his alleged advocacy of violence against fur farmers and animal researchers. From Gary's perspective, the animal liberation movement was the "most peaceful" liberation movement. To him, that was a problem. They needed to embrace tougher tactics, including violence.

***

But it wasn't just the ALF. There were several other animal rights and animal liberation groups that sprang up and were influential in the 1980s through the early 2000s. Two notable groups that targeted specific aspects of animal liberation were the Sea Shepherd Conservation Society and Stop Huntingdon Animal Cruelty.

Paul Joseph Watson formed the Sea Shepherd Conservation Society in 1977. Watson had been part of Greenpeace at its founding in the early 1970s. Back then it was an organization that used advocacy and nonviolent civil disobedience to protect and educate the public on environmental issues. There's a debate as to whether Watson was a co-founder or just a core member of Greenpeace.[13] Regardless, he became disillusioned with what he felt was Greenpeace's passivity and unwillingness to engage in more confrontational tactics especially related to seal-, whale-, and shark hunting.[14] It was at this point that Watson formed the Sea Shepherd Conservation Society. With its small fleet of ships flying their version of the Jolly Roger—a skull with dolphins crossed with a trident and shepherd's crook—Watson and his Sea Shepherds rammed whaling vessels, disrupted seal hunts, and cut fishing nets in ocean waters around the world from the 1980s to the mid-2000s.[15] They advocated an aggressive form of nonviolence. Watson's activities brought a large amount of attention, including celebrity supporters such as Martin Sheen, Mick Jagger, and Uma Thurman, among others. Not suprisingly, whalers and fishermen were vocal critics of Sea Shepherd, arguing that their boat-blocking tactics put sailors' lives at risk.[16] Watson even faced criticism from some of his old Greenpeace allies.[17]

One of Sea Shepherd's most famous actions occurred in November 1986. Two Sea Shepherd activists, Rod Coronado and David Howitt, posing as tourists, "infiltrated" Iceland's whaling industry. They took sledgehammers and wrenches to a whale-processing facility where they smashed windows, machinery, and the logistics systems. Coronado and

Howitt then went to the Reykjavik harbor where two of the four whaling ships in Iceland's whaling industry were docked. Once aboard the two ships, Coronado and Howitt then opened the seacocks, allowing water to rush in, sinking both ships. In less than 24 hours, Iceland's whaling industry had been brought to its knees. Watson bragged that he had been the mastermind behind the whole action.[18]

***

Ted was one such animal rights and environmental activist whose path took him into the orbit of Paul Watson and the Sea Shepherds.[19] I remember chatting with him on the phone in between his shifts at the wildlife sanctuary he was managing. Ted grew up on the West Coast and as a kid idealized the swashbuckling Watson and Greenpeace. He quickly joined up with Watson and the Sea Shepherds; devoured the Ed Abbey environmental activist bible, *The Monkey Wrench Gang*; and began carrying out small-scale actions. Ted also started hearing whispers about the ALF and their direct actions, and so he headed over to England. The time in England was transformational for him. There he saw how activists were engaged in anarchist, autonomous action. As Ted told me, he realized that he "could just take personal, radical, direct action. It just made sense (to me)." There weren't formal organizations, or sign-up forms, and he didn't have to do letter writing campaigns or lobbying before being able to escalate things. He could just act on his own. Back in the United States, Ted began targeting animal laboratories, for which he would eventually spend time in prison in the 1990s. It was from his time in the ALF that Ted also found his way into the radical environmental movement, teaming up with Earth First! activists for hunt sabotages and linking the animal rights and environmental movement.

***

Stop Huntingdon Animal Cruelty (SHAC) was formed in 1999 in the U.K. Its goal was to bankrupt and shut down Huntingdon Life Sciences, one of the largest animal testing companies for biological and commercial research.[20] Animal rights activists had made Huntingdon Life Sciences the corporate face of animal cruelty. In the United States, SHAC engaged in an aggressive campaign of targeting both workers for Huntingdon Life Sciences. But they also pioneered something new:

they went after the company's financial backers. SHAC activists didn't just name and shame those associated with Huntingdon Life Sciences; they also posted personal information about and addresses of their targets on their websites. SHAC encouraged direct action against them with labels such as "Target of the Week" and "Ongoing Targets." On those same websites, they also reported both legal and illegal direct actions that activists had carried out against Huntingdon Life Sciences and other targets. To its critics, the American branch of SHAC were using the same tactics as anti-abortion extremists—doxing animal researchers and those associated with Huntingdon Life Sciences, and encouraging violence against them by their anonymous followers.[21] Seven activists, known as the SHAC 7, were eventually arrested in 2004 under the Animal Enterprise Protection Act of 1992 for their campaign against Huntingdon Life Sciences. They were charged with conspiracy and stalking the company through their SHAC campaign website.[22] The 1992 law stated that an animal enterprise consisted of anything from a circus to a fur farm to a medical laboratory that used or sold animals, and it made it a crime to disrupt or damage such an enterprise. In response to SHAC, as well as to the increasing use of hidden videos by animal activists, Congress eventually passed the Animal Enterprise Terrorism Act in 2006. It amended the 1992 law and gave the federal authorities even greater authority to go after animal rights activists.[23]

***

While the Sea Shepherd Conservation Society and SHAC focused on specific campaign targets—whaling and overfishing, and antivivisection, respectively—they both had their roots in animal liberation and ALF tactics. In many ways, the animal liberation movement was more hardcore and less compromising than the radical environmental movement. And that makes sense. If you believe that animals are living beings just like humans and deserve the same freedom from cruelty, then every factory farm is a scene of mass murder, every animal experimentation lab is a torture chamber, and you are compelled to act.

Starting in the 1990s, the distinct ideas of animal liberation, ecocentrism, and anarchism began to cohere into a general philosophical movement known as total liberation.[24] Some activists focused on the environmental aspects of total liberation and referred to themselves as green anarchists.²⁵ But a core part of this movement of total liberation was a preference for civil disobedience and direct action, and sabotage in particular, over conventional politics.²⁶

From the beginning, the animal liberation movement was entwined with the hardcore punk subculture. Both animal liberation and the punk scene hit England in the late 1970s. Ronnie Lee, the founder of the ALF, formed a punk band in 1979 called Total Attack. Other bands, like Crass (1977–1984), preached animal liberation, anarchism, and environmentalism. Many U.K.-based ALF activists were part of the punk scene. Lee even pointed to the shared culture and symbiosis between ALF and animal liberation activists and the punk scene. Both preached autonomy and had a do-it-yourself ethic, anarchist and leftist politics, and an anti-establishment ethos. This created a "crossover" in the movements, with punks doing animal liberation, and animal liberation activists making punk music.²⁷

Punk arrived in the United States in the early to mid-1970s. By the early 1980s, in the punk scenes in New York and Washington, D.C., the straight edge subculture within hardcore punk began to take hold. Straight edge was a reaction to the alcohol and drug-fueled nihilism that characterized much of the early punk scene.²⁸ Minor Threat, the Washington, D.C. hardcore punk band, penned the 1981 song "Straight Edge," which became a foundational anthem and gave the movement its name.²⁹ This burgeoning hardcore straight edge punk scene promoted a lifestyle of no alcohol, no drugs, and clean living. Within the straight edge movement, a notable offshot of vegan straight edge adherents, who promoted animal rights, veganism, and anarchist politics, emerged.³⁰ The vegan straight edge movement was supported by pamphlets and underground literature collections called "zines" that were passed out at shows. The lyrics of bands like Vegan Reich (formed in 1986) and Earth Crisis (formed in 1989) promoted veganism and direct action in support of animal and environmental liberation. Prominent vegan straight edge zines published articles designed to provoke outrage or encourage direct action, and many times they included a list of recent acts of sabotage or actions carried out by activists.³¹ At the punk shows of prominent bands, there would be zines and merchandise supporting radical direct actions. The Syracuse-based Earth Crisis often wore camo fatigues when they performed to emphasize their militancy. In a 2015 interview, Earth Crisis's lead singer, Karl Buechner, said, "When the Animal Liberation Front, Earth First! or the Sea Shepherds save lives, we [want to] let people know through our music [that we support them]."[32] This subculture of veganism, animal- and eco liberation, leftist politics, and punk confrontation served as a gateway for many activists.

Robert, whom we met at the beginning of this chapter, also got into animal liberation activism through the vegan hardcore punk scene. He emphasized the role that zines played in the scene and in his own political awakening.[33] To Robert, the zines that were circulated before and after shows were as important as the bands on stage spreading the animal liberation message. Zines with names like *Militant Vegan* and *Destroy Babylon* listed actions against targets, encouraged others to commit actions, and were an important part of the subculture.[34] As Robert told me, "A single 30-page photocopied zine could change the direction of an entire local scene, or even the subculture as a whole."

Luke was another activist who came in through the punk scene.[35] He's an animal rights activist and a self-described "cranky asshole," who spent time in prison as part of his actions with SHAC. When we spoke, Luke had his hair slicked into a slight pompadour, wore hipster glasses, and was a fast talker. Luke got involved in the hardcore punk rock music scene in the Pacific Northwest. He was in Seattle in the late 1990s, and he said "it was a perfect storm of being introduced to radical politics through music." Luke described this time and place in quasi-religious terms. At punk shows there were zines, people were tabling for political causes, and the bands were preaching from the stage. It was a mix of younger, energetic punk kids and older activists that created this vibrant scene.

Luke emphasized that there was a direct connection between his punk pathway into the movement and the kind of tactics he and his fellow activists carried out. He told me about one memorable pressure campaign that he was a part of to get a department store to stop carrying fur. The campaign against the store started with letter writing, and then activists passed out literature to customers in front of the store. Luke told me that this didn't stop the department store from selling fur, and so they escalated their tactics: "We went inside the store and did an effigy burning. And within three months they got rid of the fur salon." With that success they targeted a bigger department store, locking themselves inside the store. After six months, that store stopped selling fur, too.

When Luke was associated with SHAC in the early 2000s, online activism was just starting to take off. Luke and his fellow SHAC activists decided the SHAC website should function like an information clearinghouse. As Luke told me, "Anyone could send us an email: whether they passed out literature, smashed a window, threw paint—it wasn't our space to say what was acceptable or not." One of the things that he and other SHAC activists had to contend with was what to do when people carried out unethical actions, like threatening violence and harm against possible targets. Luke said there were discussions among SHAC folks, and they decided they would "put headers on posts (actions) that they disagreed with." For Luke, the line was physical violence against humans or animals. But Luke and others also felt it wasn't their place to censor actions that they disagreed with. The tactical experimentation was a good thing, since it helped activists "figure out what was a good tactic and what is a bad one and not ethical." Luke also collaborated with several eco activists in the radical environmental movement on hunt sabotages. He began to see SHAC-style tactics and communication pop up in the environmental movement, with clandestine actions followed by anonymous communiques justifying the tactics and choice of targets. Clearly, the animal liberation movement was sharing ideas, tactics, and even activists with the environmental movement.

***

One of the cagiest people I talked to was an activist named Stephen.[36] We chatted on the encrypted app Signal a few times before he felt comfortable talking with me in person. At the outset of our interview, Stephen asked me point blank, "What's the purpose of your book? Are you just trying to tell a salacious story?" I told him, "I don't have a specific angle; I am an academic trying to understand what happened to the radical environmental movement." Stephen relaxed a bit after my response. But he had good reason to be cagey. He was involved with the ALF and had spent several years in prison, having been charged under the Animal Enterprise Terrorism Act.

Stephen came into the movement a generation after Luke, in the early 2000s. But like Luke he also came in through the hardcore scene. However, Stephen grew up in a midsized city on the East Coast where the hardcore punk scene was nowhere near as big or as developed as in the Pacific Northwest in the 1990s. He had a few vegan straight edge friends. But it was online websites showing examples of animal abuse and ALF direct actions that were crucial to Stephen's political awakening. He told me that when he was about seventeen years old, he saw some people at a hardcore punk rock show tabling for the ALF. "[At the show] I picked up a direct action guide . . . and it talked about small-scale sabotage and gluing locks." Stephen continued: "I was [already] doing sabotage—smashing windows, gluing locks—all on my own," but the ALF gave him a more coherent ideology, and even better for Stephen—a list of targets.

Eventually, in the mid-2000s, Stephen headed out to the Bay Area, where he hooked up with other ALF activists. During this time, the hardcore punk pathway was still open to Stephen, but it was a combination of in-person concerts and zines, as well as online activities, that brought him into the movement. The mid-2000s through the early 2010s was a period of flux for both the animal liberation and radical environmental movements. As Stephen recounted, "I came in right at the time the below-ground movement was coming under threat [from government repression] and things were happening more aboveground; this was like post-SHAC 7 [the trial] and just the end of Green Scare [the name activists use to describe the heavy repression of the early 2000s, which we will talk more about in Chapter 5]."

***

As Stephen mentioned, the vegan straight edge scene had a big influence on the radical environmental movement, bringing it both energy and militancy. You had a bunch of kids who were already primed with anti-authoritarian, fuck-the-system attitudes. Added to this was the sense of immediacy that animal liberation demands. If there are no differences between animal rights and human rights, then industrial animal agriculture is torture and mass murder, and it demands direct action to stop the cruelty and killing. This kind of ethos bled over into the radical environmental movement.

My discussions with Grant—the academic and activist whom we met in the previous chapter—about the effects of the straight edge scene and animal liberation on environmental activism were fascinating.[37] Grant was a longtime environmental activist. But he also had gotten a PhD and studied social movements and extremism, so he was able to offer insights both from his scholarly background and his intimate familiarity with the scene. Grant grew up in the Pacific Northwest, and in the 1990s he was regularly attending punk shows. He explained to me how intense and political the punk scene was: "At my first punk show there was a major fight between neo-Nazi skinheads and antifascist punks, and a neo-Nazi almost got killed." Grant also talked about this interesting dichotomy in the Pacific Northwest when he was becoming a politically active punk. There were left-wing anarchists and punks, but "it was also a fertile environment for the far-right" and for neo-Nazis.

Grant described how these separate movements—punk anarchists, "Green radicals/Earth First!ers," the antiglobalization movement, and the animal liberation movement—all coalesced in the Pacific Northwest in the late 1990s. When "the green people [environmentalists] from the forest and the radical black bloc anarchist folks"[38] joined forces, activists became more accepting of intense tactics like property destruction. Or as Grant put it: "[The movement] became about smashing things."

Brett, a direct action activist who has been involved in the antiglobalization, animal liberation, and environmental struggles, echoed what Grant said about the coalescing of the punk, animal, and environmental scenes.[39] He also grew up in the Pacific Northwest in the 1990s. Brett was a vegan and a punk but didn't necessarily identify as vegan straight edge, even though he was friends with a lot of people in that scene. As Brett recounted, "In general in that era [the 1990s,] in the Pacific Northwest punk rock subcultures were so intertwined with anarchy, veganism, animal rights, and eco defense culture." It wasn't just bands and ideas, but a vibe. Yes, the animal and eco wings were distinct, but the subcultures shared a lot of ideas and people. To Brett, during this time there was a heavy crossover between the eco and animal subcultures in terms of how they communicated, who their targets were, the kinds of zines they wrote, and their willingness to engage in direct action. Punk was the bridge between these two movements. As Brett said, the "Venn diagram [intersection] between animal and eco movements was pretty significant . . . they were definitely related."

One point that Brett emphasized when we talked was that in his opinion the animal liberation movement was bigger and more widespread than the radical environmental movement. He said, "I know the animal liberation was much more widespread [than the eco movement]. I remember seeing [all those animal liberation] zines when I was a teenager. There were hundreds of actions listing animal releases all over the country/world—releasing minks, supergluing locks at fur farms. It was big movement." And the radical environmental movement would draw from this wellspring of animal liberation activists.

***

I got to know Jesse, an activist and former spokesperson for the ELF, fairly well during the writing of this book. When I first talked to Jesse, I was a bit disarmed.[40] He was in his mid- to late forties but looked younger, and I couldn't square his soft-spoken, mellow skater and slacker vibe with his radical past. But the more I chatted with him, the more I began to see glimpses of the intensity of his beliefs. Jesse and I chatted several times while I was working on this book, and he even Zoomed in a couple of times to my classes to talk to my students about his pathway into activism.

The throughline from Earth First! to the ELF goes through the punk scene and the ALF. And Jesse's trajectory follows that. He grew up in the Northeast and came in through the hardcore punk scene in the early 1990s. He loved skateboarding and aggressive music. He described himself as straight edge and vegan, but initially not that political. But then he "got handed a bunch of zines/manifestos on animal rights at punk shows. That's all it took [for me to radicalize]." He started to listen to radical bands like Earth Crisis and was attracted to their militant animal liberation and radical environmental message. This was around the time of the Persian Gulf War (1990–1991), and Jesse also became active in the antiwar movement.

Eventually, Jesse headed out to the West Coast to pursue skateboarding, but once he arrived, he found the skateboarding scene lame. He connected with other punk activists involved in civil disobedience against animal testing and vivisection. Jesse told me he "was on a mission to try to find the Animal Liberation Front and the monkeywrenching Earth First!" Jesse was arrested a few times for civil disobedience and low-level property destruction, none of which he felt was too serious, since he wasn't charged with felonies. Jesse didn't want to just wear a t-shirt with a slogan. He wanted to do "radical and illegal stuff," and he was looking for the most radical groups around. "The things that were most exciting [to me] were the Animal Liberation Front and underground Earth First!" And it was here in the Pacific Northwest that Jesse would eventually link up as spokesperson for the most radical of factions that would emerge from this scene—the ELF.

***

The influence of the straight edge hardcore punk scene and animal liberation would reverberate in the radical environmental movement. It would give rise to more confrontational forms of direct action and lead to an escalation in tactics associated with the ELF, which we will talk more about in the next chapter. But the importance of this scene for subsequent environmental activists raises important questions. Why did the vegan straight edge scene cease to be an important source of radical environmental activists? And why is there less symbiosis between the animal liberation movements and current radical environmental activists?

Robert, the animal liberation activist and prisoner whom we met at the beginning of the chapter, had a lot to say about why the hardcore punk and the vegan straight edge scenes were no longer as influential as they once were.[41] There were fallouts in the late 1990s and early 2000s when big bands like Vegan Reich (1999) and Earth Crisis (2001) broke up.[42] Others, in Robert's view, sold out "by not being vegan or straight edge anymore." With the declining primacy of animal and eco-liberation in the straight edge scene, bands became more niche. But one point that Robert made, and one that others echoed, too, is that the broader animal liberation movement stopped encouraging direct action and total liberation. Instead, it went from, in Robert's words, "a movement to an identity." Activists became more focused on policing their fellow activists' food choices and on how strictly vegan they were rather than on animal and eco-liberation.

Vegan animal rights activists also alienated a lot of people in both the animal rights and environmental movements. Critics said that they cared more about the politics of personal choice—whether you were a vegan—than about what people were doing for the movement. Ted, the ALF activist we highlighted earlier in this chapter who was involved with Sea Shepherd and spent time in prison in the 1990s, could barely hide his disgust at the shift in strategy within the animal liberation movement. He referred to most of the activists as "white people with privilege" who lacked "backbone" and cared more about their own veganism than about engaging in risky direct action like animal releases.[43] Ted decried that the ALF had in his words turned into a "vegan advocacy movement." This radical change in turn had alienated the animal rights movement from the radical environmental movement.

Gary, the ALF spokesperson and activist whom we also met earlier in this chapter, had a different take on why the animal liberation and radical environmental movements were no longer as close as they used to be.[44] He mentioned that he still kept in contact with folks into both animal liberation and radical environmentalism. He used to do hunt sabotages with Earth First! but said that it was awkward. For example, he'd be trying to save animals, and then the Earth First!ers would sit down and have burgers after actions. In Gary's view, this prevented more serious alliances from taking place in both the present climate and animal liberation movements. He mentioned that Greta Thunberg, the prominent Swedish climate activist, was vegan too, which to him was an obvious choice. As Gary told me, "If you are interested in saving the planet and fighting against global warming [then], you have no business eating meat."

It's worth stepping back to reflect on a few key points. First, punk and animal liberation went hand-in-hand. And by the 1980s and 1990s, this punk–animal liberation scene developed into a potent activist training ground. Animal rights activists were also remarkably effective: veganism went mainstream, animal testing was scaled back, and wearing fur in public became a socially dicey proposition. But their influence didn't stop there. They also helped usher in new kinds of sabotage, and leaderless cells and an anarchist punk ethos into the radical environmental movement.

The infiltration of groups like Earth First! by anarchists was something that early leaders like Dave Foreman and Mike Roselle lamented. It was driven in part by the rise of the animal liberation and vegan straight edge scene, but internal schisms, state repression, shifts into other movements, and the success of their own campaigns gradually diminished the central role of anarchists. In the years that followed, the animal liberation punk scene would cease to be an important pathway into the radical environmental movement. And when the punk animal liberation activists moved on, they took much of their confrontational militancy with them.

But not before helping give rise to the most one of the most infamous of the radical environmental groups, the Earth Liberation Front.

4

Kaczynski's Shadow and the Rise of the Earth Liberation Front

IT WAS MAY 2024, AND I was meeting Adam for coffee in Eugene, Oregon.¹ Adam was in his early eighties. He had a silver beard, a mop of hair to match, and wire-rim glasses, and he wore a denim shirt, shorts, and some hiking sandals. Adam had picked New Day Bakery for our meeting place. It was exactly what you would expect of a funky Eugene bakery and cafe. The exterior was painted in warm pastel colors, and it had a spacious outdoor area shaded with umbrellas, picnic tables, and some metal chairs and tables. The inside was filled with the smell of warm breads and pastries, mingled with coffee and tea. It was a beautiful day in Eugene—the temperature was in the mid-70s, and the sky was clear and sunny. So Adam and I chose to sit outside on the deck to enjoy the warm air.

Adam described himself as an "anarcho-primitivist." He had lived in Eugene for a long time, but he got his start in activism in the Bay Area in the 1960s.² As he put it, he had the "good fortune" to come of age in the Bay Area during the heyday of the radical 1960s activism. He worked in labor organizing, and he also started but didn't finish a graduate program in history. Adam was soft-spoken, and he had a great sense of humor. But the anarchist in him would seep through in his phrases and ideas. For example, he had a penchant for referring to the police as "pigs."

While sitting at the bakery, Adam and I chatted about our families, our writing processes, and the frustrations that come with trying to publish books. But I was mostly there to understand what happened in the late 1990s and early 2000s in Eugene. Why did it become the epicenter of the radical environmental movement and give birth to the ELF?[3] Adam finished his coffee and said, "If you want to understand what was going on [in Eugene], let me show you. We are right in the middle of where it all happened."

Adam pointed out that the New Day Bakery was in the Whiteaker neighborhood of Eugene. The Whiteaker, or as some people called it, the "Whit," was a mix of funky bungalows and large trees framing straight streets. On one of the streets in the neighborhood, a local artist had carved an animal sculpture from a rotted tree stump. And what I at first thought was a piece of plastic trash in the crook of the sculpture was a plastic bag that contained free condoms.

Adam walked me around and showed me the local co-op, as well as a few places where he and other activists had clashed with police. When we first talked, Adam told me that what made Eugene—and especially the Whiteaker neighborhood—so special was the collision of different kinds of activist energy: environmentalists, punk anarchists, and animal rights advocates all converging in one place.[4]

Tim Lewis, a longtime environmental activist, filmmaker, and resident of the Whiteaker, described the neighborhood similarly in a 2012 interview with the local newspaper as "a place that homeless people, poor people, anarchists, [and] a wide variety of types of freaks that existed in that area could go and not spend money."[5]

To Adam, the 1990s Whiteaker was humming with anarchists, hippies, and different affinity groups. There was a palpable energy, and Icky's Teahouse was its center. Icky's Teahouse was a mainstay in Eugene's counterculture scene during the brief time it was open in the mid-late 1990s.[6] As Adam told me, it was in kind of a grimy location in the Whiteaker neighborhood, and it served free food, fixed bikes, held punk shows, and served as a meeting place for Eugene's hippies, anarchists, and burgeoning forest defenders and eco-radicals. A 1996 concert at Icky's gives a glimpse into the Eugene scene. The concert was a punk show and a benefit concert. That wasn't unusual. However, the "cause" raised a few eyebrows. It was a concert to honor "Uncle Ted," as his supporters called him. But he was better known as Ted Kaczynski, the Unabomber.

While we were talking, Adam told me that there was an incident that marked a turning point for mid-1990s radical activism in Eugene.[7] In 1997 the city agreed to chop down forty trees to make way for a parking lot downtown. To try to block the trees from being cut down, activists from Cascadia Forest Defenders and Earth First! climbed the trees and began a tree-sitting protest. On June 1, 1997, Eugene police moved in to clear the activists. Riot police and a chain-link fence held back supporters of the tree-sitting activists, as police used pepper spray to remove the activists perched in the trees. After each activist was arrested, their tree was immediately cut down. Jim Flynn was the last tree-sitter left. Tim Lewis, the local documentarian, captured the scene with his video camera as it unfolded. Two police officers and a fireman blasted Flynn with multiple bottles of pepper spray for over an hour. They even cut his pant legs to spray his bare legs directly. Finally, they brought him down and hosed him off with a firehose. The footage, which appeared in the local news broadcast, was shocking even to those not as sympathetic to the activists. I remember watching this brutal scene in the documentary about the ELF, *If a Tree Falls: The Story of the Earth Liberation Front*. Adam made the point that this was one of the watershed events for the Eugene radical environmental scene. The activists from the woods had made their way back to the city.

The previous chapter highlighted the importance of punk and hardcore to the animal liberation movement, and the Eugene scene was no exception to this constellation; Eugene's punk community cross-pollinated with anarchists, animal liberation activists, and forest defenders, creating a unique, radical ecosystem. The music preached a message of no compromise. And as we'll see with the ELF, the activists who emerged from this scene embraced that same uncompromising ethos.

Adam was one of the main reasons I had traveled to Eugene. And it's not just because he was a good tour guide and host. It was because Adam and his writings were key to understanding what happened in the Eugene scene. As an anarcho-primitivist, he was one of the key voices pushing against civilization and technology. For a while Adam was even a close confidante of Ted Kaczynski after he was arrested. Adam supported Kaczynski and visited him in prison. But Adam and Kaczynski had a falling out over ideological directions in the revolutionary movements, rather than over Kaczynski's tactics (sending mail bombs). Adam's writings and marriage of anarchism, environmentalism, and anticivilization tendencies gave intellectual heft to Eugene's radical environmental scene of the 1990s.

To tell the story of the ELF, we have to trace two currents that existed in the mid-1990s. The first was the influence of Kaczynski's bombing campaign and manifesto on ecoradicals. The second was the marriage of forest defenders, anarchists, and punks in Eugene. And Adam stood at the center of both. When I asked Adam what explained the rise of the ELF, he paused for a moment and then said: "It was a confluence of the forest defenders, the tree sitters, and the urban crust punk scene [in Eugene], which was young and quite radical. I remember thinking that if they ever joined up, it would get interesting, and that's what happened."[8]

***

On April 24, 1995, Gilbert Murray, a forest industry lobbyist and president of the California Forest Association, picked up a heavy brown package about the size of a shoebox at the association's Sacramento office.[9] The moment he lifted it, the package exploded, killing Murray and causing significant damage to the building, which was just blocks from the state capitol.

Murray wasn't the person to whom the package was addressed. But the general target—a timber lobbying group—and the use of a sophisticated homemade bomb bore the hallmarks of a familiar suspect: the Unabomber. The unidentified suspect was given this name for his early focus on universities and airlines (UNiversity and Airline BOMbing).

This was the sixteenth bombing that would be attributed to the Unabomber, one in a spree of seemingly random mail bombs targeting university academics, technology companies and scientists, and forestry officials dating back to 1978. An interagency task force led by the FBI, with assistance from the Bureau of Alcohol, Tobacco, Firearms, and Explosives (ATF) and the U.S. Postal Inspector, was formed in 1979. But by 1995 it was no closer to finding a suspect. The Unabomber used sophisticated devices and didn't leave many clues. He took great pains to use everyday materials and scrap items as bomb components—and the victims seemed to be chosen at random.[10] The Unabomber investigation morphed into one of the longest and costliest in FBI's history, and yet even after the Murray bombing, they were no closer to finding a suspect.

In the days following the Murray bombing, the Unabomber mailed letters to several media outlets, including *The Washington Post* and *The New York Times*. In the demand letter addressed to *The New York Times*, the Unabomber insulted the FBI (calling them a "joke"). To try to throw investigators off his trail and make the FBI think that the bombings were the work of a large, underground group, the Unabomber also claimed that a terrorist group "FC" (Freedom Club) was behind the bombings. Finally, the Unabomber said that he was willing to "permanently desist from terrorist activities" if a major media outlet like *The New York Times, Newsweek*, or *Time* published his included 35,000-word manifesto entitled: "Industrial Society and Its Future."[11]

With the blessing of law enforcement—who were hoping publication of the manifesto would provide new clues from the public for the moribund investigation, and financial support from its newspaper rival, *The New York Times*—*The Washington Post* eventually published the Unabomber manifesto as a supplement to its paper on September 22, 1995.

The opening lines from the manifesto laid out the Unabomber's worldview:

> The Industrial Revolution and its consequences have been a disaster for the human race. They have greatly increased the life-expectancy of those of us who live in 'advanced' countries, but they have destabilized society, have made life unfulfilling, have subjected human beings to indignities, have led to widespread psychological suffering (in the Third World to physical suffering as well) and have inflicted severe damage on the natural world.[12]

To the Unabomber, technology and progress made life unfulfilling, atomized society, and led to destruction of the environment.[13]

He borrowed heavily from the French philosopher Jacques Ellul, but he also shared anticivilization views that were common in deep ecology circles among radical environmentalists.[14] The FBI had hoped that publication of the manifesto would lead to somebody from the public recognizing the writing. And that's exactly what happened. Linda Patrik told her husband, David Kaczynski, that the writing sounded like his brother, Theodore "Ted" Kaczynski, a reclusive former math professor who lived in an isolated cabin in Montana.[15] David went to the FBI with his suspicions about his brother. These suspicions were confirmed by the FBI, and Ted Kaczynski was arrested in his rural cabin in Montana in April 1996.

The arrest of Ted Kaczynski was a massive story. Details emerged that he had been a math prodigy and at the age of 16 attended Harvard, where he participated in more than 200 hours of brutal and humiliating experiments by the Harvard psychologist Henry Murray. These experiments were designed to stress and break down individuals by challenging their worldviews. Kaczynski got his PhD at the University of Michigan, and then in 1967, at twenty-five years of age, he became the youngest assistant professor at the University of California, Berkeley. He abruptly resigned two years later.[16]

Kaczynski's unusual background allowed many to dismiss him as an evil, misanthropic, reclusive genius. His story seemed to fit this archetype perfectly. He terrorized the country with his bombing campaign. And his threat to media organizations to publish his manifesto "or else" did little to dispel the idea that he was an evil genius. To save him from the death penalty, Kaczynski's own attorneys argued that he had a mental illness. They did this over Kaczynski's own objections that his actions were perfectly sane.[17] In January 1998, just before his long-delayed trial was to begin, he pleaded guilty and was sentenced to consecutive life sentences without the possibility of parole. In an article discussing the guilty plea, a staff writer for *The Washington Post* summed up the popular view of Kaczynski as a "schizophrenic hermit filled with rage against technological society" and a "terrorist . . . who killed three and maimed dozens more in a deranged campaign."[18] In June 2023, Kaczynski—who was suffering from late-stage cancer—committed suicide at the age of eighty-one in his prison cell.[19]

In radical environmental circles, Kaczynski's manifesto and actions were met with mixed reactions. To some within the radical environmental movement, particularly the deep ecology wing, Kaczynski represented an extreme but coherent worldview: technology and industrialization were not just threats to wilderness and nature but also to humanity. Few activists openly supported his use of bombing and violence against humans. Rather, many attempted to distance the movement from his actions. For instance, following Kaczynski's arrest in 1996, Craig Beneville, an editor at *Earth First! Journal*, said: "The Unabomber has been bombing people for a lot longer than Earth First! has even been in existence. There's no incitements to violence in the *Earth First! Journal*. It's exactly the opposite."[20]

When an ABC World News report in April 1996 linked Kaczynski with Earth First!, the *Earth First! Journal* editors responded with an open letter that began as follows:

> On Friday, April 5, the ABC news program World News Tonight with Peter Jennings aired a report linking the non-violent environmental group Earth First! with Theodore Kaczynski, the alleged Unabomber. The piece was riddled with distortions and inaccuracies and can only be described as a hit piece on Earth First! and the environmental movement. ABC's sensationalistic coverage has done serious damage to the reputation of the Earth First! movement, based on the word of Barry Clausen, an individual employed by the timber industry.[21]

But it was hard for activists to say that Kaczynski's ideas had nothing to do with radical environmentalism, when one of Kaczynski's core arguments was that more radical action was needed to protect wilderness. This idea had support within many pockets of the environmental movement. This partial embrace of Kaczynski, or Uncle Ted to his supporters, owed much to the growing influence of green anarchism that was popular in the Pacific Northwest environmental circles. And it's crucial for understanding the emergence of the ELF, whose first actions would take place in late 1995 and 1996—the period when the Kaczynski manifesto was first published and when he was eventually arrested. The green anarchism that was swirling in the Pacific Northwest advocated for more than simple monkeywrenching; it argued for active campaigns of sabotage. There's even evidence that Kaczynski tried to communicate with the green anarchists and anarcho-primitivists popular in the Pacific Northwest before his arrest.[22]

In this late 1990s and early 2000s, some activists began to openly embrace anarcho-primitivism, the idea that civilization stifles fundamental human needs and destroys nature. Many of its devotees were champions of Kaczynski and his actions and read *Green Anarchy* magazine, which was based in Eugene, Oregon, and was active from 2000 to 2008.[23]

John Zerzan, the Eugene-based anarcho primitivist, was one of the chief intellects behind *Green Anarchy*.[24] Zerzan was an influential voice for those fighting against civilization and technology. His 1994 book, *Future Primitive and Other Essays*, was widely read and cited by activists.[25] During the Kaczynski trial, Zerzan's support for and meetings with Kaczynski fostered wide notoriety for the ideas of green anarchy and primitivism.[26]

In 1995 Zerzan published a polemic entitled "Whose Unabomber?". Zerzan, while not endorsing all of Kaczynski's actions, criticized activists like Judi Bari, who tried to distance the movement from Kaczynski. He said:

> In fact, except for his targets, when have the many little (Nazi Adolf) Eichmanns who are preparing the Brave New World ever been called to account? . . . Is it unethical to try to stop those whose contributions are bringing an unprecedented assault on life? Or is it unethical to just accept our passive roles in the current zeitgeist of postmodern cynicism and know-nothingism? As a friend in California put it recently, when justice is against the law, only outlaws can effect justice.[27]

In 1999, Theresa Kintz, a former *Earth First! Journal* editor, interviewed Kaczynski from prison and wrote up her impressions in an article. The article was rejected by *Earth First! Journal*, but it later appeared in *Anarchy: A Journal of Desire Armed* and in the U.K.-based *Green Anarchist* magazine.[28] When Kintz asked Kaczynski about his influences, he responded: "I read Edward Abbey in mid-eighties and that was one of the things that gave me the idea that, 'yeah, there are other people out there that have the same attitudes that I do.' I read (Abbey's) *The Monkeywrench Gang*, I think it was. But what first motivated me wasn't anything I read. I just got mad seeing the machines ripping up the woods and so forth."

This ambivalent attitude toward Kaczynski reflected the broader crosscurrents present in the Pacific Northwest scene in the mid- to late 1990s. Earth First! had made large inroads in the 1980s and 1990s, but the burgeoning green anarchist movement had a harder edge to it.

My interview with Max, an academic, self-proclaimed antifascist who was involved with *Earth First! Journal*, helped clarify what was happening.[29] Max grew up in Texas, but as an anarchist he ended up squatting in apartments in New York City before making his way to *Earth First! Journal*. As he told me, there was all this energy in the Pacific Northwest in the late 1990s. Anti-civilizational green anarchism was taking shape and was being influenced by John Zerzan and others in Eugene. The ideas of green anarchism and *Green Anarchy* magazine were very "different than the hippy-ish *Earth First! Journal*," which took a more "social justice approach" and favored nonviolent tactics. As Max told me, the emergence of green anarchism in the mid-1990s led to a shift in tactics. People advocated explicitly insurrectionist tactics like arson and intense forms of sabotage beyond simple monkeywrenching, squatting buildings, robbing banks, and the like. For example, CrimethInc— an autonomous anarchist network that published zines and became prominent in the punk scene in the United States in the mid-1990s—also advocated for more militant direct action.[30]

And as Max told me, that's where the green anarchist scene that was taking root in Eugene and other parts of the Pacific Northwest diverged from Earth First! "They wanted to fight with cops. They [the green anarchists] had no interest in nonviolent civil disobedience. Their whole thing was to avoid getting arrested while doing as much damage as possible."

Kaczynski was a curious figure for the green anarchy movement. His actions and parts of his primitivist ideology were cheered and seemed to echo some of the deep ecology roots that had found their way into the green anarchy wing. But when you read Kaczynski's manifesto, *Industrial Society and Its Future*, you see his open contempt for leftists. Right after his introduction, which focuses on the problems of technology, he launches an extended diatribe against "leftists" in his section entitled "The Psychology of Modern Leftism." He refers to leftists as a "manifestation of craziness" (6) and "masochists" (20). And as Kaczynski himself said wrote in his 2008 book, *The Road to Revolution*, published from prison, "Whenever a movement of resistance begins to emerge, these leftists (or whatever you choose to call them) come swarming to it like flies to honey until they outnumber the original members, take it over, and turn it into just another leftist faction, thereby emasculating it. The history of Earth First! provides an elegant example of this process" (p.17).[31]

For all its nods to primitivism and deep ecology, green anarchism was fundamentally a leftist, liberatory, and anti-authoritarian ideology. And Kaczynski's actions behind bars at the ADX Florence Supermax in Colorado further raised questions among the green anarchists. He was housed with Timothy McVeigh, who carried out the 1995 Oklahoma City Bombing, and Ramzi Yousef, the mastermind of the 1993 World Trade Center bombing. Kaczynski became friendly with both, and their wing of the prison was known as "Bombers' Row."[32] Kaczynski bonded particularly with McVeigh over their love of survivalism and hatred of the government. In a letter to reporters Lou Michel and Dan Herbeck, Kaczynski gave his impression of McVeigh. While saying he disagreed with McVeigh's tactics in bombing the Alfred P. Murrah Federal Building, Kaczynski largely spoke positively of McVeigh, saying he was friendly and smart, and that he didn't believe McVeigh was a racist.[33]

***

The issues with Kaczynski soon became harder for radical environmental activists to ignore. Gavin, a self-described primal anarchist writer, was familiar with Kaczynski and his influence on the anarchist wing of the movement.[34] Gavin was a tough person to interview. We texted several times, and after I assured him that I was not writing a hit piece on the movement, he said he was willing to talk on the phone. Between doing chores around his house, Gavin recounted how he got involved in activism. He grew up in the suburbs in the Midwest and had a special relationship with the woods and forests around his house. He told me he first became politically active as a kid, when these woods were cut down to make room for a strip mall and new houses. Gavin also got involved in the local anarchist punk scene, and eventually he found his way to the green anarchy scene. He became a confidant of Kaczynski's while Kaczynski was in prison. But after a while Gavin began to see Kaczynski in an extremely negative light. He called him an inflexible "Maoist." And he cut his ties completely with him over his attitudes "on homosexuality, the patriarchy, and Ted's ignorance on social issues." Ted, as Gavin called Kaczynski, seemed more interested in trolling leftists, excusing the racism of McVeigh, and trying to understand Nazis than in actually fighting against authoritarians and the capitalist machine.

The uncomfortable truth was that while Ted Kaczynski wasn't part of the radical environmental movement, he drew heavily from its ideas, and he exerted a powerful influence on many activists. He read *The Monkey Wrench Gang* and *Earth First! Journal*, and he shared a deep suspicion of technology and modernity. His tactics were widely rejected by radical environmentalists, and many disagreed with his anti-leftist ideology. Yet at the same time, his writings were discussed and debated in zines and journals across the movement.

Max, the antifascist and academic, had a front-row seat to this paradox while involved at *Earth First! Journal*.[35] He saw Kaczynski and the deep ecology wing of the movement as potential gateways to more explicitly right-wing and ecofascist currents. To Max, these ideas had echoes of the pseudo race science of Madison Grant, the early 20th-century American conservationist and eugenicist. Max told me that Kaczynski's ideas and ecofascism couldn't be totally ignored by environmentalists. "The ecofascist side was always too close [for comfort to the radical environmental movement]. We never understood it. [Also,] Ted Kaczynski was this creepy Uncle Ted who was still around [like a relative] who we don't like. Yet he was still in our family, and we don't know what to do about it."

We'll return to this tension in Chapter 7, in which we examine how Kaczynski's ideas have been repackaged and embraced by parts of the extreme right and the ecofascist fringe. And in Chapter 9, we'll discuss how Kaczynski's critiques of technology are finding new resonance.[36]

In June 2023, I again reached out to Adam, the Eugene-based anarcho-primitivist with whom we started the chapter. I wanted to get his thoughts about Kaczynski's suicide in prison.[37] While mentioning his academic disagreement with Kaczynski over what precivilization society was really like, Adam told me that he felt that Kaczynski's antitech ideas were even more relevant now, with the recent emergence of AI and large language models (LLMs). Adam told me that we were "so fully engulfed by onrushing technology," and that he continues "to endorse *Industrial Society and its Future* to one and all; [it's] needed more than ever."

***

In the early morning hours of October 19, 1998, the Vail Ski Resort in Colorado was engulfed in flames. The night before, activists had set fire to the resort's ski lifts and lodgings. It took more than seventy firefighters from around the region to eventually put out the flames, but not before the arson had done $12 million in damage—making it one of the costliest acts of eco-sabotage in U.S. history.[38] The resort was targeted by activists associated with the ELF. Shortly after the arson, the activists sent the following communique from a Denver library:[39]

> On behalf of the lynx, five buildings and four ski lifts at Vail were reduced to ashes on the night of Sunday, October 18th. Vail, Inc. is already the largest ski operation in North America and now wants to expand even further. The 12 miles of roads and 885 acres of clearcuts will ruin the last, best lynx habitat in the state. Putting profits ahead of Colorado's wildlife will not be tolerated. This action is just a warning. We will be back if this greedy corporation continues to trespass into wild and unroaded areas. For your safety and convenience we strongly advise skiers to choose other destinations until Vail cancels its inexcusable plans for expansion.[40]

The communique was signed "the Earth Liberation Front (ELF).

This anonymous environmental activist group calling itself the ELF had burst onto the scene two years earlier, in October 1996. Their first action took place at the Detroit, Oregon, station where they set a small fire that was easily put out, and they spray painted "Earth Liberation Front" on the walls. Two nights later, they succeeded in burning down the Oakridge U.S. Forest Ranger station.

Both arsons occurred within a short drive of Eugene, Oregon, and both used homemade timed incendiary devices fashioned from gas cans and milk jugs. The damage to the ranger station was substantial—close to $5 million.[41] Even more than the damage, it represented an escalation in tactics from the days of forest defense and monkeywrenching. And it was all happening in the Pacific Northwest, around Eugene, the hotbed of green anarchism.

Many of the activists who became part of the ELF had cut their teeth on prior forest defense campaigns. The 1995–1996 Warner Creek forest defense campaign was one of the largest and most intense.[42] Less than an hour outside of Eugene, activists dug in to prevent the logging of old-growth forests. Over nearly a year, and through the bitterly cold and snowy winter, the activists set up an encampment and blockaded the forest road. They dug trenches and they chained themselves to heavy concrete barrels to prevent the U.S. Forest Service and lumber companies from gaining access to the forest. Eventually, the encampment was cleared, but the forest was saved. Warner Creek was a victory for activists and was even turned into a documentary titled *Pickaxe* (1999).[43]

The name Earth Liberation Front comes from the early 1990s in the U.K. A group of disaffected Earth First! activists referring to themselves as "Elves" created a separate umbrella under which they could carry out and claim more intense actions, like property destruction and arson.[44] This was an escalation from the tree-sits and small-scale sabotage that characterized Earth First!–style monkeywrenching. ELF cells eventually began popping up in the United States, particularly in the Pacific Northwest in the mid-1990s. From the beginning, the ELF was not a formal organization with membership rosters and a defined hierarchy. Rather, fitting with the green anarchy ideology, it was a leaderless group of autonomous cells that would agree on a tactic and a target, and then carry out an action. Much like the ALF, anybody could carry out actions in the name of the ELF if they adhered to the following principles:

(1) To cause as much economic damage as possible to a given entity that is profiting off the destruction of the natural environment and life for selfish greed and profit,

(2) To educate the public on the atrocities committed against the environment and life,
(3) To take all necessary precautions against harming life.[45]

Given its underground, clandestine nature, it's hard to say precisely how many attacks the ELF carried out. For instance, a 2013 U.S. Department of Homeland Security (DHS) report counted 239 arsons and bombing attacks, 55% of which they attributed to the ELF and 45% to the ALF.[46] In the dataset I put together for this book, I counted more than 150 actions carried out by the ELF, most of which occurred between 1999 and 2002 (the peak of the data from Figures 1 and 2 in Chapter 1).

Some of the most notable attacks carried out by the ELF include:

- The 1998 Vail, Colorado, ski lodge resort arson
- The December 1999 arson at the Monmouth, Oregon, headquarters of Boise Cascade Timber
- The December 1999 arson at a Michigan State University agricultural research lab conducting research on genetically engineering crops
- The August 22, 2003, destruction of more than a hundred sport utility vehicles at dealerships and other sites in California's San Gabriel Valley.

The ELF's calling cards were arson and anonymous communiqués to claim responsibility. The group was divided between those who carried out actions and those who spoke publicly. After an action, ELF activists would send unsigned communiqués to the aboveground spokespeople to publish. The communiqués explained the motivation, the choice of target, and the tactics, and would claim the action in the name of the Earth Liberation Front.

From the late 1990s to the early 2000s, Leslie Pickering and Craig Rosebraugh—two Portland-based activists who lived just 110 miles north of Eugene—served as these aboveground spokespeople for the ELF via the North American Earth Liberation Front Press Office (NAELFPO). Both Pickering and Rosebraugh frequently gave interviews to local papers and national media organizations about the ELF.[47]

A U.S. House committee even subpoenaed Rosebraugh to testify about the movement in 2002.[48]

It's important to emphasize that during the crucial period of 1995–2005, there was considerable overlap between the ELF and the ALF. It's true that the origins of the ALF in the Bands of Mercy were very different from those of Earth First! But the Northwest in the mid- to late 1990s was awash in ideas of total liberation—human, animal, and environmental. And the influence of animal liberation on the ELF was undeniable.

Many actions during this period that were carried out by ELF were also jointly claimed by ALF. In my dataset, I counted more than thirty actions jointly claimed by both groups. And many of the activists in the largest ELF cell who were arrested in 2005 had backgrounds in animal liberation.[49] Both Craig Rosebraugh and Leslie Pickering also got their start in animal liberation, and Rosebraugh himself was a spokesperson for some of the ALF's actions.

The federal government dubbed the leaderless ELF and ALF clique "The Family" and accused them of being behind several prominent attacks, notably the Vail Ski Lodge arson attack in 1998. These ELF and ALF activists came from a variety of backgrounds. They included disaffected Earth First!ers, animal liberation folks, and anarchist punk kids, and their epicenter was Eugene, Oregon.

For instance, the ELF activist Joseph Dibee, who fled the country after being indicted in 2006 for burning a horse slaughterhouse and was later extradited in 2018 from Cuba, was active in environmental causes before the ELF.[50] Others, like Kevin Tubbs and Daniel McGowan, were animal rights activists before getting involved in the ELF.[51] Chelsea Gerlach was born into a hippy activist family and grew up in Oregon. Her parents even got *Earth First! Journal* and mailings from Sea Shepherd.[52] As a young high school environmentalist, Chelsea helped maintain hiking trails, but after witnessing clear cuts of her beloved forests by timber companies, she became an activist. Jacob Ferguson was a punk anarchist kid from Eugene. He had a heroin habit, which law enforcement would eventually use to turn him into an informant.[53] Bill Rodgers, aka Avalon, had a background in Earth First!. He had participated in tree-sits and forest defense campaigns across the West, including those in Cove Mallard, Idaho.[54] It was at the Warner Creek forest defense from 1995-1996 that the core of these activists would form the ELF/ALF cell dubbed "the Family" by law enforcement.

The ELF/ALF actions were also happening against the backdrop of a broader anarchist movement in the Pacific Northwest. Many Eugene-based anarchists were active in other left-wing causes, and several attended the massive 1999 World Trade Organization protests in Seattle, referred to as the "Battle of Seattle" by activists. The protests were carried out by a mix of union activists, anarchists, and anti-globalization activists and were attended by more than 35,000 protesters.[55] Ahead of the WTO summit, protesters engaged in civil disobedience chaining themselves together downtown, while a small group of anarchists dressed in black smashed windows and vandalized property.[56] Many criticized the Seattle police response to the activists as heavy handed, especially their liberal use of tear gas and mass arrests.[57]

To anti-globalization activists, the 1999 WTO protests were a success. They had disrupted the WTO meeting, built a tentative alliance with certain labor groups, and flexed their anti-globalization muscles. In many ways, it represented a highwater mark for the radical Pacific Northwest scene.[58] Anti-globalization was one plank in the broader liberation platform popular among green anarchists. The ELF activists were sympathetic to the Seattle WTO protests and the broader anti-globalization moment. Following the 1999 Seattle WTO protests—which many Eugene anarchists attended—Eugene's Republican Mayor Jim Torrey referred to his city as the "anarchist capital of the world."[59] There was some truth in the mayor's statement. Five months prior to the WTO protests, Eugene had its own anti-globalization protest turn into a riot, where nearly 300 anarchists and activists clashed with police, leading the Eugene police to tear-gas the protesters and arrest fifteen of them.[60]

***

I remember my interview with Nathan vividly[61]—mainly because it was so hard to interview him in the first place. Nathan was a former activist involved in the direct action movement, and he moved in the same circles as the ELF. We had been emailing back and forth. Several activists had vouched for me with Nathan, but judging by his noncommittal responses to my emails, in which he repeatedly wrote, "maybe" and "I'm busy, don't have the bandwidth to chat right now," he was skeptical.

After a few months passed, it turned out that I had interviewed enough people who Nathan knew that he said he was willing to chat. I liked Nathan right away. He was blunt. One of the first things he asked me was whether I was actually going to write this book. He said he'd spoken with a few academics before, done interviews, and nothing ever came of them.

Nathan grew up on the East Coast and was involved in human rights work after college. He initially thought of "human rights and the environment as separate [issues]." After college, he was living in a city, and he was walking through a park one day when he was approached by a woman who tried to get him to sign a petition to protect dogs and cats. She gave him some literature, which he read. Nathan had always had a soft spot for animals, and he agreed with much of the literature. Pretty soon he found himself in an animal rights activist group, regularly protesting outside of fur stores. From animal rights activism he started going to a radical anarchist bookstore where he discovered Dave Foreman's classic book on monkeywrenching, *Ecodefense: A Field Guide to Monkeywrenching*, as well as *Earth First! Journal*. Nathan quickly became hooked on activism. He went to an Earth First! gathering, was arrested for civil disobedience, and then in the mid-1990s made his way out to the Pacific Northwest, the hub of where it seemed everything was happening.

Nathan also emphasized that he was primed for "direct action from the get-go." Despite it being his pathway into activism, he wasn't interested in tabling for groups like the Sierra Club or PETA. Direct action for him was simple: you had to put your body on the line to stop the bad thing from happening. And as Nathan saw it, the bad things and bad people were those who were abusing animals and destroying or polluting the planet. While we were chatting, Nathan was also quick to point out that he was different from some of the folks in the ELF scene. He said that he "didn't identify as an anarchist and wasn't from the punk scene."

As Nathan spent more time in the Pacific Northwest scene, he realized that he wanted to make the biggest impact, and that's how he said he "ended up involved in arson." He told me, "I liked the idea we [activists committing arson and sabotage] could be a deterrent . . .

a kind of eco defense, become a pain in the ass [to the companies and polluters], and invisible. This was the 'Elves' thing [what ELF activists sometimes called themselves]." Nathan also emphasized that clandestine action suited him. He wasn't drawn to public actions, but rather saw himself as an activist "worker bee" who wasn't in it for the glory. Nathan said he felt satisfaction seeing his and others' actions publicized in the zines and *Earth First! Journal.* He told me that pre–social media, this "DIY (do-it yourself) politics" aesthetic was crucial to its success.

Nathan also made three points that really stuck with me. First, he said that the ELF was carrying out "highly technical actions," using timed incendiary devices. For instance, a fire at a University of Washington horticulture lab in 2001 was started by a device that was constructed using digital timers, parts from model rockets, and road flares all wrapped in matches.[62] But Nathan said these sophisticated devices were not easily replicable, and that the actions were harder to carry out than the earlier ELF actions, which just involved gas cans and a lighter.

Second, he said something that surprised me. Nathan recounted that part of what attracted law enforcement attention to the ELF was that on the heels of the Unabomber, "there was a fear that we [the ELF and other activists] would graduate to killing people." Nathan didn't just write this off as nonsense. The ELF had a stated goal of not harming living things. But Nathan told me that there was a certain momentum and escalation to the ELF tactics. He implied that if things went on long enough, members might target corporate CEOs or others harming animals or the environment.

Finally, Nathan said that the clandestine nature of activism was grinding. "Living underground . . . it's exhausting to lie [to your friends and family]. I had to say I was going camping or hiking [all the time]. The recon [of targets] and the lying was exhausting."

***

When I met with Nicole, the activist lawyer introduced in the Preface, during a visit to Eugene in May 2024, she echoed Nathan's point about the double lives of many in the ALF/ELF's cell.[63] She told me the simultaneous arrests of these ELF core activists in December 2005 shocked her. Nicole had been in and around the Eugene activist scene since the late 1990s, while in law school. When she saw the list of those arrested, she was taken aback. How could these people be involved with the ELF? She thought it was "a horrible witch hunt." In Nicole's words, "I was in my mid-twenties, the same age as many of the ELF folks. I worked as a law clerk and ran out to do tree-sits on the weekend with these folks—they were peers; I thought they were my peers. I just was a lawyer, and they were activists." But it turned out that some of these activist peers were living double lives and involved in a clandestine group that the government labeled the number-one domestic terror threat after 9/11.[64]

Cameron—the former soldier turned activist I met in the Pacific Northwest in 2024 and whom we first encountered in Chapter 1—had a lot to say about the ELF.[65] Why was the ELF able to sustain such an intense period of action? To him the answer was the geography and energy of the Eugene scene. As he said, "the ELF and the ALF were primarily on the West Coast in the U.S. But there was a culture built in Eugene and Olympia, Washington, that was built like a community and home. One could ask the question how could some of the most radical and militant actions come out of the weird confluence of events in the Pacific Northwest? If I were to design the perfect campaign, it would be a place-based campaign, and that has all the mechanisms, and you drive two hours to a target and go home." And that's what the ELF had in the Pacific Northwest.

***

The bulk of the people I interviewed for this book were activists. This was by design. I was interested in understanding the movement and its strategies through their eyes. But the Pacific Northwest, and the Eugene scene specifically, were so important and the target of such intense law enforcement that I wanted to get a different perspective.

I reached out to Jack, a veteran Eugene police officer who was involved in investigating the ELF cases.[66] I wanted to know how law enforcement viewed the anarchist hotbed of Eugene. Jack had salt-and-pepper hair, glasses, and a soft-spoken, but plain way of speaking that belied his decades of experience in law enforcement. He was born in Colorado, but he eventually made his way to Eugene in the 1980s. One of his first assignments was carrying out intelligence for the organized crime unit in Eugene. They were going after the last vestiges of Weather

Underground–like, leftist activity. But then Jack transferred out of the unit. It wouldn't be until the mid-1990s that he started making his way back into the intelligence unit in Eugene. And by this time the activist landscape had changed, and anarchists and radical environmentalists were attracting the attention of law enforcement in a big way. Jack told me about the 1996 burning of the Oakridge Ranger Station, an hour outside of Eugene.[67] He said that he heard whispers of this "pocket... of the ELF and the ALF [activists] that combined resources [of the two groups]." Put this together with the "radical anarchist ideology" and talk of revolution, and the Eugene Police Department had a big problem on their hands.

Jack mentioned two other things during our conversation. First, he emphasized that the ELF and the ALF activists were just one part of a much larger, thriving anarchist scene in Eugene. He and other law enforcement officers knew that activists from Eugene had participated in the 1999 WTO protests in Seattle, as well as in local actions. "The anarchists were doing nightly raids, small-scale [arsons], and protests [in and around Eugene]."

The second point Jack made was more unexpected. He brought up the activists involved in the Warner Creek blockade from 1995 to 1996. This was the protest that lasted over 300 days and ultimately succeeded in stopping the logging of Warner Creek.[68] It was also where many of the core ELF/ALF activists cut their teeth. Jack made it clear to me that he found much of the ELF and ALF ideology to be "ultra-radical anarchist junk," and he considered the use of arson unforgivable. But when talking about the Warner Creek blockade, he showed grudging admiration. He told me, "They [the activists] were trench dwellers, they grew up in the forests, they were comfortable in that environment, they were earth muffins, it was a special group of people who had the wherewithal to stand the cold." And then he made the most surprising statement of the interview:

> It's kind of interesting, looking back at clearcutting of old-growth forests [here in Oregon]. Had it not been for them [and other activists], we wouldn't have any old-growth forests [left]. Stopping some bad forest-management tactics.... It wouldn't have happened, honestly, if they [the activists] hadn't been so radical.

Here was Jack, a veteran law enforcement officer who helped put many of these same activists in prison, expressing admiration and even grudging support while looking back on their forest defense tactics at Warner Creek.

After we talked, Jack put me in touch with his friend and fellow police officer, Rick, who was deeply involved in the ELF investigation. Rick was hired out of college by the Eugene Police Department and assigned to their bomb squad. He told me that was how he first became aware of the ALF and the ELF.

"It was Christmas morning in 1995; I get a phone call that we got some [incendiary] devices that we needed to render safe. The ALF had spray-painted 'meat is murder,' and this was before anybody had any idea what ALF was. We thought it was a disgruntled employee. And then about two years later, the national press office of the ALF and media [began publicizing actions], and that's when they started claiming everything."[69]

As a bomb squad officer in Eugene, Rick grew to recognize the ELF's signature in certain incendiary devices: "Two 1-litre bottles, with a sponge soaked with fuel, and then it was all wrapped with an incense stick.... that was their first generation [of devices]."

Like Jack, Rick described how Eugene in the mid-1990s was an activist hotbed: "[You had people associated with] the *Earth First! Journal* and *Green Anarchy* magazine. It was a hybrid–mix of everything–anarchists, the ELF, the ALF, and deep green folks." He even talked about the first day that he was assigned to the special investigation unit that would start focusing on the ELF and the ALF cell dubbed "The Family." "June 18th, 1999, was my first day in the special investigation unit. We lost the city, during a massive riot, dealing with all of the anarchists. We lost. They [the anarchists] took over. That was my welcome to the unit." Rick was referring to the Eugene riot that preceded the 1999 WTO Seattle protests by a few months.

We will come back to Jack and Rick in the next chapter, when we talk about their role in Operation Backfire and the crackdown on the radical environmental movement in the early 2000s.

***

One of the ELF's calling cards was their use of communiqués to claim responsibility and explain their actions. And that's why I wanted to talk to Blake.⁷⁰ He was a longtime ecoactivist and documentary filmmaker and was involved with publicizing the ELF's communiqués. While a student in Portland in the early 1990s, Blake got his start in activism protesting the Persian Gulf War. From there he moved into animal rights and environmental activism. He was arrested a few times in the mid-late 1990s for carrying out civil disobedience targeting fur stores and anti–animal abuse actions.

In 1996, Blake began to receive communiqués from the ALF. To him it was easy to support the ALF actions, and he agreed to publicize them. Blake wanted to let "the public know there was a purpose behind a particular mink release. . . .[The] ALF opening cages was easy for me to support—it was just supporting [petty] theft, vandalism, or trespassing [to save animals]." Shortly after publicizing the ALF actions, Blake and others began receiving some of the first communiqués from the ELF. He told me he was a bit more ambivalent about the actions. "When the first communication came in from the ELF, that involved fire. There were some moments of conflict [internally]. As long as no-one was harmed, I felt I should still put it out. . . . I wanted to let people know what happened and why."

While Blake felt some queasiness about arson as a tactic, he didn't see it as terrorism. "The nonviolent thing was always tenuous. Nobody was hurt, but fire is violent. It's [also] categorically different from McVeigh or Kaczynski. The whole notion of [non-]violence was never a clear line with the ELF (to me)."

Yet, Blake could also sympathize with the ELF activists. Later he found out who was involved in the ELF following the arrests in 2005. These were folks who had also been involved in forest defense and civil disobedience. He empathized with their dilemma. "If at some point your strategies and tactics are not working—what do you do after XYZ? It's relative, based on your opinion. But it's almost a form of insanity to keep doing these nonviolent, ineffective tactics. You either give up or [you] decide to do something else. And they [the ELF] tried to take the fight to a new level and to influence directly the companies responsible for the destruction of the environment."

Yet along with the repression that the ELF tactics triggered, Blake looked back at many of the ELF's strategic choices as mistakes. "They [activists] can't just be an isolated wing [like the ELF]. It will happen to any movement that has a splinter movement." But to Blake, the mistake was that the ELF operated like a vanguard movement and didn't want or build a mass movement.

But not everyone shared Blake's view of the ELF. Jesse—the punk skateboarder introduced in Chapter 3, who later became a spokesperson for the group—had a very different take.[71] Unlike Blake, he didn't see all ELF tactics as a mistake. He largely saw the ELF and the other anarchist impulses around the WTO as a winning strategy, challenging the power of the state and corporations. To Jesse it was largely successful:

> The fact that we built our movement as a gut movement and passion and even a base understanding of intersectionality and anticapitalism—that was pretty sound. There was bad stuff and personal behavior that wasn't great, but to me, I think that's how social change is made. You can get little things by being polite. But if you are talking about an overthrow of the established order or end of the exploitation of the environment, that takes radical action.

And to Jesse that's exactly what the ELF brought. He couldn't resist taking a shot at mainstream activists, saying, "It's only liberals who would think that [peaceful protest] is the way the world works and who limit themselves to being kind and civil when there are lives [on the line] and the whole world is being annihilated [by climate change]."

Jesse also wanted to correct my view that the radical environmental movement had disappeared. Think about "Antifa," he said, "it's the same movement [and many of the same people] from the Earth First!, ELF, WTO [1999 protests] days . . . the people tearing down Confederate Flags at Black Lives Matter marches, and the people who smashed police cars after George Floyd's murder [in 2020]. It is the same movement . . . and the ELF was a part of that."

It's worth noting that Jesse's notion of a movement is quite different from mine. He views all broadly left-leaning movements that engage in sabotage or property destruction as the same. In contrast, I see a movement as a group of individuals who share (1) a common worldview and ethos, (2) a subcultural background and social network, and (3) an agreed-upon set of tactics.

The disagreement between Jesse and Blake over the ELF's tactics echoes debates in other movements over the risks versus reward of radical action. For example, during the U.S. Civil Rights Movement there were fierce arguments about whether militant Black activists helped the cause by making mainstream actors appear more reasonable. Or did they hurt it by allowing opponents to paint the entire movement as "radical"?[72] There was a similar tension within the antiwar left. In the late 1960s, the Weather Underground splintered from Students for a Democratic Society (SDS) out of frustration with what they saw as inaction—convinced that only more confrontational tactics could bring about revolutionary change.[73]

The pace of the ELF actions and the level of notoriety they achieved ensured that activists to this day are still debating their tactics and impact. I interviewed Cedric, an Earth First! organizer who was active during the ELF era.[74] He told me that he was "on the other side of the ELF" debate that was happening in *Earth First! Journal* and was openly critical of the ELF's broader vanguard strategy. As Cedric told me, "Much praise for the ELF, but it's a politics of despair—when people had given up on building a mass ecology movement, and lacked the discipline to build a mass base, and target fault lines, and [instead] there was a 'story of the righteous few' [the ELF]."

Cedric was not alone in his critique of the ELF strategy. Dylan, a gray-haired academic and activist who was a follower of Murray Bookchin, the social ecologist, saw the ELF tactics as a mistake.[75] Dylan said that with the "ELF [came] the fetishization of property damage, [and] that's when things go off the rails."

***

During my research, many people brought up the book *How to Blow up a Pipeline*, by Swedish author and academic Andreas Malm. In this book, Malm argues that the stakes of climate change call for sabotage and massive civil disobedience to halt global warming and stop fossil fuels.[76] His book was made into a film that was released in 2022, but it wasn't a documentary film. Rather, it was a slick, fictionalized thriller about a group of young people from different backgrounds and with different motivations who decide to blow up a pipeline in Texas.

In his book, Malm also offered a sharp critique of the ELF. He argued that their actions were largely ineffectual because they weren't connected to a broader mass movement and thus lacked impact.[77]

As you can guess, many ELF-affiliated activists had strong opinions about Malm. Nathan, the activist who was associated with the ELF, grew visibly frustrated when I brought up Malm's name during our interview. He pointed out Malm's inconsistency: Malm, he said, was a revolutionary writer who didn't have the stomach for actual activism and was no better than "an armchair asshole."[78]

Jesse, the former ELF spokesperson, also was visibly irritated when I brought up Malm's name and his critique of the ELF. He told me that Malm fundamentally didn't understand the ELF and anarchism more generally. "Malm is a Leninist, and he is an authoritarian, and he's not an anarchist. He endorses eco sabotage and he wants to prod the state into solving–the state to do what it should be doing."[79]

It is important to keep in mind that post-2001 ELF and ALF actions were happening against the backdrop of the 9/11 security state and the Global War on Terrorism. Increasingly, the government and law enforcement referred to the ELF and the ALF as ecoterrorists. Eric Devericks, a cartoonist with *The Seattle Times*, even published an editorial cartoon in 2008 comparing the ELF to Al-Qaida. In the cartoon, an ELF activist holds a gas can next to a smoldering building while Osama Bin Laden looks on. The cartoon ELF activist says, "the ends justify the means," and the cartoon image of Bin Laden replies, "Amen, brother."[80] Devericks in his op-ed noted that "Earth Liberation Front members are no better than Al Qaida terrorists. In my opinion, they are terrorists. They have an established pattern of using destruction and fear to bring about a change in behavior.... When this tactic doesn't work, how do they escalate it? Is it really such a stretch to imagine one of these cowards targeting those they consider the most egregious environmental offenders for death."[81]

There's a larger debate about whether property destruction even qualifies as terrorism.[82] But the rhetoric of labeling the ELF and other radical environmentalists as terrorists did have an effect. Not only did the terrorism label bring increased law enforcement pressure on activists, but it also put mainstream environmental activists into a bind.

Brett, the direct action organizer whom we met in Chapter 3, echoed this point about the chilling effect of the ecoterrorism label:[83] "People's fear of being associated with the terrorism word—particularly for a lot of labor movements and non-profits who were into direct action but were scared of being called into Congress and being called a terrorist: that's the bulk of the reason for the demise [of the radical movement]."

I asked Charles, an academic who has studied and written extensively on radical environmental activism during this period, what effect he thought the ELF and the ecoterrorism label had on the broader movement.[84] He opined that "mainstream activists had to always worry whether they were being recorded—is there a chance somebody snaps a picture of me with an 'ecoterrorist.' People need to be careful about bringing down state repression on a movement. And the irony is, that's exactly what happened with the movement. The radical actions of the ELF and others brought the power of the state down on them."

As we close this chapter, it's worth returning to the importance of place and to the scene that made the ELF possible. Eugene in the 1990s was awash in radical ideas: Kaczynski's anti-tech message, green anarchism, punk, animal rights, and forest defense. This mix helped spark one of the most intense and militant waves of environmental activism in U.S. history.

To its supporters, the ELF achieved both symbolic wins and plenty of notoriety. Their tactics were bold. Their communiqués kept the media and public engaged. And law enforcement was unable to arrest them. This combination pushed the ELF and ALF to the top of the FBI's domestic terror threat list.

As I discuss in the next chapter, this notoriety came at a high cost. It would draw the attention of law enforcement and make activists the target for crippling repression.[85]

5

Repression and Operation Backfire

"Can I see your faculty ID?"

I replied, "excuse me, you want to see my faculty ID?" I was a bit taken aback, but I dug into my wallet and pulled out my faded faculty ID. I hadn't used it since locking myself out of my office on the American University campus a few months prior. I held my ID up to the screen of the Zoom call, and I said, "Does this work?"

Grace said, "Sure, that works. It appears you are who you claimed to be."[1] She laughed a bit as she said this, but I could also tell she wanted to check. I was puzzled. Grace was an advisor for youth climate justice activists in the Pacific Northwest and didn't strike me as particularly radical as far as activists go. I would find out later that Grace had done a bit more than just advising. She had even spent a brief stint in jail, stemming from her participation in an oil pipeline blockade.[2] But still, the faculty ID request took me by surprise.

***

Several activists I spoke with told me that I had to talk to Nicole—the activist lawyer based in the Pacific Northwest, who had been involved in the movement since the height of the ELF and whom we met earlier in the book. One activist said to me, "Look, if you want to understand the depth of repression and legal entanglements [faced by the movement], you have to talk to Nicole. She's seen it all."[3] In the spring of 2024, when I knew I was going to be traveling to the Pacific Northwest, I had one of my activist contacts reach out to her to set up a meeting. Nicole responded and told me that she would be delighted to meet in person when I was out there. I responded "great!" and sent her a Google Calendar invite for the agreed-upon date. Nicole quickly rejected the Google Calendar invite and said, "Sorry, we don't use Google products for security reasons" but assured me that she had put our meeting in her calendar. She also said that the publicly listed address of her office was just a mailing address and that they kept their real address private for "security reasons." She passed along the real location of her office.

Fast-forward a few weeks. I finally arrived at Nicole's office on the outskirts of a college town in the Pacific Northwest.[4] As advertised, her office was in a nondescript neighborhood, and there was nothing on the building to indicate that it was an activist law office. I rang the secure doorbell and Nicole answered. She had long blonde hair and a laid-back demeanor. Her office was comfortable and had pictures of various actions on the wall, supporting other activist campaigns. There even was a small poster from the documentary film about the ELF, *If a Tree Falls*.

Nicole's calm demeanor was underpinned by a fierce commitment to activism. While we chatted, I noticed a large, beautiful husky-type dog that lay on the floor of her office. Nicole started off our conversation by mentioning what a crazy time it was to be in her position as a "movement lawyer." She was advising campus activists about their rights in relation to the crackdowns during the Israel-Palestine protests in 2023 and 2024. She was also advising defendants in Georgia who were ensnared in a series of legal cases related to the protests to halt construction of a police training center in the forests south of Atlanta, known as the Stop Cop City movement. Finally, Nicole chuckled and said, "Oh yeah, and there's the 2024 election coming too." I then asked about her previously mentioned aversion to using Google products, and the unmarked office. She smiled and told me that it wasn't that she was paranoid, as some of even her friends accused her of being. She was just cautious because she was familiar with the history of the movement and because of her own "lived experience."

As isolated incidents, my interactions with Grace and Nicole would simply be considered unique anecdotes that come from interviewing people. Yet, these kinds of security-conscious interviews became part of a pattern throughout my fieldwork for this book. Some of the environmental activists asked me how my interviews with them differed from those I'd conducted in other places with political conflict, like Ukraine, Turkey, or Israel. I would usually respond: "You guys are a lot more paranoid." That would get a laugh, and I would say, "I am semi-kidding, but not really." And then their response would invariably be some form of, "Have you read up on [what happened with] the Green Scare?" The Green Scare "definitely affected how I thought about the world, and I have a lot of thoughts on that shit."[5]

The Green Scare, as mentioned earlier, refers to the period in the 2000s when the federal government declared radical animal rights and environmental activists the number-one domestic terror threat.[6] At the center of this crackdown was Operation Backfire (2004–2006), which involved a multi-agency task force made up of Oregon state and local police, the FBI, and the ATF. The task force targeted, and ultimately dismantled, the ELF and ALF cell operating in the Pacific Northwest, a group that the government called "The Family."

As we'll see, the Green Scare crippled the movement and continues to cast a long shadow over activists to this day.

***

It's hard to pinpoint the exact start of the Green Scare, but a hearing before the innocuously named "House Resources Committee, Subcommittee on Forests and Forest Health" in February 2002 set the stage. The hearing took place a little over five months after the 9/11 terrorist attacks. The topic of the hearing was domestic extremism. But the focus wasn't on Salafi-jihadism, or right-wing extremism. Rather, the topic was "ecoterrorism." This hearing would serve as a preview for the coming Green Scare.

In prepared remarks during the hearing, the FBI Domestic Terrorism Section Chief, James F. Jarboe, laid out to members of the House committee the growing threat from "special interest extremism, as characterized by the Animal Liberation Front (ALF) and the Earth

Liberation Front (ELF)."[7] Jarboe described how the FBI defined ecoterrorism as "the use or threatened use of violence of a criminal nature against innocent victims or property by an environmentally oriented, subnational group for environmental-political reasons, or aimed at an audience beyond the target, often of a symbolic nature." The key piece of the FBI definition was the inclusion of the word "property." Thus, when activists carried out vandalism or property destruction, it could be considered terrorism. Jarboe further said that the FBI had estimated that the ALF and the ELF had committed more than "600 criminal acts" leading to more than $40 million in damage since 1996. During his testimony, Jarboe also listed several prominent arrests of environmental and animal rights activists, but he also emphasized the difficulty in penetrating these "ecoterrorist" groups. In his conclusion Jarboe said that more law enforcement resources were being put into these ecoterrorism cases, and they were hopeful about results.[8]

But it wasn't just FBI officials like Jarboe who testified. Craig Rosebraugh, the spokesperson for the ELF, also delivered prepared remarks.[9] In a long statement citing Thomas Jefferson's ideas of liberty, the oppression of Black and Indigenous peoples by the U.S. government, and the importance of forests, Rosebraugh bashed the very idea of the hearing and the concept of "ecoterrorism." Rosebraugh said that to him terrorism meant violence, which meant actually harming humans. "Yet, in the history of the Earth Liberation Front," he said, "both in North America and abroad in Europe, no one has ever been injured by the group's many actions." To Rosebraugh, the hearing was a farce. He then listed his run-ins with law enforcement since becoming the ELF spokesperson: seven grand jury subpoenas, two raids on his home and work, confiscated property, and constant surveillance by federal agents—all without any charges or any information to aid FBI investigation. Rosebraugh concluded his testimony by saying that both law enforcement and the committee seemed bent on "harassing and targeting [him] for simply voicing [his] ideological support for those involved in environmental protection."

The 2002 hearing laid out the stakes. Ecoterrorism was a major domestic terror threat, and the full weight of federal law enforcement would come down on activists. Activists even distantly associated with the ALF and the ELF would eventually feel the pressure of law enforcement. This repression would leave a deep scar and reshape the broader movement.

***

The Operation Backfire investigation, like many successful criminal investigations, hinged on good luck and bad life choices. In early 2003, law enforcement were looking into a series of arsons carried out on behalf of the ELF, but they had hit a brick wall. There was little evidence to go on. But going back through their notes, investigators noticed that shortly after a 2001 car dealership fire carried out by the ELF, a woman filed a police report claiming her former housemate, Jacob Ferguson, had stolen a truck. The woman later withdrew the report. But another woman followed up to check on the status of this withdrawn report. The police started to get suspicious, and they decided they should give Ferguson a closer look.[10]

Ferguson's appearance wasn't exactly subtle. He was heavily tattooed, including a pentagram on his forehead, and had piercing eyes.[11] Having participated in the Warner Creek blockade, he was already on the Eugene police's radar.[12] Law enforcement had a hunch that Ferguson might have had something to do with the ELF. So they began following him, hoping he might interact with other suspects in Eugene.

By 2004, federal grand juries were subpoenaing witnesses, and the investigative pressure was building. It also turned out that Ferguson was a struggling heroin addict. Law enforcement brought Ferguson in for questioning several times and threatened to charge him with arson. While they didn't have enough evidence to do that, they could charge him with lying to federal investigators. Using the threat of imprisonment and Ferguson's addiction, investigators were able to turn him into an informant.[13] In exchange for a dramatic reduction in jail time and treatment for his addiction, Ferguson agreed to wear a wire. However, the timing was not without irony. By 2003, the ELF/ALF cell had gone quiet. Tired of living double lives, the pressure from law enforcement, and disagreement with each other over tactics, they had largely ceased carrying out covert actions.

Ferguson's cooperation gave law enforcement the break it needed. And so Operation Backfire was born. Within two years the operation bore fruit. On December 7, 2005, simultaneous raids were carried out by the FBI's Joint Terrorism Task Force in Oregon, Washington, Arizona, Virginia, and New York.[14] The prosecutors focused on eleven activists associated with the ALF/ELF cell law enforcement called "The Family."[15] The pressure and charges against the ALF/ELF cell led several defendants, including Chelsea Gerlach and Stanislas Meyeroff, to sign cooperating plea agreements. Another alleged ELF conspirator, Bill Rodgers, also known as "Avalon," committed suicide in his Arizona jail cell two weeks after his arrest. Within two years of Operation Backfire forming, most of the activists associated with the ALF/ELF cell were in prison. Several of the defendants were threatened with decades-long prison sentences due to terrorism enhancements, and as a result, most pleaded guilty.[16] In all, more than nineteen activists received sentences of between three and nearly twenty-two years in prison.

There were two notable missing fugitives from the ALF/ELF cell. Joseph Dibee, one of the alleged members, went on the run and was captured in Cuba in 2018. He was later sentenced to 1,000 hours of community service and $1.3 million in restitution—but no jail time.[17] The second, Josephine "Sunshine" Overaker, one of the cell members indicted in 2006, remains on the run and is on the FBI's Most Wanted List.[18]

Operation Backfire marked a turning point: the pace of arson, sabotage, and vandalism carried out by radical activists declined precipitously afterward.[19]

But what was it like to be labeled the number-one domestic terror threat by the federal government? What did that do to the movement and to the people within it? How did it change activists? What happens when a once-vibrant scene, like the one in Eugene and the Pacific Northwest, dies out?

This chapter also examines a less well-known, but equally consequential prosecution: the 2006 case against the Stop Huntingdon Animal Cruelty (SHAC) activists, known as the SHAC 7. How did the growing criminalization of ALF-style tactics reshape the broader movement?

***

Jack, whom we met in the previous chapters, was a Eugene police officer who was intimately involved in Operation Backfire.[20] His eyes lit up when he told me how he and others in law enforcement were able to turn Jacob Ferguson into the key informant. Jack said it was the result of a fortuitous series of events. He and others on the task force were looking back at old case files from around the same time as the car dealership fire in 2001. He recalled the weird case of the woman who reported a stolen car right around that time, accusing Ferguson. She then withdrew her stolen car report, but then another woman followed up to check on the report.[21] To Jack it seemed suspicious. So, he and others started to look more closely at Ferguson. Jack said that, in many ways, Ferguson was the perfect informant. He was an idealogue, but he had "personal problems—he was a heroin addict, and he had a kid, and he had a lot to lose if he were sent to prison. And that's a great handle to have on someone." Then Jack got a big smile on his face and told me that Ferguson "was much better positioned [inside the ALF/ELF cell] than we even thought."

Rick, whom we also met in Chapter 4, was Jack's partner in the Eugene Police Department. He was also heavily involved in Operation Backfire.[22] Rick told me that he felt that turning Ferguson was key to the investigation. Rick said he had a grudging admiration for the "tradecraft" of the ELF/ALF folks. They didn't talk about past actions, and they intentionally recruited people who could keep their mouths shut. After 2002, the pace of arson and sabotage slowed down, and the investigation was stalled. But then Rick told me, "They went quiet for a while [in 2002. But then] we got Jake Ferguson on our side as an informant, and we started knocking them [the ALF/ELF cell members] off one by one." And this was all because of Ferguson and the power of informants. Rick told me that before the informants, people in the ALF/ELF cells thought they could trust everyone in the movement. But once the arrests happened and people started to cooperate with prosecutors, "every single person talked."

Jack and Rick, both former law enforcement officials, believed that informants were key to the success of Operation Backfire. Activists who lived through that period agreed—though they saw the repression through very different lenses.

Nicole, the activist lawyer who was part of the Eugene scene at the time, told me how disorienting it was to be there when the Operation Backfire arrests began. She couldn't believe that Jake Ferguson had been working with law enforcement.[23] There was rampant speculation in the activist community that law enforcement was engaging in undercover investigations. Yet, Nicole was still shocked: "[We all thought] Jake Ferguson was the last person who would become a snitch." He seemed so hardcore. She talked about one of her friends and clients who had a bizarre interaction with Ferguson at an Earth First! gathering. Ferguson was asking her friend a bunch of questions about "The Family." Nicole's friend thought the whole thing was strange, since he'd never heard anyone use that name. But after the arrest, they both realized that Ferguson wasn't just acting weird; he was trying to get them on tape saying incriminating things for law enforcement. Nicole also said that the whole concept of "The Family" was "ridiculous" and that it was an angle to make the ALF/ELF activists seem more sinister than they were. To her the ELF/ALF cell was just a group of friends and activists who had bonded through campaigns like the Warner Creek blockade and had a fierce anarchist ethos. They weren't cult members or some crime family.

Mark, one of the original Earth First!ers whom we met in Chapter 2, had a lot to say about the ELF.[24] It was fascinating to hear him express a mix of grudging admiration for and frustration at what he saw as a disconnect between how his generation of activists built their movement and how the ELF operated. To Mark, the ELF activists, many of whom had been involved in Earth First! previously, "formed a little cult" within the group. Mark felt that given some of the pressures on old-growth forests in the Pacific Northwest, ELF members were right to escalate their actions. And he described the ELF era from 1995 to 2008 as "an amazing run." But he also viewed the group as ultimately "controlled by animal rights activists." And to Mark the cardinal sin the ELF activists committed was that they started carrying out actions (arson, etc.) that required a "security bubble." As soon as that bubble was pierced, people started ratting each other out, and the whole thing collapsed.

***

What was it like for the activists themselves to be targeted during the Green Scare? Nathan, the activist whom we met in the previous chapter, whose path crossed the ELF, was eventually arrested and went to prison as part of the broader crackdown associated with the Green Scare. When we talked about Operation Backfire, he grew animated.[25] Nathan was in Eugene, Oregon, in 2002, and the pressure from law enforcement was overwhelming. "There were undercover agents and it felt like a Green Scare.... it was a multi-agency effort [to bring us down]." He felt that he and other activists were just being "fucked with" by law enforcement. Nathan then mentioned Jacob Ferguson, calling him "the rat," and his voice noticeably shifted, his contempt for Ferguson barely disguised. He described Ferguson as the main hub in the ALF/ELF cell. Once he was taken down by law enforcement, the rest of the spokes were done. To Nathan, this Pacific Northwest green anarchist scene headquartered in Eugene was also important. The ELF depended on the punks and their do-it-yourself (DIY) ethos, the anarchists, and the above-ground environmental activists. Operation Backfire didn't just arrest the ELF/ALF activists; it led to the demise of the broader scene.

But it wasn't just Operation Backfire that crushed ELF/ALF. It was also 9/11 and the increasing focus on terrorism that made activists like the ELF and their supporters question their tactics. Other radical environmental activists were exhausted from living underground and aged out, or they shifted their focus to other movements like the antiwar movement, which was heating up in opposition to the U.S. invasion of Iraq in 2003.[26]

***

I asked Blake, whom we met in Chapter 4 and who was involved in publicizing the ELF actions, how the Green Scare affected activists. I was curious about his answer because he had experienced firsthand the effects of Operation Backfire. Blake was in the Pacific Northwest, and he had been subpoenaed, followed, and, in his view, harassed by law enforcement for more than five years leading up the arrest of the ALF/ELF cell members. When I asked Blake this question about the effects of Operation Backfire he said,[27] "I'm fairly certain about why it [the Green Scare] did [work and crushed the movement]." He cited the prosecutions of the ELF/ALF activists in 2006, and the dismay that some activists "received long [prison] sentences, and [those who cooperated with the federal government] got nothing." Blake also cited Jacob Ferguson, "who was an integral member [of the ELF], but he wore a wire and received no jail time." The use of informants led to infighting and created bad blood in the movement. Or, as Blake said, activists "wanted to kill each other"—particularly those who cooperated.

Blake went on to say that after 9/11, the "resources to fight terrorism were endless." The sentences that ELF activists were facing, especially with terrorism enhancements, were "insane." He highlighted the case of Marius Mason, an ELF activist. Marius's husband, Frank Ambrose, eventually cooperated with federal law enforcement and testified against Marius, implicating him in a string of arson attacks in Michigan, including one at a Michigan State University agriculture research facility in 1999. Marius received a 22-year prison sentence in 2009.[28] Blake got emotional and said that that was more than many convicted murderers get. So in his view the repression worked.

But not everyone agreed with Blake's take on the Green Scare. Just as was the case with the question of whether the ELF's tactics were effective or not, Jesse had a different view from Blake. This was ironic because both Blake and Jesse worked together publicizing the ELF's actions, and both were under intense scrutiny from law enforcement. Jesse agreed with Blake that repression had broken the back of the ELF and had snuffed out the broader Eugene–Pacific Northwest scene. But to Jesse, it wasn't only the prison sentences. The first thing, he said matter-of-factly, was that "it's hard to stand up to state repression."[29] After 9/11 it was even harder. Jesse said that there was "a ton of money flowing into the feds and police after 9/11." And the idea that "we were just radical environmentalists [stopped when] we became the number-one terrorist threat." Even activists remotely sympathetic to the ALF/ELF were treated like terrorists. But one key point Jesse made was that Operation Backfire was just a symptom of the broader repressive crackdown. As he told me, it wasn't Operation Backfire itself. Rather, it was the federal and local grand juries that "subpoenaed every activist who was remotely connected to the movement. People were threatened with contempt [if they didn't testify], and those that could were in the wind [and left the Pacific Northwest], and the movement died."

The interview with Jesse helped me understand a few key points about the Green Scare and the broader environmental movement. Yes, prison sentences were long and scary. But harassment of activists was just as critical to the collapse of the Pacific Northwest scene, if not more so. The ELF depended on the Pacific Northwest and the Eugene scene, and when those people who supported the radical environmental movement were targeted, the scene dissipated.

***

Much of the popular focus of the Green Scare centered on the ELF and Operation Backfire. It's true that some ELF members also carried out actions under the ALF banner, and, as many activists pointed out, there was significant overlap: some got their start in the animal rights movement and used similar tactics. But the ELF was distinct from the purely animal rights–focused wing.

Around the same time as Operation Backfire, animal rights activists experienced their own wave of repression. In particular, the SHAC campaign—first discussed in Chapter 3—became a major target. SHAC aimed to shut down Huntingdon Life Sciences, a company deeply involved in animal testing. This campaign overlapped with the tail end of the ELF actions and with Operation Backfire. SHAC activists set up a website in the early 2000s to publicize illegal actions carried out against targets, including Huntingdon Life Sciences, as well as other groups or individuals who profited or supported the company.

Like the ELF, SHAC was a leaderless campaign, but its targets were much more focused.[30] In March 2006, six of the SHAC activists and the group itself were convicted of violating the Animal Enterprise Protection Act of 1992 and were later sentenced to three to six years in federal prison for stalking and inciting violence.[31] One unusual aspect of the trial was that the SHAC members weren't accused of carrying out the acts themselves. Rather, they were convicted of enabling and encouraging violence. In response to the SHAC trial, the federal government amended the 1992 law and in 2006 passed the Animal Enterprise Terrorism Act, which broadened protections for "animal enterprise" businesses and research labs and stiffened the penalties for activists who sought to disrupt them.[32]

***

We first met Luke, the hipster glasses–wearing animal liberation activist and vegan in Chapter 3. Luke was intimately involved in SHAC and later ended up serving significant time in federal prison because of it.[33]

When I asked him what it was like being the target of an intense federal investigation, he first said that it was amazing being part of a radical campaign. In Luke's view, ALF and radical animal rights activists were "actually winning in the 1980s." So, industry and the federal government started passing new repressive laws like the Animal Enterprise Protection Act of 1992 and were trying to figure out strategies "to take down the animal terror movement." Luke said this didn't stop activists. In Luke's view, there were bigger lab raids, more direct actions—and the data on direct actions support Luke's view, with the pace of direct actions increasing throughout the 1990s.

Luke viewed the repression faced by ELF and SHAC as quite similar. The FBI decided that it wanted to "cut the heads off the snakes" of the radical animal rights movement and arrest the key players, and that's what they did. The FBI tapped SHAC's phones and tried to infiltrate the group. In a nod to Jacob Ferguson's cooperation with law enforcement, Luke also said that law enforcement "got lucky with snitches [with the ELF]" but that snitches weren't as effective against SHAC.

But it was Luke's thoughts on how prison affected the movement that were most insightful. He noted that the prison sentences faced by SHAC activists had three effects. (1) Activists were labeled as "terrorists"—something nobody wanted to be called after 9/11; (2) they faced serious jail time, and, finally, (3) activists were scared. Luke believed that prison sentences empowered people in the animal rights movement who were suspicious of direct action and militancy and preferred mainstream approaches. These mainstream activists encouraged educational outreach or converting people to veganism, and thus the lasting effect was to cripple support for direct action within the animal rights movement.

Luke then put me in touch with Ross, who had also spent time in prison as part of the broader crackdown on SHAC.[34] I was eager to talk to Ross because I thought that as a self-confessed anarchist who had experience with SHAC and the animal rights movement, he would be able to provide a unique perspective. Ross and I emailed back and forth several times, but finally, he declined to talk face-to-face, saying that he had said everything he wanted to say. I was disappointed but not surprised. Many of the activists I wanted to chat with were skittish about talking, and others just wanted to put it all behind them. Ross did put me in touch with several folks whom I ended up interviewing. But before declining to chat with me, Ross replied to my questions with his own thoughts on the effects of repression.

Ross said that repression was something that young activists didn't understand, and academics who write books about the movement like me "often get wrong." He went on to say that it was difficult to describe what it was like to be under constant surveillance; subjected to trumped-up charges, prison time, and house raids, and find out "that people you care for are FBI agents or informants." He felt that, given the brutality of law enforcement and the strength of industry lobbies that opposed them, what they had accomplished was "truly impressive." And, he emphasized that for a bunch of kids in their twenties, it was "incredibly hard to navigate."

Ross ended his email to me with one of the bleakest and most haunting views of radical environmentalism. He expressed his fears that increased temperatures from global warming would permanently destroy the ability of the planet to sustain life, "but I hope that isn't true." Ross then added that he placed little to no faith in the mainstream environmental movement, which he viewed as incredibly naïve. To Ross, his own failure and that of other radical activists to radically change things could mean that life as we knew it would not be feasible at some point. This was what gnawed at him. He concluded his email, writing that there wasn't "a day that goes by that I don't wonder what we should have done instead and regret my part in our errors. I don't have much in the way of answers."

***

The legacy of Operation Backfire and the Green Scare was imprinted on the movement. Activists became security conscious, and many turned away from the more intense actions that characterized the ELF, particularly arson.

Stephen, the ALF activist who spent time in prison and whom we first met in Chapter 3, helped me put the legacy of the Green Scare in perspective. He was part of a generation of animal rights activists who joined following this period of repression. Stephen and I traded messages on Signal, the encrypted messaging app, a few times before he was open and willing to talk.[35] As he viewed it, everyone involved in the ALF and the ELF were "nonviolent" and wouldn't harm humans or other living things. Nor did he think arson and property destruction should qualify as violent tactics. But following the Green Scare, Stephen shifted his tactical approach. He "wasn't willing to fuck around with arson to face life in prison" for property destruction. Like a well-trained activist lawyer, he told me he was always willing to engage in burglaries, break-ins, sabotage, pouring bleach into gas tanks—anything that didn't involve fire. He wanted "to do as much damage as possible [to targets] without tripping the sentencing guidelines for arson."

It is interesting to compare Stephen's experience to that of Robert, a fellow ALF activist and prisoner whom we first met in Chapter 3. I always liked talking with Robert for his quick, sardonic view of activism, as well as his penchant for saying seemingly flippant but also insightful things. But Robert's semi-trollish comments usually contained a kernel of truth. It's why I liked inviting Robert to talk to my classes. He wasn't boring, and he always challenged my students in how they viewed high-risk activism. During one of our conversations, I asked him what he thought about the Green Scare."[36] He got an exasperated look on his face, as if he was now being asked to talk about his least favorite person in the world. He said that the use of the term "the Green Scare" was one of the worst things to happen to the animal and environmental movements. He called the term "activist clickbait" and said that he talked to kids who were worried that if they wore a shirt with a militant message on it, they would be placed on a list and labeled a terrorist. The Green Scare, he noted, created this crippling climate of fear. Other activists, he emphasized, hearing of the lengthy sentences given to the ALF/ELF cell, assumed that all types of clandestine actions would get those same stiff sentences. But newer activists didn't realize that these sentences were handed down for arson specifically. "The average activist," Robert said, "doesn't read the law."

Robert even labeled the Green Scare paranoia as the number-one reason the movement declined in the early 2000s. He called this belief that the government was going to come after every activist "movement self-sabotage." To Robert, the paranoia of activists did the government's work for them. He said the shift following the Green Scare was palpable. In the 1990s, when he first got into activism, Robert saw the animal rights movement as operating offensively and as willing to challenge corporate and government interests. But post-Green Scare, its activism became very defensive. The new attitude was, don't get tripped up by the government, be careful what you say, and don't trust other activists too much. To Robert "it was a one-fucking-eighty [degree shift]" and it was a bad thing.

***

Why did the radical environmental movement collapse in the early 2000s? If we had to point to one factor, it would be repression. And the effects of the repression were numerous. Repression led to the arrests of many of the core activists in ELF, who were driving the most intense actions in the Pacific Northwest. Repression ensnared many people with grand jury summonses. Repression raised the penalties for activism and brought greater law enforcement resources to fight "ecoterrorism." Repression led activists to leave the Eugene and Pacific Northwest scene altogether.

A further insight I took away from talking to activists was just how important a sense of place and a scene was to the movement. The Pacific Northwest, and Eugene in particular, served as the incubator for all these radical ideas and people. It was where punk anarchists, Earth First! eco-activists, and the animal liberation activists all met, reinforcing, radicalizing, and encouraging each other. The Green Scare and Operation Backfire marked the end of this scene. The scene might have burned out on its own. Many of the ELF's actions had cooled off by 2002 anyway, and some members had moved from the area or had shifted their interest to the burgeoning anti-Iraq War movement around 2003. But it's clear that the prosecutions hastened the scene's demise.

In the absence of a broader scene, the pathway of hardcore punks and animal rights anarchists into radical environmental activism ceased to be as important. Animal rights and environment activists had always been uncomfortable bedfellows, with debates about the personal politics of veganism always lurking below the surface.[37] Some activists, like Robert, saw the purported synergy between the ALF and the ELF as "revisionist history" and as quite marginal. But the number of activists I interviewed from this era who came in through the animal liberation hardcore punk scene was undeniable. After the Green Scare, the animal rights-to-radical environmental movement pipeline wasn't the same. The movement had shifted and changed.

* * *

In June of 2023, *The New York Times* ran a story about Craig Rosebraugh, a former spokesperson for the ELF.[38] As a spokesperson for the ELF, he claimed not to know the identities of the ELF activists. But in the early 2000s the federal government believed otherwise. During this time of intense federal scrutiny and repression, Rosebraugh was working on a book manuscript detailing his time in activism. Literary agent Robert Eringer, who had published spy novels and other memoirs, eventually approached him about his book. Rosebraugh initially agreed to work with Eringer, but he later read articles that suggested that Eringer might have been involved in a shady campaign against a journalist, so in February 2003, Rosebraugh, already paranoid from his time under federal surveillance, ended his relationship with Eringer. More than 20 years would pass, but Freedom of Information Act (FOIA) disclosures and a 2023 story in *The New York Times* confirmed that Eringer had been tasked by the FBI with trying to get Rosebraugh to give up more information on the ELF (which Rosebraugh didn't have) through his memoir. Eringer the agent was also Eringer the FBI informant.

When I saw the Eringer–Rosebraugh story, I sent it to several activists whom I'd interviewed. Some of them simply wrote it off as "a dumb sting operation," but most shared Rosebraugh's reaction to the revelation: "Everything I was paranoid about—and more—actually happened."[39] It led me to rethink my initial views on Grace, the activist who asked to see my faculty ID before we chatted. Maybe she wasn't paranoid after all; she had just been around the movement long enough.

6

From the Ashes of Backfire to the Pipelines, Forests, and Roads

I MET BERNARD AT A coffee shop in May 2024, in Portland. We had talked previously a few times. Bernard could wax poetically about the transformative power of being in the forest and about his spiritual connection with the natural world. He had a soft-spoken way about him. But Bernard had also spent quite a bit of time thinking about activism, where things went wrong, and his own place in the movement. I spoke with him for the first time two years earlier.[1] It had not been easy to connect with him, partly because of his health. Periodically, Bernard would get quite sick and be sidelined for a few weeks. His health issues had forced him to give up his frontline direct action activism. But, as he saw it, his health issues also gave him time to reflect on what had happened to the movement.

Bernard grew up in what he termed a "religious cult" in the Mountain West but eventually escaped as a teen. He was homeless in the mid-1990s, hopping trains around the country, and ended up in Austin, Texas. It was in Austin that Bernard started reading *Earth First! Journal* religiously. "Religiously" was an apt term. Bernard eventually made his way back out west and had begun spending a lot of time in the forest, which served as the site of his "conversion" (as he called it) to environmental activism. But by the start of the Green Scare in the mid-2000s, he had become disillusioned with activism. He had picked up a nasty heroin habit and was shooting up in Portland. It took him several years to crawl out of the addiction hole, but he eventually got clean and resumed activism, focusing less on wilderness and more on shutting down the fossil fuel infrastructure (trains, refineries, etc.), or, as he put it, "the apparatus of destruction." But he had to give it all up in 2019 when his body started to fail him.

So here we were in 2024, meeting for the first time in person for brunch in Portland.[2] Bernard was tall and had a lithe, limber build. He had a slightly weathered face and thinning hair, and he was wearing black pants and a black tank top; he had tattoos up and down his arms and shoulders. My first impression was that he looked exactly like what I thought a veteran Portland anarchist forest defender would look like. We shook hands, and both of us commented on the weather. It was in the high 80s that day, and Bernard remarked that "Ten to fifteen years ago, we never had weather like this . . . climate change in action."

I told Bernard that when we first chatted and he referred to the forest as a sacred, religious space, I thought it was a bit of "hokey bullshit." But having just hiked in the Willamette National Forest and seen the massive old-growth forests, I kind of got it. Bernard then told me that back when he was deep into frontline activism, there was an old Earth First! adage that until somebody spent enough time in the woods to have a spiritual, religious experience, they weren't ready to carry out direct action or sabotage.[3] Bernard noted that it was not surprising that the Pacific Northwest was the incubator for the radical environmental movement. As an activist, "you would go spend time in the forest, your sacred space, and then you would see these massive logging trucks passing you—and you knew they were taking something that was sacred to you."

I really enjoyed my time with Bernard, and it didn't hurt that the brunch was quite good. But much of our conversation revolved around the grief that Bernard had experienced. He told me the story of his friend, Carson McCann, who went by the name "Sparrow." He was a fellow forest defender and activist who committed suicide in 2003 in the forest.[4] What made Sparrow special, Bernard mentioned, was that "while [Sparrow was] willing to put all his waking energy into ecological politics, he kind of strangely floated above all the controversy and factionalism, etc., that made so many people so perpetually bitter." He then called Sparrow "a remarkable soul." I brought up the fact that when we first talked, Bernard commented that he lived "in a constant grief for the collapse of the eco movement." He acknowledged that it was still true. He told me that his upbringing in the religious cult gave him a very jaded but realistic view that "people can justify everything if they need to. And climate [collapse] is one of those things." He used words like "fatigued," "lethargic," and "depressed" to describe the current state of the climate movement.

Bernard was getting by with the money he made from writing and podcasting, as well as with support from fellow activists who had participated with him in the pipeline blockades. He had a lot of medical expenses because of his health issues. He jokingly referred to the support he received from activists as "veterans benefits for activists."

Bernard's outlook and his body are an apt metaphor for the Pacific Northwest scene. It was weaker than it had been, and much of the radical organizing energy had dissipated, moved to other more mainstream movements, or was too battered and broken to continue.

But as the scene in the Pacific Northwest cooled off, new campaigns and organizations emerged. In 2007 climate activist Bill McKibben formed 350.org with the goal of using protest and lobbying to influence climate policy.[5] There was also an increasing focus on blocking oil pipelines. The Indigenous-led Dakota Access Pipeline protests at the Standing Rock Indian Reservation in North Dakota in 2016 and 2017 captured national attention.[6] Another group of pipeline activists emerged who called themselves "Valve Turners." They illegally shut down valves on pipelines to stop the flow of oil.[7] In 2018, Swedish climate activist and teenager Greta Thunberg helped spark a new type of global, youth-focused climate movement; she encouraged her supporters to raise awareness for climate change by skipping school. There were also new, place-based campaigns. For example, the Stop Cop City protest in Atlanta, which began in 2021, sought to prevent the building of a police training center in the South River Forest just outside of Atlanta.[8]

Many of these campaigns echoed the tactics used to protect the old-growth forests in Oregon decades earlier. For example, both the Dakota

Access Pipeline protests and the Stop Cop City movement in Atlanta used blockades, tree spiking (in Atlanta), and sabotage.[9] But as we'll see, these new movements were different from the earlier ones. Standing Rock was an Indigenous-led movement, and environmental concerns were subsumed under the banner of Indigenous land rights. And Stop Cop City fused the ideas of green anarchism and total liberation with ideas from prison abolition and the Black Lives Matter movements.

Several activists I interviewed argued that antifascists' use of property destruction and sabotage in Portland after the George Floyd protests in 2020[10]—and by abortion rights activists following the overturning of *Roe v. Wade* in 2022[11]—reflected the same tactical legacy as earlier radical environmentalists. Others argued that for many leftist activists, issues like racism, police brutality, and U.S. foreign policy demanded more immediate attention than the environment. And we can't forget that the threat of repression from the Green Scare still hung over the radical environmental movement.

***

Bill McKibben, with his angular chin, toothy wide smile, and wire-rimmed glasses, is an odd person to become one of the leading figures in American environmentalism. He was a graduate of Harvard in the early 1980s, where he was president of the college newspaper, *The Harvard Crimson*. For several years in the mid-1980s he worked for *The New Yorker* as a writer and journalist.[12] He later quit *The New Yorker* and wrote the highly influential book *The End of Nature* in 1989.[13] The book was one of the first to lay out for general audiences the threat from global warming, arguing that it was endangering both our planet and the future of humanity.[14] McKibben also argued that science wouldn't rescue humanity, and he even called for reduced reliance on technology and lower population growth, echoing the deep ecologists who held sway at that time.[15] Since the early 2000s, he has been a scholar and teacher at Middlebury College.

But we aren't talking about McKibben because of his writing or his teaching. What makes him important is the crucial role he played in forming a new model of NGO-based activism that would become the hallmark of the climate movement. This new strategy called for climate NGOs to mix climate advocacy with nonviolent civil disobedience.

In contrast to past radical environmental groups, McKibben encouraged closer ties to the mainstream movement. The goal of these new climate NGOs was to capture enough attention to persuade wealthy, sympathetic donors to fund their effort and hopefully sway policy. That meant that certain tactics, including property destruction and arson, were taboo.

McKibben helped found the NGO 350.org in 2007. The number 350 was not just a random number. It came from the amount of carbon (in parts per million) that climate scientist James Hansen in a presentation in 2007 stated was the safe upper limit for the planet—a limit that had already been crossed by that time.[16]

The goal of 350.org was to encourage collective protest and put pressure on policymakers to level off emissions and stop building more fossil fuel infrastructure. The organization would support and fund grassroots chapters across the world, and their actions would be targeted toward reducing reliance on fossil fuels. One of their first protests was a large-scale climate protest in October 2009, launched ahead of the 2009 UN climate summit in Copenhagen. The 350.org protests around Copenhagen were a huge success, with more than 4,000 protest events held in more than 170 countries.[17]

When I talked about this period with Tim, a direct action organizer who has been involved in the environmental movement since the early 2000s, he brought up an important point.[18] Despite the repression, the period after the Green Scare (post-2008) was a time of optimism for many activists. President Barack Obama was in the White House, and, unlike President George W. Bush and Vice President Dick Cheney, he wasn't seen as beholden to the fossil fuel industry. Tim called it the "hope and change" era. Many activists thought President Obama would do the right thing by the environment and "get the right people in government agencies so we could make progress [on climate change]." But to Tim and other activists, Obama's presidency was a massive disappointment. As he told me, "Boy, were we wrong."

In February 2013, activists associated with 350.org and other environmental groups performed one of their most dramatic acts of civil disobedience. More than forty activists, including Bill McKibben, climate scientist James Hansen, actress Darryl Hannah, Robert F.

Kennedy Jr., leaders from the Sierra Club, and civil rights veteran Julian Bond were arrested in front of the White House.[19] Some of the activists used plastic zip ties to bind their hands to the fence, and others refused to leave. Their goal was to put pressure on President Obama to cancel the proposed 1,200-mile-long Keystone XL pipeline that would carry oil from Canada to the Gulf of Mexico. This wasn't the first time McKibben had been arrested at the White House over the Keystone XL. In 2011, McKibben and more than 1,200 others were arrested for a series of sit-ins protesting the pipeline.[20]

McKibben and 350.org set the blueprint for much of the radical activism to come. There would be less monkeywrenching and property destruction and more civil disobedience. There would also be less focus on pure wilderness and more focus on stopping pipelines. And all the subsequent campaigns would make aggressive use of social media.

In some ways, this pressure campaign worked. President Obama eventually paused the Keystone XL pipeline in 2015. President Trump reversed it when he came into office in 2016. But then President Biden canceled a key permit when he came into office in 2020, and the developer of the Keystone XL pipeline eventually canceled their plans entirely in 2021.[21]

Marianne had a lot of thoughts on 350.org and Bill McKibben when we chatted.[22] She's a self-described longtime ecoactivist who got involved in Earth First! and ecodefense after the Green Scare. Around 2008, right after she completed college, she had a "spiritual awakening" in the old-growth forests of the Pacific Northwest. From there, she began her activism journey. To Marianne, the fight against fossil fuels was an urgent, generational fight for the future in the planet. She was involved with numerous civil disobedience actions for which she was arrested—mostly for blocking pipelines for fossil fuel development and transportation. I asked Marianne why activists, post-2008, were less radical and engaged in fewer instances of property destruction. She reminded me that she came into the movement after the Green Scare. She said activists weren't willing to carry out actions such as arson that could get them branded as terrorists and lead them to spend twenty years in prison—"repression works for a reason."

Marianne then added something that surprised me. She said that in addition, activists were mindful of who has money. These "middle-of-the-road" environmental NGOs provide funding and support for activists (including Marianne). They wanted activists to do "non-radical" things, like civil disobedience. They wouldn't support property destruction and would condemn any activist who carries out these kinds of actions. She then added, "I might not care about 350.org [and Bill McKibben], but I don't want 350.org to come out against us for shutting off a pipeline." Marianne felt that McKibben and his NGO followers used their disapproval and their control of money to constrain the space for radical actions. In contrast to the Earth First! ethos of a generation earlier—which had been built around the mantra "No compromise in defense of Mother Earth"—many activists now had to compromise if they didn't want the funding to dry up.

Leila, a younger climate change organizer, had a different view.[23] She grew up in the American Southwest, and as a "younger Millennial," drought and climate change were never far from her mind. She told me that from as early as she could remember there were wildfires caused by climate change, or neighbors who had no water in their well. This knowledge gave Leila an environmental consciousness from an early age. As a young teenager in 2009, she saw Bill McKibben give a talk about climate change. She was mesmerized and organized her own small protest in October 2009 with others as part of 350.org's International Day of Climate Action. As Leila told me, "Being a part of that, and looking at all the pictures from around the world [of other 350.org activists], and seeing these creative images, and demonstrations, and the culture and solidarity–it was mind-blowing." This was Leila's gateway to action. She ended up participating in pipeline protests to try to halt the Line 3 pipeline expansion in Minnesota,[24] and she found herself working more with Indigenous activists.

Marianne's and Leila's stories are part of the post–Green Scare phase of the radical environmental movement. Newer, younger activists were brought into the movement to combat climate change and end fossil fuels. Wilderness was no longer the main focus. Increasingly, civil disobedience became the preferred tactic. And monkeywrenching and sabotage became less common in reaction to concerns over repression and the desire to not upset NGO funders. The movement also began to grapple with and focus on other social justice issues related to racism, policing, and Indigenous rights.

***

The 2011 350.org White House protests marked a strategy shift in the effort to stop pipelines. But there were other shifts as well. The nearly year-long protest at the Standing Rock Indian Reservation (2016–2017) was led by the Indigenous activists. The Standing Rock Sioux Tribe was protesting the proposed path of the 1,200-mile-long Dakota Access Pipeline that would go through their main water source and sacred tribal lands.[25] While there were blockades and other forest-defense tactics at Standing Rock, the environmental cause was second to the cause of Indigenous rights.[26]

The Standing Rock Protests attracted a lot of outside attention and media coverage.[27] Much of this attention was due to the intense clashes between protesters and local security and law enforcement, which resulted in large numbers of arrests.[28] Actress Shailene Woodley was arrested in October 2016 and charged with trespassing and engaging in a riot. In September 2016 private security guards hired by Energy Transfer Partners, the pipeline company, used dogs and pepper spray on protesters. In November of that same year, law enforcement used tear gas and water cannons on protesters in below-freezing temperatures.[29] While President Obama paused construction on the pipeline in 2016, President Donald Trump authorized construction by the U.S. Army Corps of Engineers when he assumed office in 2017, and the pipeline was completed that June.[30]

The Standing Rock Protests exemplify several trends in the radical environmental movement. Activists showed deference by centering Indigenous rights, elevating Indigenous claims, and following Indigenous leaders on tactics. Tim, the longtime direct action organizer, mentioned the training of activists as part of the Stop Line 3 pipeline protests against a proposed expansion on Indigenous lands, this time in Minnesota.[31] The outside activists who supported and protested Line 3 were explicitly instructed not to engage in sabotage or in property destruction, which would go against the wish of the Indigenous tribe. Even the phrase used by activists protesting the pipelines was different—they were called "water protectors." The key point is that these were not chiefly environmental campaigns. Rather, they were Indigenous land defense struggles in which environmental activists participated not as leaders but in solidarity.[32]

***

Not all pipeline protests eschewed sabotage and monkeywrenching. From November 2016 until May 2017, a spate of sabotage attacks occurred along the length noted twice already–and recently Dakota Access Pipeline. A bulldozer was set on fire, and blow torches and rags doused in gasoline were used in more than eleven arson attacks to damage various valve sections of the pipeline.[33] But these pipeline sabotage attacks were different from past Earth First! or ELF actions. They weren't anonymous actions claimed through a communiqué.

Rather, at a press conference in July 2017 held in front of the Iowa Utilities Board, two women affiliated with the Catholic Workers Movement—Jessica Reznicek and Ruby Montoya—announced that they were responsible for the sabotage actions. Reznicek and Montoya made the following statement:

> After having explored and exhausted all avenues of process, including attending public commentary hearings, gathering signatures for valid requests for environmental impact statements, participating in civil disobedience, hunger strikes, marches and rallies, boycotts and encampments, we saw the clear deficiencies of our government to hear the people's demands. . . . Our conclusion is that the system is broken and it is up to us as individuals to take peaceful action and remedy it.[34]

Reznicek eventually pleaded guilty and was sentenced to eight years in prison with a terrorism enhancement charge. Ruby Montoya got six years in prison, also with terrorism enhancement charges.[35]

The Reznicek and Montoya pipeline sabotage happened on the heels of another campaign against pipelines. In coordinated actions on October 11, 2016, five climate activists—Michael Foster, Leonard Higgins, Emily Johnston, Annette Klapstein, and Ken Ward—simultaneously shut different emergency valves on pipelines in four different states.[36] It was one of the largest coordinated acts of civil disobedience in the history of the environmental movement, and again it differed notably from previous actions. First, many of the activists were in their fifties and sixties, with children and grandchildren. The five activists known as the "Valve Turners" welcomed their arrest, as they planned to use their trials to argue that their criminal sabotage actions were necessary to prevent the greater harm of fossil fuels and climate change. While several defendants weren't allowed to argue a necessity defense, only one of the Valve Turners, Michael Foster, faced significant prison time (three years). In response to the Valve Turners' actions, the American Legislative Exchange Council (ALEC) pushed bills in several states to stiffen penalties for protests and sabotage of "critical infrastructure."[37]

***

Violet was one of the first people I reached out to when I started writing this book.[38] She ran a prisoner solidarity support network for those who had been arrested for civil disobedience, particularly around pipeline protests. But as we started talking, she revealed that she wasn't just doing prisoner support but also was a frontline activist herself. Violet had gone to graduate school for environmental economics, and she had worked in a policy-related NGO. But like some of the earlier Earth First!ers, she found the NGO world unfulfilling, and she quickly became disillusioned. She said her turning point was reading Naomi Klein's 2013 book, *This Changes Everything*.[39] In her book Klein argued that the problem with climate politics was not about carbon, but about capitalism, and that to solve the problems of climate change we need to drastically reshape the world and the way our economy functions.

Shortly after reading Klein's book, Violet made her way to the Dakotas, joining other activists at the Standing Rock Protests for several months in 2016. Violet talked about how transformative it was and described it as "lightning in a bottle" for activists like herself. She saw "the injustice of the energy industry and the power of struggles rooted in Indigenous solidarity." To Violet, there was something courageous and empowering about allying with the Standing Rock Tribe, who were challenging those who were "poisoning their water system." Violet "had never seen anything like that before, especially not in the policy [NGO] spaces where [she] had worked previously."

Violet described the nitty-gritty, tactical side of her activism. At Standing Rock, she said they would mobilize 200–300 people to occupy a site at a time. She described it as a "military-like" operation, with logistics, walkie-talkies, and coordination with dozens of activists at a time while trying to avoid the police. Violet also talked about the lockdowns, in which people would chain themselves to strategic equipment and machines, while others would "pray and hold space." She found the experience intense and awe inspiring. There was a range of activists at Standing Rock, and Violet found it dizzying but amazing that every encampment had its own way of doing things. As she described it, her encampment was consensus-based. If most people didn't feel comfortable with a tactic or a strategy, they wouldn't do it.

Violet also was part of a group associated with the aforementioned Jessica Reznicek, who was later arrested for sabotaging the Dakota Access Pipeline. They were both part of the Mississippi Stand movement, led by a group of activists and water protectors seeking to prevent the Dakota Access Pipeline from being built. Violet protested and engaged in civil disobedience in Iowa. As she told me, the Mississippi Stand movement was "scrappy and [we were] figuring out things as we went along."

It was while carrying out this anti-pipeline activism that Violet was arrested. She locked herself to a piece of equipment before police forcibly removed and arrested her. Violet spent several months in jail. It was a scary but formative experience. As she told me, "I stand by everything [I did] . . . I have a real sympathy for people fighting fossil fuels." To Violet, the experience at Standing Rock and her connection to Indigenous pipeline struggles were the guiding forces behind her activism and willingness to risk arrest.

Dan's introduction to pipeline activism was a bit more circuitous than Violet's, but it also involved the NGO world.[40] As a student, he had been active on various environmental campaigns. He worked with Ralph Nader, the perennial Green Party presidential candidate and environmentalist, in the 1990s.[41] He then found his way to Greenpeace activism. Dan told me, half-laughing and smiling, "I tried and failed at Greenpeace. I was a consultant for various NGOs and climate organizations, and I was awful." He saw all sorts of new possibilities for organizing that Greenpeace didn't offer, and he was interested in going after the system related to climate change.

And that's how he found himself involved with the Valve Turners, the group of activists who in October 2016 turned the emergency shut-off valves on pipelines in four states. As Dan said, the goal was not only to shut down the pipelines but also "to be as annoying as possible." Dan even admitted that he and the other Valve Turners wanted to get federal charges, so that they could make the trial as big of an event as possible. They wanted to make the argument that their actions of sabotage against pipelines were necessary because the threat of climate change was such a big deal. In other words, they wanted to make a necessity defense. Dan didn't get his wish for a federal trial, but he was able to avoid serious jail time.

He then told me something curious. He said that he "didn't want to be a martyr." Dan said that he had been engaged in this kind of activism for eight years, but he didn't want to be the lone person shutting off valves or chaining himself to a bulldozer. He said he wanted, and that there needed to be, a critical mass of people willing to sacrifice themselves and risk jail time to "try and change society."

At the end of our interview, Dan discussed what he thought climate activists were up against. He said that unlike other issues, such as poverty or racism, climate change was uniquely hard to convince people to act on. "People don't want to face how bad it [climate change] is." The scale of the threat is enormous. But the time lag between when society needs to act, which is now, versus when the really awful effects of climate change start to come into play in ten to twenty years, makes it "daunting" to mobilize people.

Throughout much of our conversation, Dan talked in the classic language of nonviolence and civil disobedience. But he dropped that language when he told me what it was like going up against entrenched fossil fuel interests. He told me, "We don't really understand the sophistication of the enemy [fossil fuel companies]." To Dan, the fossil fuel companies are evil entities that learn through crises and use corporate manipulation and split the public. He decried the level of climate disinformation.

***

While Violet and Dan were open about their actions and thoughts on the movement, and were willing to talk, others were more reticent. I struggled to find anyone affiliated with the Mountain Valley Pipeline protests who was willing to talk. The protests were aimed at obstructing the more than 300-mile-long pipeline carrying natural gas between West Virginia and Virginia.[42] Activists had experimented with a variety of tactics—peaceful marches, sit-ins, road blockades, and chaining themselves to equipment—to block or slow down the project. The pipeline had been expedited in a deal between President Joe Biden and Democratic West Virginia Senator Joe Manchin in exchange for raising the debt ceiling limit in 2024.[43] There had been dozens of arrests of mostly peaceful activists, some facing serious jail time under new laws targeting those seeking to obstruct "critical infrastructure."[44]

I had originally planned to drive down to southwest Virginia, where many of the Mountain Valley Pipeline protests were located. It was only a four-hour drive from Washington, D.C. But I chatted with one of my contacts who knew people who were at the protests, and he advised against it. He cautioned that a lot of law enforcement pressure was being brought down on the Mountain Valley Pipeline protests, and so activists were leery of outsiders, including academics like me. Instead, he put me in touch with an activist who I could talk with via the encrypted messenger app Signal. A few days later, Sadie messaged me on Signal saying she was willing to chat.

Sadie and I messaged back and forth and arranged to do a video call on Signal. Sadie was in her mid-twenties and was wearing a baseball cap and a t-shirt. At the beginning of our call, she was nervous.[45] She paced around the woods outside of her work while we chatted because she didn't want people listening and because of the legal charges she was facing. Sadie identified as a direct action organizer affiliated with the Mountain Valley Pipeline struggle. She had grown up and spent all her life in Central Appalachia, the nexus of eastern Kentucky and Tennessee, and southern Virginia and West Virginia. Sadie's environmental activism wasn't motivated by the antiwar movement or national policy debates on renewals. Those were distant concerns for her. As she told me, "Seeing mountain top [mining] removal, and pipelines [being built in my woods], and people getting cancer from polluted water. That trauma radicalized me."

She had been involved in the Yellow Finch Tree-sit, a nearly three-year tree-sit campaign that lasted from 2018 to 2021 in Montgomery County, Virginia, on the path of the Mountain Valley Pipeline.

Activists constructed platforms nearly fifty feet off the ground in trees on steep slopes that made it difficult for law enforcement to extract the rotating group of tree-sitters.[46]

When I asked Sadie what kind of tactics made sense, she gave a very anarchist response. She said she believed in a "diversity of tactics" and said it was up to each small, autonomous group to figure out where their line was. To make her point, she told me, "I don't think killing someone for political change is generally OK—but in Nazi Germany it was definitely OK to kill Nazis. It depends on the context."

But Sadie was crystal clear on what was holding the movement back from taking more radical actions. It was repression, and the daunting prison sentences that awaited activists if they were caught. As Sadie said, "I have faced multiple felonies for a direct action with no property destruction and no sabotage." She told me how activists associated with the Mountain Valley Pipeline protests had faced felony abduction charges for simply blockading the path of a construction vehicle. At first I thought Sadie was exaggerating, but then I confirmed that it was true.[47] She contrasted other countries where property destruction was more common among anarchists and leftists (like Greece, Italy, and Germany), and where activists faced only a few years in prison at most, compared to the long prison sentences for activists like the ELF in the United States. She said that "our [the U.S. legal] system is designed to repress property destruction."

Sadie then said something I wasn't ready for: "the thing academics [like you] and Malm [author of *How to Blow Up a Pipeline*] don't get is that flashy actions like blowing up a pipeline bring a lot of attention [from law enforcement] and make a big stink, but there are other tactics that are effective and also subtle." I wasn't prepared to be lumped in with Andreas Malm, but Sadie then continued. She said activists could set a bulldozer on fire and get in a ton of trouble, or they could do other, subtler things, like put sugar in the gas tank of a bulldozer. Sadie said you wouldn't find out about the tactic because it's not as "flashy" and fossil fuel companies wouldn't publicize actions like this because they don't want to encourage other activists to do the same thing.

It's helpful to stop and consider the paths Violet, Dan, and Sadie have followed. They are all pipeline activists. They've all been arrested for carrying out civil disobedience, but their pathways into the movement were different. Violet came in through the Indigenous environmental struggles and saw herself as a water protector, whereas Dan came from the nonviolent civil disobedience world, and Violet saw herself as an Appalachian environmental activist with anarchist tendencies. To all of them the pipelines were a symbol of the actual problem behind climate change and environmental degradation. But digging deeper, it's clear they had very different worldviews and varying willingness to use more extreme tactics.

***

It's hard to pinpoint the exact moment when the Youth Climate Movement began. But a good place to start is August 2018 in Sweden.[48] That's when a little-known fifteen-year-old named Greta Thunberg skipped school and stood outside the Swedish parliament to protest government inaction on climate change. She was soon joined by teachers and other students. In March 2019, following Thunberg's example, more than 1 million students in over a hundred countries walked out of their schools to protest climate inaction. The movement was dubbed Fridays for the Future, and it encouraged students to skip school on select Fridays. In September 2019, what many regard as the biggest climate protest ever took place. Following Thunberg's call, an estimated 4 million–plus students, union workers, and others in more than 150 countries joined protests calling for a cut in fossil fuel emissions, and for action on climate change; this coincided with the 2019 UN Climate Action Summit in New York City.[49] Thunberg became the symbol for this new youth-led climate movement.

Other nascent, youth-focused climate movements took a different direction. The Sunrise Movement was formed in the United States ahead of the 2018 midterms. The goal of Sunrise was to pressure Democrats in the primary, and then later in the general election, to support the Green New Deal—a comprehensive set of economic and social justice policies that would cut emissions to zero by 2050.[50] Sunrise's goal was to shift the range of acceptable policy options—the Overton Window—on climate legislation. They knew they wouldn't get everything they asked for, but they believed they could push Democratic politicians to the left on climate policy. In November 2018, Sunrise activists organized a sit-in at Nancy Pelosi's office, calling for more action on climate change. These activists were joined by New York Democratic Representative Alexandra Ocasio-Cortez. While more than fifty activists were arrested in Pelosi's office, it was more of a pressure tactic than a rowdy sit-in. The Inflation Reduction Act of 2022 was signed into law by President Biden in August of 2022. It was a significant piece of climate legislation that contained more than $350 billion in funding for clean energy and electric vehicles and was seen as one of the biggest federal investments ever to deal with climate change. For many activists and progressive Democrats like Ocasio-Cortez, these tactics worked. As Ocasio-Cortez posted in a tweet lauding passage of the bill, "Four years ago, the Green New Deal was called 'unrealistic.' Last year, we fought for climate action in the IRA. That fight resulted in the largest piece of climate legislation in American history. 'First they laugh at you, then they fight you, then we win.'"[51]

This youth climate movement differed from radical environmental movement of the past in several ways. First, it was younger. Many of the activists got their start in high school, and some even in middle school.[52] In fact, the Sunrise Movement explicitly limited its membership to those under the age of thirty-five.[53] The demographic of the climate movement was also different. It was majority White, female, and highly educated.[54] The movement also focused on connecting the climate to issues of economic, racial, and social justice. This youth movement was also policy focused. Unlike radical Earth First!ers, they were focused on using civil disobedience to nudge the policy and political process. For instance, many of the Sunrise activists also did regular political canvassing and door-knocking for their preferred candidates.[55] So even though the youth climate movement shared many of the same environmental concerns as earlier radical activists, they were more willing to compromise to achieve policy change—and most weren't prepared to engage in sabotage. At least, not yet.

Other groups that emerged around this time took a more contentious approach. There was the U.S. wing of the U.K.-founded group Extinction Rebellion. Its main tactics included mass civil disobedience and disruption. For example, in New York City in October 2019, activists associated with Extinction Rebellion used fake blood and staged a mass "die-in" outside of Wall Street, blocking traffic, all to call attention to the threat of climate change.[56] In April 2022, fifteen Extinction Rebellion activists were arrested in New York City for blocking the printing presses of *The Wall Street Journal* and *The New York Times*.⁵⁷ A group of scientists even formed an offshoot civil disobedience group called Scientist Rebellion. Peter Kalmus, a prominent climate scientist associated with Scientist Rebellion, was arrested with several others in April of 2022 for blocking the entrance to the Los Angeles office of JP Morgan Chase.⁵⁸

***

Even within more mainstream activist circles, a new question was emerging: Did the threat of climate change justify more confrontational tactics? And that's where Sam comes in.

During a conversation with one of my contacts from previous research in Ukraine, I mentioned that I was interviewing activists for a new book I was writing on the radical environmental movement. She told me that I had to talk to her friend Sam, a climate activist and organizer. She put us in touch, and we scheduled a time to talk.

Sam told me that he had gotten into student organizing as an undergrad, around the time of the Dakota Access Pipeline and Students for Standing Rock.⁵⁹ He then got pulled into the climate justice movement, where several of his friends helped found Sunrise Movement. Sam was mindful of the history of the radical environmental movement, and the Earth First!, eco-centric, wilderness-first approach. But he saw the wilderness focus as a mistake. He ascribed to the climate justice movement worldview. The climate struggle was one part of the broader struggle for global justice, and he favored civil disobedience to sabotage.

Yet Sam's commitment to civil disobedience wasn't absolute. During our chat, Sam also brought up Malm's *How to Blow up a Pipeline*. He then said, "The fossil fuel industry has done an incredible job deflecting blame. The majority of people in the climate movement are not disrupting the bottom line of the fossil fuel company." Sam said this was a "big problem," and the part that Malm got right and mainstream NGOs got wrong. Sam believed that fossil fuels are a "cancer" on society. If they are a cancer, then what should activists do? And here is the answer that surprised me. Sam favored civil disobedience in general. He told me that as a student activist he was raised on the writings of Erica Chenoweth, the well-known political scientist and author who argued for the strategic advantage of nonviolence.⁶⁰ Sam said he recognized that "You need a mass movement built on civil disobedience [nonviolence] to have the moral high ground." But "you also need people who are willing to work clandestinely [engage in sabotage] . . . it's a winning combination." Sam saw the utility of mixing civil disobedience with a more radical flank.

While Sam had come into the movement through his student activism, Stacey took a different path.⁶¹ Stacey was an anarchist active in social justice causes just north of Dallas. She and others opposed the fracking boom that was happening across the state in the 2000s. In 2011 and 2012, she got involved in the Tar Sands Blockade in East Texas to try and block portions of the Keystone XL pipeline that moved through Texas.⁶² Stacey said that being a climate activist and anarchist in Texas wasn't easy. They had succeeded in having some local fracking bans put in place in Denton, the home of the University of North Texas. But in 2015, Governor Gregg Abbott signed a bill that blocked any local restrictions on oil and gas production from taking place.⁶³ In a Republican-controlled state like Texas, that meant that in practice there would be no way for activists at the local level to use policy pushback on fossil fuels. Stacey told me that after that, it was frustrating for activists; "we were completely out of legal options . . . it was really radicalizing for a lot of ordinary folks. People saw direct action as the only way [forward]."

Stacey said that direct action meant a whole "toolkit," including tree-sits, lockdowns, blockades, and stoppages. The strategy was for "direct action to delay [the bad thing]" and let activists and their legal strategy "catch up." In other words, direct action went hand-in-hand with legal maneuvers. But Stacey also had a cynical view of more mainstream environmental NGOs. As she told me, "The Green non-profits like the Sierra Club, 350.org, Greenpeace, and other groups, they suck the oxygen and resources, especially money, out of grassroots and radical environmental organizations. And they don't really do much." This jaundiced view of mainstream environmental NGOs could have come from Dave Forman or any of the other founders of Earth First!.

Faith was another climate activist I interviewed. She was a junior in college when we talked and a self-described climate justice activist.⁶⁴ Faith told me she had been radicalized by Al Gore. I laughed and asked, "Former Vice President Al Gore, really?" She told me she was seven years old when she first read his book *An Inconvenient Truth* (2006), which came out along with a documentary on climate change.[65] She got involved with the Sierra Club as a young kid in the Midwest, biked everywhere, and cared deeply about reproductive rights and abortion access. As a college student in Washington, D.C., she went to a punk show where she met activists associated with the Sunrise Movement. In September 2019 she was part of a group of activists who blocked more than fifteen intersections in Washington in a campaign known as Shut Down DC. The goal was to force "the whole city to a gridlocked standstill" and push politicians to pay attention to climate change and climate justice.[66] As Faith told me, "Ever since, I've been hooked."

Faith had a knack for vividly describing the different generations of environmental activists: "You have the older veterans from Greenpeace who never are going to understand they/them pronouns." And then she said there were the Generation-X and Millennial activists, "who were introduced to activism during the anti-Iraq War protests and Occupy Wall Street Movement" in the early to mid-2000s. Faith said, "My generation is Greta [Thunberg] and Youth Climate Strike [events inspired by Greta and Fridays for the Future]."

But Faith also made a distinction about activists who had come into the climate movement after the Black Lives Matter (BLM) protests, following the murder of George Floyd in 2020. She saw this divide as even more important. To Faith, those who came in via Black Lives Matter were "very different." Those activists whose first taste of street protests was in 2020 faced a more aggressive police repression—they were tear-gassed, kettled, and so on. Faith said, "they were more confrontational" but also more concerned and preoccupied with security and communicating via encrypted apps. Faith said that it was sometimes hard to bridge these divides. "When you are working with Boomers and Gen X, their experiences weren't shaped by trauma as much as the George Floyd/BLM folks [activists']."

***

On January 18, 2023, state and local law enforcement in Georgia launched a raid on an encampment of environmental activists opposed to the building of a police training center in the Weelaunee Forest just south of Atlanta. During the raid, police shot more than fifty times and killed Manuel Esteban Paez Terán, a queer environmental activist also known as "Tortuguita." Law enforcement claimed that Tortuguita had opened fire on them first—a Georgia State Patrol officer was wounded during the exchange.[67] But it remains unclear whether Tortuguita shot the officer or whether it was friendly fire from other law enforcement officers, as activists claim. An autopsy conducted by Tortuguita's family suggests that Tortuguita's hands were raised when they were killed.[68] Several days after the shooting, on January 21, 2023, activists held a vigil for Tortuguita. While the vigil itself was peaceful, other activists later set a police car on fire and smashed windows.[69]

The murder of Tortuguita was a watershed event. It was the first time in modern U.S. environmental protest history that an environmental activist was shot and killed by law enforcement during a protest.[70] But the Stop Cop City movement also represented a broader shift. The goal of the movement, which began in 2021, was to prevent police from building a massive new training center in a forest outside Atlanta. And the eventual protests and encampments that surrounded the movement represented something different. It fused activists and ideas from the green anarchy and total liberation movements with those from prison abolition and the Black Lives Matter movement.[71] Some of the Stop Cop City activists had cut their teeth on previous forest defense and pipeline protests. Echoing this throughline from past environmental defense campaigns, many of the anarchists who camped out in the forest near the proposed construction site were known as "forest defenders." As in past forest campaigns, activists used blockades, non-hierarchical structures, sabotage, and even tree spiking.[72] But there were key differences. Many of the activists involved in Stop Cop City didn't come out of the environmental movement. Instead, they had first become active during the 2020 uprisings following the murder of George Floyd and the resurgence of Black Lives Matter. This fusion of movements and causes—racial justice, environmental defense, anti-policing—became a defining feature of contemporary radical environmental activism.

Throughout the Stop Cop City protests, activists camped out in the forest near the construction site, vowing to block construction of the facility. Law enforcement periodically tried to clear the forest encampment. In fact, they were attempting such a clearing when they shot and killed Tortuguita. In March 2023, activists held a concert to rally support for the Stop Cop City movement. But during the concert, a separate group of activists set fire to construction equipment and clashed with police. Close to two dozen activists were arrested and charged with violating Georgia's domestic terrorism laws.[73] In addition to the domestic terror charges, in August 2023 more than sixty activists associated with the Stop Cop City movement were arrested and charged under Georgia's Racketeer Influenced and Corrupt Organizations (RICO) laws. In a press conference announcing the indictments, Georgia Attorney General Chris Carr called the activists who were part of the Stop Cop City group known as Defend the Atlanta Forest "[an] anarchist, anti-police, and anti-business extremist organization."[74] In an unusual step, those who were not even part of the protests but simply organized bail funds for activists—a common occurrence in protest movements—were also indicted on RICO charges. Though the charges for organizing bail funds were later dropped, the main case moved forward.[75] As of May 2025, the main RICO trial against 61 Stop Cop City activists was moving forward, making it one of the largest RICO cases in U.S. history.[76]

It was clear that authorities were using the RICO charges and threat of serious jail time to stop the movement in its tracks. The park was eventually closed completely, and construction went ahead, clearing the land for the police training facility. While the activists had lost the battle for Cop City, they created an estimated $20 million in delays and attracted national attention.[77]

I had a chance to talk with Brandon, who was involved in Stop Cop City, twice on Signal. The first time was in April 2023, a month after the concert and while activists were feeling the pressure of law enforcement.[78] Brandon was in his mid- to late thirties and took our Signal video call from his dimly lit room. He told me he didn't identify as an environmental activist. He referred to himself as an anti-repression organizer. That description mirrored his pathway into activism. Brandon said he had been involved in protests and social movements ever since he was a teenager. He was attracted to any movement that was "critical of capitalism and hierarchical power." Brandon found his way into the early anti-globalization movement and then, later, Occupy Wall Street. He was also heavily involved in organizing and protesting during Black Lives Matter protests throughout the summer of 2020. He told me that "ecological concerns were just one symptom of [broader] issues in society." Brandon was interested in any movement that advocated for people and attracted state repression; to him that meant the movement was doing something right. I asked Brandon about the Green Scare and how it related to what was going on in Atlanta with Stop Cop City. He answered that the "intensity of repression" was similar. Anytime activists like those in Atlanta tried to hurt the bottom line of business or a government project, the government reaction was likely to be swift. Brandon also emphasized that several large corporations, such as Waffle House, Delta, and Home Depot, had contributed $60 million to police foundations and training facilities across the U.S., including the one in Atlanta.[79]

When talking about the repression, Brandon noted that "people [activists] are familiar [with the idea] that the cops are going to try to fuck you up when you go to protests that the cops don't like." But to him the level of repression activists faced as part of Stop Cop City went "beyond what's normal." He cited the extremity of domestic terrorism charges people were facing and the killing of the activist Tortuguita.

One notable difference between the repression faced by Stop Cop City, the Green Scare, and Operation Backfire was who was going after activists. Operation Backfire investigations were led by federal law enforcement. In contrast, in Atlanta, the arrests tied to Stop Cop City were led by local and state police, and activists were being prosecuted under Georgia's RICO statute, not federal law.

Brandon had mixed feelings on the effect of the repression. On one hand, he seemed heartened by the fact "that repression usually leads to people scattering, or people get scared, and that doesn't seem to be happening [with Stop Cop City]." But in the next breath, he told me that he and other activists were particularly worried about the slew of charges activists faced—even those not directly responsible for property destruction. "The big and scary change is that they [the state] are charging people with RICO, not even people who do stuff, but those associated can be charged. That's scared people."

Brandon's concerns about charges were eerily prescient. I chatted with him a second time, a year later, in April 2024.[80] He had been part of a large round-up of activists and was facing charges, even though he wasn't accused of being involved in any of the violence. Brandon was a bit circumspect, considering his legal troubles. He couldn't comment on the specifics on the charges he was facing, but he was surprisingly open. He said the past year had been an emotional "roller coaster" for him. He told me that the arrest had shaken him. "They used a SWAT team on us and broke down on our door with a battering ram—it was like you see in the movies. Totally scary and surreal." The charges scared Brandon. But he also spoke to a few lawyers who told him they didn't think the charges against him would stick. The lawyers were right; the most serious charges he was facing were eventually dropped. But Brandon saw the RICO charges as a "circus" and the tactic of over-charging activists as a state strategy to put fear into other activists and potential supporters in an effort to break the back of the movement. Brandon felt the repression had partially worked and that he and other activists "had to make their own mental health a priority." Yet, Brandon also took heart in the fact that support for the Stop Cop City movement had attracted the attention of activists from all over the country. There was even a Stop Cop City Summit held in Tucson, Arizona, in February 2024.[81]

Brandon said he didn't think that the Stop Cop City movement would reach its end goal of blocking construction of the police training facility. The repression had been "devastating" for both him and many of his activist friends who had been intimidated or arrested. He finished our conversation on a somewhat optimistic note. Brandon told me that when he was in jail, he asked himself "whether the momentum [of the movement] was gone." But he added that the solidarity he received from other activists across the country gave him hope "that there could be a resurgence on the horizon."

Luann could not have been more different from Brandon and many of the other activists I talked to.[82] For one thing, she was neither an anarchist nor a radical environmentalist. She was older, and she was one of the few longtime Black environmentalists, having been involved in the Atlanta area's environmental issues since the mid-1990s, including Stop Cop City. When she first got into activism, she said, the other activists were "all White." Luann talked about how the concept of environmentalism was seen as a White person's problem. So, the idea of wilderness didn't have as much resonance for Black people living in urban areas. As she told me, "There's a gap between White environmentalism and the Black experience. Until people and activists started understanding the concept of environmental justice"—that Black people in cities deserved clean water and air free from pollution, too—there would continue to be a gap. This critique echoed those of scholars who argue that environmental problems are social problems, and that environmentalists have long had a blind spot for racism and other forms of oppression.[83] Luann felt that activists had to care about social justice and to think intersectionally.[84]

Luann made it clear to me that she saw both the positive and the negative aspects of the anarchist forest defenders. On a positive note, she viewed the forest defenders as doing a good job of keeping Stop Cop City in the news. The clashes with police attracted national media attention, which resulted in more resources for the protesters. On the other hand, there were drawbacks. To Luann, the police and the supporters of the training facility in the Atlanta Mayor's Office were able to say, "OK, it's a bunch of White, anarchist outsiders trying to agitate.... The anarchists in the forest [messaging] obscured the real opposition within the [Black] community and the community impacts" of the police training facility.

Luann expressed a combination of anger, sympathy, and resignation for the plight of the forest defenders. She said, "There are a bunch of young folks who are in prison over some terrorism bullshit." But she also saw the forest defenders as having different end goals than she did with respect to environmental justice. "I let the Defend the Forest folks fight their fight, but it's not my fight."

I asked Luann, given everything that was going on with Stop Cop City, what she saw as the path forward for the environmental movement. Luann said that folks, especially White folks, were in denial about the environmental and climate justice changes that needed to be made. "Most [ordinary White] folks aren't willing to make changes, and they figure they will be dead before it happens [climate change problems]."

After I talked to Luann, I spoke to a forest defender named Parker. And yes, he was White. We chatted in May 2023. Parker was in his mid- to late twenties, and he was tinkering with his bicycle in his garage while we spoke via video call on Signal. Parker was also quite nervous.[85] Given all that had happened in Atlanta with the March 2023 protests and sabotage, as well as the increasing threat of arrests, this was understandable.

When I asked Parker how he got into activism, he told me he was aware of environmental issues from a young age and always felt an "intimate connection with the natural world." He oscillated between hating humans for what they had done to the world and focusing on trying to protect the natural world. Parker's participation in Black Lives Matter protests in 2020 marked a turning point for him. "I had participated in protests before," he said, "but it was the George Floyd uprising that activated me politically."

Much of my conversation with Parker centered on tactics. He said that many of the actions he and other forest defenders carried out were less about the larger strategic goals of the movement, and more about what needed to happen in a particular moment or day. "While we were in the woods [the Weelaunee Forest], the actions just stemmed from the need to stop contractors and police from entering the woods, and that was the metric for importance." He believed in a vanguard approach to activism and use of tactics like property destruction. "Even if it doesn't happen immediately, eventually the public will come around to such tactics [if the cause is worthy enough]."

Parker also contrasted the tactics used in the forest in Atlanta to those of other forest defense campaigns and Earth First! blockades. He saw them as fundamentally different, when operating in an urban forest like the Weelaunee Forest in Atlanta. Parker said the standard kind of forest blockage–occupying a road (like in Warner Creek in the mid-1990s) or a group of trees–didn't work because there were multiple entrances to the park, and "after the first couple of [police] raids we realized we were sitting ducks [if we stayed] in the treehouses."

Parker then brought up the sabotage that occurred during the Stop Cop City charity concert in March 2023, when during the concert multiple construction vehicles were set on fire. Parker said that "being able to use the cover of the charity concert was incredibly effective to allow people [activists engaged in sabotage] to operate and take actions while it was happening. The forest was a buffer zone, and it was hard for the police to track folks [who had committed the violence]." More than twenty people were arrested shortly after the concert and charged with domestic terrorism that March.[86] Parker further believed that the repression—while hard to fathom and difficult to deal with—was ultimately helpful to the movement. "As fucked up as repression is, I think it galvanized people. In the wake of the repression, there were more eyeballs on Atlanta."

At the end of our interview, Parker told me that he had experienced major depression all of his life and that at multiple points he had been suicidal. After one "close call with suicide," he got connected to the "movement." He then said, "This movement makes life worth living. The more people that are disaffected, alienated, or on the brink (the better) . . . nihilism can be freeing. Living as if you are already dead can be empowering. There's a freedom there."

***

While I was working on this book, other protest movements emerged, not always rooted in environmental politics. These movements captured the attention of left-wing activists, and many of the those I interviewed also got directly involved in these protests. For example, in early May 2022, the U.S. Supreme Court decision in *Dobbs v. Jackson Women's Health Organization* was leaked to the media.[87] It became clear that the Court was overturning decades of precedent stemming from *Roe v. Wade* and that many women, particularly in Republican states, were about to have their abortion rights greatly restricted. Shortly after the decision was leaked, the office of an anti-abortion group was set on fire in Madison, Wisconsin, by activists calling themselves Jane's Revenge. In their communiqué to the public, the activists made the following statement:

> This was only a warning. We demand the disbanding of all anti-choice establishments, fake clinics, and violent anti-choice groups within the next thirty days. This is not a mere "difference of opinion" as some have framed it. We are literally fighting for our lives. We will not sit still while we are killed and forced into servitude. We have run thin on patience and mercy for those who seek to strip us of what little autonomy we have left. As you continue to bomb clinics and assassinate

doctors with impunity, so too shall we adopt increasingly extreme tactics to maintain freedom over our own bodies.[88]

The firebombing and the language used in the communiqué echoed those of the ELF more than twenty years prior. Following this initial attack, there was a string of at least ten arson attacks and acts of vandalism. These attacks targeted anti-abortion groups and crisis pregnancy centers—facilities that try to discourage women from getting an abortion. An anonymous group of activists calling themselves "Jane's Revenge" claimed responsibility for the actions[89] Right-wing pundits decried the left-wing abortion extremists.[90] In addition, a U.S. Department of Homeland Security memo described Jane's Revenge as "loosely affiliated suspected violent extremists."[91] In 2023, law enforcement arrested four activists on charges related to vandalism and threats against a crisis pregnancy center in Florida. The four activists were initially indicted under federal laws meant to protect access to abortion clinics from anti-abortion activists. The irony was not lost on those on the left who decried the Supreme Court's decision to restrict abortion rights.[92] Three of the activists eventually pleaded guilty, with two sentenced to 30 days in prison, and another, against whom charges were more serious, getting 1 year and a day in prison.[93]

Faith, the youth climate activist whom we met earlier in this chapter, was involved in protests related to abortion rights. She told me that following the leaked decision that overturned *Roe v. Wade*, she and other activists had been attending weekly demonstrations outside the suburban Maryland home of Supreme Court Justice Brett Kavanaugh, one of the justices who voted to overturn *Roe v. Wade*. As Faith explained to me, when people questioned how she would feel if right-wing activists protested outside of Supreme Court Justice Sonia Sotomayor's house, she said, "I wouldn't like it." But she said you couldn't separate the tactic from the target. As Faith told me, "I like it when we [left-wing activists] show up outside of the U.S. Capitol—it's good, but it's not good when the fascists did it on January 6th."[94]

But Faith also brought up a curious point. She said that since *Roe v. Wade* had been overturned, mainstream abortion rights activists had become super security conscious. As Faith said, there was a place for security culture among activists engaged in property destruction or clandestine sabotage. "But now people say you can't go to a Planned Parenthood march without a burner phone." Faith felt this hurt the movement. As she said, "That's not what you want to do and how you want to approach city hall when you're trying to guarantee access to Plan B [emergency contraceptive]."

Nathan, the activist associated with the ELF whom we met in the previous chapter, emailed me a few weeks after we talked in June 2022. At the end of our conversation, I had asked him why, given the threat from climate change, there hadn't been a return to more intense actions like those of the ELF. In his follow-up email, he referenced this question and wrote, "Maybe the kids are busy elsewhere." He then linked to a *New York Post* article about a crisis pregnancy center near Buffalo, New York, that had been firebombed.[95] I responded that I was curious to see if those activists responsible for the Buffalo bombing had come out of the broader left-wing or environmental movement. Nathan responded a few minutes later: "I hope we don't find out."

***

On October 7, 2023, Palestinian militants associated with Hamas launched a coordinated and surprise attack from the Gaza Strip on Israel proper. More than 1,200 Israeli soldiers and civilians were killed, and more than 250 were kidnapped and taken back to the Gaza Strip as hostages.[96] The Israeli response was swift. As the war escalated, the Israeli military cordoned off much of the Gaza Strip and began a fierce bombardment of the territory in an attempt to rescue Israeli hostages controlled by Hamas, but also to destroy the militant group's fighting capacity. Estimates vary, but the Gaza Health Ministry reported that by August 2024, with the fighting still raging, more than 40,000 Palestinians in Gaza had been killed by the Israeli incursion—many of them women and children. Additionally, Israel's actions displaced 85% of the Gaza Strip population.[97] Given the fierce fighting and the vast displacement, international aid groups and experts reported that Gaza was at a high risk of famine.[98] Israeli critics, pro-Palestinian activists, and leftist activists accused Israel of waging genocide against the Palestinians. To Israeli supporters, many of these claims were antisemitic, especially given the scale and scope of the Hamas attack on October 7. But to pro-Palestinian activists and sympathizers, supporters of Israel were using charges of antisemitism to distract from and excuse Israel's conduct.[99]

The brutal nature of Hamas's violence on October 7 and the swiftness and intensity of Israel's response mark one of the worst periods of violence in the long history of the Israeli-Palestinian conflict. It's not surprising—given the strong Jewish and Palestinian diaspora communities in the United States and the increasingly partisan nature of support for Israel—that activists were mobilized.[100] There were widespread protests, particularly on college campuses throughout 2023 and the spring of 2024.[101] These protests sparked harsh and aggressive police responses at schools like Columbia University and the University of Texas at Austin. Pro-Palestinian activists across the country engaged in civil disobedience actions as well. For instance, in April 2024 pro-Palestinian activists blocked the Golden Gate Bridge.[102]

Many climate justice activists saw the Palestinian issue and the plight of Gazans as intimately connected to their broader environmental struggle for liberation. For example, in May 2024, pipeline activists trying to block construction of the Mountain Valley Pipeline in Virginia locked themselves to construction equipment. They held a sign with a picture of a Palestinian flag that read, "Free Palestine No Pipelines No Prisons No Genocide."[103] In 2024, pro-Palestinian and climate activists protested outside of CitiBank as part of the "Summer of Heat on Wall Street" campaign. Activists wanted the bank to stop financing fossil fuels and supporting Israel; as one activist said, "We understand that there is no climate justice without a free Palestine."[104] For many climate activists throughout 2023 and 2024, the pro-Palestinian movement became the most important cause to support.

When I talked to Brandon, the Atlanta-based activist associated with Stop Cop City, in April 2024, he told me that it felt like "every protest is about the Palestinian genocide and also about Cop City."[105] Being in Atlanta, he regarded the Cop City protests as a local-based campaign where he had a personal connection, whereas Palestine, he said, was more of a "symbolic international pressure campaign" to fight oppression.

In April 2024, one of my key contacts, Tim, the longtime direct action organizer, put me in touch with a younger climate activist, Alicia, who he said would be able to give me the youth climate perspective. He was close with Alicia, so I thought I would hear back from her relatively quickly. After two weeks and several unanswered emails, I reached out to Tim and told him I hadn't heard back from Alicia. Tim then told me that Alicia was super busy with pro-Palestinian activism at the movement and was involved in a recent blockade of the Golden Gate Bridge.

A few weeks later, Alicia apologized for her radio silence, and we eventually agreed to meet in Portland in May 2024, when we would both be there.[106] We met up at a hip café that had a spacious interior. Alicia was short, had medium-length brown hair, and was wearing a Joshua Tree hat. She was also carrying a large Nalgene bottle filled with water and ice cubes, given how hot it was in Portland that day—close to 90 degrees. The door to the café was open, and inside it was hot, borderline stifling. Alicia and I almost considered not staying, but the chocolate cookies were too good to pass up. I asked a person working there if they couldn't turn on the fans to cool it down. She responded with a slight smile—"they are on, our AC is just broken."

Alicia and I then sat down and talked. She told me that she grew up in the Bay Area and was the daughter of immigrants. As a first-generation kid, her parents warned her about protesting or getting involved in politics. And she was worried that any protest activities might put her parents' immigrant status at risk.

She then told me how she got into activism. "My roommates radicalized me, no for real, that's the truth." She said that in her mid-twenties she was living with a bunch of friends who were active in the Sunrise Movement. She noted that she "was around all these activists, and it was during the election [in 2020], and [her] roommates would be having three different meetings." Her roommates would also periodically ask Alicia for help with presentation slides or with a flyer design, and before she knew it, she was working on communications for the climate movement. It was also during the height of the Black Lives Matter protests and the COVID-19 lockdowns. She said there wasn't much else to do but protest. So Alicia and some of her friends and roommates did exactly that. Alicia said that she vividly remembered her "first time putting [her] phone away at home (to prevent being tracked) and writing a jail support number on [her] hand." Waiting to be "kettled by the cops," she said, was both scary and exhilarating, and she became hooked on activism.

When I asked Alicia about the Palestine protests, she told me about being in Atlanta for the Stop Cop City protests in the spring of 2023. She connected the repression she felt in Atlanta to the Palestinian cause. As Alicia saw it, "the climate justice is majority-White, but when I think about Palestine, people who are Brown, or have intergenerational trauma ... it feels more powerful." To Alicia the Palestinian cause was a broader symbol of liberation against imperialism and climate change—"'Free Palestine' means free them all," and that's why it was so big and important, she said.

When the conversation shifted to tactics, Alicia made a provocative statement: "I do want to blow up a pipeline, for the record." I paused to make sure I had heard her correctly. And then she followed it up with, "But then I have to think about the cleanup, the insurance [that covers the property loss for the pipeline company], the new security [that the pipeline people will hire], and that I might rot in jail." She then said, for climate change, for George Floyd and Black Lives Matter, and Palestine, "I want to do direct actions where the actual elite people making decisions have nowhere to hide. I want to do home demos, I want to turn the AC off on the hottest day of the year of the elites' homes, I want them to not feel safe."

Yet the most memorable part of my conversation with Alicia came toward the end of our chat. She told me that she had recently attended a major fossil fuel industry conference and had plans with a few other activists to disrupt it. Alicia said that the night before the action she went on Tinder and matched with someone whom she realized was also attending the conference. She agreed to go on a date with him, and then, instead of small talk or romance, she "actually confronted him about working for a fossil fuel company." She asked him if "he was happy, and where he saw himself in five years." To Alicia "it wasn't a date, it was a conversation to save lives" by changing the mind of those who profit from fossil fuels. Alicia told me she thought she had partially persuaded him and was still in touch with him. Diversity of tactics, indeed.

**

One thing I was left pondering after talking to activists who have been involved since the Green Scare is that, for many of the protest movements they participated in, climate change and the environment were not the main issues. For instance, many climate justice activists were active in the Black Lives Matter movement in 2020. Others participated in Stop Cop City, in which the environment was an issue, but Black Lives Matter and police abolition were more front and center. In addition, several activists told me that in the spring of 2024 they had a hard time getting a few hundred activists to come out to a climate rally, whereas they could get thousands to march for Palestine.

What does it say about the modern radical environmental movement that its biggest issues aren't even the environment? A charitable reading would be that these are all different struggles for liberation against racism, imperialism, capitalism, policing, and the like, and that they are all linked. So, it's simply an update of the total liberation philosophy of the 1990s and the social ecology view of environmentalism. In fact, Jesse, the former spokesperson for the ELF, made exactly that argument to me.[107] To Jesse, the antiwar movement in the early 2000s, Occupy Wall Street, Antifa–it's all the same movement. He said the Stop Cop City and "blockade with the Atlanta Forest Defenders is a mixture of the ELF and Black Lives Matter . . . I know people involved in these movements, and it is the same people, the same resources, the linkages between Antifa and the ELF . . . people [just] shifted struggles." Jesse was emphatic about this point. He said activists like himself don't just care about one thing and walk away from others; "we care about a collection of ideas." The idea that activists participate and show solidarity across multiple movements isn't new. The ELF and the anti-globalization movement made common cause in the late 1990s and early 2000s. And as we've seen in this chapter, for many of the younger environmental activists, Black Lives Matter, Free Palestine, or Stop Cop City was equally important.

But not all activists approved of this fusion approach. Bernard, the former Earth First!er who was struck with grief and despair and whom we met at the beginning of this chapter, had a different view when I broached this topic with him. He got excited and a bit upset. It was clearly something that had been gnawing at him for a while: "People [activists] can go all out for Palestine, abortion rights, and racism . . . and that's great. But the environment will always play second fiddle—that's a big problem!"[108] Bernard said Earth First! was able to get hundreds of people into forest defenses "in the middle of Nowhere, Wyoming in the early 1980s"—he was referring to a 500-person Earth First! rally against a proposed oil field in Little Granite Creek, Wyoming, in July 1982—with just "love of wilderness and love of Earth,"[109] and now that belief "is taboo."

Bernard said activists felt pressure to confront and talk about concrete things like jobs, racism, and material security, which are important. But on the left, "if you simply love trees and the Earth, you are seen as less-than." Bernard viewed this as a failure of the movement. People, especially activists, want to believe in the "transcendent; it's not all rational motivation."

That's the deep question. Climate change and its effects are happening all around us, and scientists warn that these effects are only going to get more intense with hotter heat waves, worse droughts, and more intense hurricanes.[110] But these same climate effects are likely to pressure food supplies from droughts and floods, heighten the risk of armed conflict in different parts or the world, and increase migration from climate-affected regions.[111] That's a lot of social problems in our future. So, will the environment always be the second-most important cause for activists? Or is there space for a purely environment-focused radical movement like the one Bernard wants to see? That's the big question and one we will return to in the final chapter.

7

From Ecofascists to Raw Milk

THIS CHAPTER ALMOST DIDN'T MAKE it into the book. When I first drafted an outline, I included a chapter on ecofascism. Some of the initial academic reviewers advised against it. One argued that ecofascism wasn't a coherent or consistent enough ideology to warrant a full chapter.

It's true that the label has often muddied the waters. Both far-right mass murderers and deep ecologists from Earth First! have been described as "ecofascists"—despite their vastly different worldviews and tactics.[1] Yet, at its core, ecofascism is a belief system rooted in the idea that overpopulation, non-White immigration, and development are destroying the planet. To ecofascists, the only solution is to return to nature and protect White nations, by force if necessary. As we'll see in this chapter, ecofascism is best understood as a fascist ideology that coopts environmental concerns. It cherry-picks ideas to justify a broader authoritarian, racist agenda.

Meanwhile, activists have had their own concerns about the idea of ecofascism. Cameron, the military veteran turned activist with whom I had become close during the writing of this book, said that he thought the notion of ecofascism was "overblown."[2] But he also warned that as the effects of climate change become more apparent, the far-right would likely adopt their own kind of environmental policy that would scapegoat immigrants and climate refugees. Cameron was particularly worried that a right-wing "asshole" acting on behalf of environmental concerns would carry out a major attack and "get the whole movement framed as terrorists."

Cameron had a reason to be concerned. In the past 10 years, there had been a spate of right-wing attacks that targeted Muslims, immigrants, and non-White people. These included the 2018 Pittsburgh Tree of Life synagogue shooting in 2018 (which killed eleven people); the 2019 Poway, California, Synagogue shooting in 2019 (killed one); the 2019 Christchurch, New Zealand, mosque shooting (killed fifty-one); the 2019 El Paso shooting (killed twenty-three); and the 2022 Buffalo shooting (killed ten).[3] Many of the perpetrators issued manifestos and long lists of grievances, and all of them were preoccupied with a shrinking White population. In 2011 in Norway, far-right extremist Anders Breivik killed seventy-seven people in two attacks that targeted the office of the then–prime minister and then a summer camp run by the ruling center-left party. In his 1,500-page manifesto, released shortly before the attacks, Breivik railed against "cultural Marxists"— feminists, leftists, and minority groups whom he viewed as the enemy of White Christian European males—and Islamists. Breivik also plagiarized multiple passages from the Unabomber's manifesto, for example replacing the word "leftism" with "multiculturalism" and "cultural Marxism."[4]

Breivik and other mass shooters were obsessed with the idea of the Great Replacement Theory, a conspiracy theory that Whites in Western countries are being systematically and demographically replaced through a combination of immigration and declining birth rates.[5] As we discussed in Chapter 1, these concerns of immigrants threatening the White race are not new to the environmental movement. They stretch all the way back to the godfather of U.S. conservation, Madison Grant, and his 1916 screed, *The Passing of the Great Race*. The villains behind this so-called replacement vary from Muslims to non-White immigrants, to a cabal of Jews. But the underlying worldview, that Whites are under threat and need to defend themselves, with violence if necessary, is the common thread.

One of the major reasons why ecofascism and the Great Replacement Theory merit discussion is that since 1996 there have been only two environmentally motivated terror attacks in the United States in which people have died: the 2019 El Paso Shooting, in which twenty-three people were killed, and the 2022 Buffalo shooting, in which there were ten fatalities. In both cases, the manifestos of the shooters stated their support for ecofascism and were driven by concerns about a "White genocide." In his 180-page manifesto, the Buffalo shooter, Payton Gendron, decried the decline in White birth rates and the increase in non-White populations. Gendron said the first Whites must deal violently with the "invaders" (non-White population) before fixing their own declining fertility. But Gendron also argued that "Green nationalism is the only true nationalism" and that there's "no Green future with never ending population growth." These concerns over runaway population growth would have been at home with many of the Zero Population Growthers in the 1970s and other conservationists concerned about overpopulation. Yet like much of Gendron's manifesto, these weren't even his words. They were stolen from the 2019 Christchurch, New Zealand, shooter Brenton Tarrant's manifesto.[6] Perhaps the biggest clue that environmental concerns were not the main driving force behind Gendron's attack is where these green nationalism ideas were located in his manifesto—page 164 out of 180.[7]

✳✳✳

"You will not replace us. Jews will not replace us. Blood and soil." These were the words of far-right neo-Nazis and White supremacists carrying torches in Charlottesville, Virginia, on the evening of August 11, 2017. They were protesting plans to remove a Confederate statue of Robert E. Lee. The next day, following clashes between the far-right protesters and counterprotesters, one of the White supremacist protesters drove his car into a crowd of counterprotesters, killing thirty-two-year-old Heather Heyer.[8] The actions of the neo-Nazi protesters and their far-right Great Replacement rhetoric were roundly denounced by politicians on both sides of the aisle. A notable exception was President Donald Trump. He famously defended some of the far-right protesters, saying there were "fine people on both sides."[9] But fast-forward a few years, and the Great Replacement rhetoric has become mainstream among key Republican elites. For instance, in 2021, prominent Fox News host Tucker Carlson accused the Democratic Party of "trying to replace the current electorate [in the United States] with new people, more obedient voters from the Third World... [it's] what's happening actually. Let's just say it. That's true."[10] During the 2024 U.S. presidential election, then Republican nominee Donald Trump echoed Carlson and baselessly accused Democrats of importing voters: "They can't even speak English. They don't even know what country they're in, practically. And these people are trying to get them to vote, and that's why they're [the Democrats are] allowing them into our country."[11] From his perch on X (formerly Twitter), which he owns, Elon Musk, the richest man in the world and a vocal Trump supporter during the 2024 campaign, pushed a constant stream of content echoing Trump and Carlson. He baselessly claimed that Democrats were importing immigrant voters and also bemoaned declining White birth rates.[12]

Was there a burgeoning ecofascism movement just waiting to break through the surface? The mainstreaming of Great Replacement rhetoric—on the heels of several high-profile mass shootings with manifestos pushing ecofascist ideas—could give that impression. *The Washington Post* ran stories on ecofascism in 2019 after the Christchurch, New Zealand, shooting and again after the Buffalo shooting in 2022.[13]

Journalists and extremist researchers also began to track various online groups and movements that were sprouting up on Twitter and Telegram. Groups like the "Pine Tree Gang," as some referred to them, emerged following a popular Netflix series on the Unabomber, Ted Kaczynski.[14] These online ecofascists held eclectic views. They rejected modernity and technology, embraced Nordic culture, and believed the environment was being polluted and the planet decimated by overpopulation—particularly by non-Whites and immigrants, whom they blamed for climate change and environmental degradation. Kaczynski's ideas and rejection of modernity were fused with other far-right accelerationist ideas such as encouraging attacks against the power grid.[15]

The ecofascist movement also found an online home among other far-right and neofascist groups that encouraged attacks with memes, fictional stories, and how-to manuals on the decentralized Telegram channels, known as "Terrogram."[16] Online fringe spaces provided an ideal place for far-right members to decry modernity and the pollution of both the environment and the nation by immigrants and minorities. In many ways this is the defining feature of the current iteration of ecofascism. It exists mostly as an online fringe subculture. The ecofascists of today post memes of bloody purges, longing for a bygone era of racial and natural purity, and esoteric and occultic symbols that harken back to Nazi mysticism and 19th-century European Romantic nationalism.[17] It is not a movement with a strong offline presence.

The concerns about ecofascism and far-right movements taking up the environmental cause also stem from a set of more uncomfortable facts for the environmental movement. All the ingredients for a right-wing offshoot have been present since the inception of the environmental movement.[18] Today, when people think of an environmentalist, they have a mental model of a person who drives a hybrid or electric car, who maybe has an "In this house we believe in science" sign, and supports progressive and left-leaning policies. Yet, as we discussed in earlier chapters, the idea of environmentalism is not just a liberal, leftist one. It's ideologically flexible. Madison Grant's views on race and immigration, and the views of Dave Foreman and other deep ecologists on immigration, serve as a reminder that right-wing ideas have been present in different parts of the movement from the start. The Nazi ideology of "blood and soil," of keeping bloodlines pure, goes along with keeping the land and environment pristine.[19] At a rally in 2023 in New Hampshire, Donald Trump echoed these points, accusing immigrants of "poisoning the blood of our country."[20]

A key figurehead in the online ecofascist space is Ted Kaczynski. In many ways, the ecofascist space functions as a bizarre fan club for the Unabomber filtered through the lens of 4Chan humor and far-right accelerationism. Pro-Kaczynski memes overflow on the ecofascist accounts.[21] His status among online ecofascists highlights the complicated relationship between Kaczynski and the radical environmental movement. FBI agents found copies of *Earth First! Journal* in Kaczynski's cabin when they arrested him, and he clearly drew some of his ideas from the deep ecologists and anarcho-primitivists who later affectionately called him "Uncle Ted."[22] But Kaczynski's disgust for modern technology was exceeded by his obsessive hatred of leftists. The word "left" and its variants appear more than 200 times in his manifesto—almost always in a critical, dismissive way. The word "environment" and its variants appear fewer than forty times.[23]

***

In 1968, ecologist Garrett Hardin published one of the most influential and widely cited essays on environmental policy: "The Tragedy of the Commons."[24] Hardin used the example of a shared village pasture. He argued that when a resource is owned by no one, individuals will overuse it—for example, by allowing their sheep to overgraze—until it's depleted, and everyone suffers. Hardin's "tragedy of the commons" has been applied to a range of environmental problems. From air and water pollution to global issues like climate change, wherever there is tension between individual actions that can deplete or harm shared resources, there are echoes of this tragedy.

Yet, Hardin wasn't just an ecologist. He was also an avowed eugenicist and close friend to overpopulation activist and nativist John Tanton, who would go on to form the Tanton network of anti-immigration groups in the United States—which Hardin supported.[25] In 1974, Hardin wrote a controversial piece entitled "Lifeboat Ethics: The Case Against Helping the Poor" in *Psychology Today*.[26] In the article Hardin introduced the lifeboat metaphor for the ethical dilemma facing the world. Imagine a lifeboat with wealthy people. Poor people swim in the water outside the boat, and maybe the wealthy people feel guilty for not letting the poor aboard. But as the number of poor people increases and the wealthy let more poor people aboard, eventually the safety of the boat is at risk. So, the wealthy boat passengers must constantly guard against the poor masses seeking to board the lifeboat and putting all aboard at risk. You can guess where this analogy is going. Hardin was talking about immigration, and the poor masses are the threat that overpopulation and immigration from the third world posed to the United States and other wealthy countries. He argued that citizens in wealthy countries had a duty to abide by the harsh lifeboat ethics—restrict immigration to save the Earth from "environmental ruin" and for posterity's sake. Hardin would continue to advocate against immigration and support eugenics and racist causes up until his death.[27]

Hardin's ideas of lifeboat ethics also resonated with Pentti Linkola, a Finnish deep ecologist with a cruel, misanthropic streak. Along with Kaczynski, Linkola is the main intellectual inspiration for the ecofascist movement. He was born in Finland in 1932 and spent summers at his grandfather's farm in Southern Finland, fishing and exploring outdoors.[28] Linkola later became obsessed with the threats posed by climate change and depletion of Earth's resources. He set about preserving Finland's old-growth forests and largely rejected modernity. He saw human overpopulation as a plague and advocated "controlled pruning" of the population through a combination of state-sanctioned sterilization, abortion, euthanasia, the death penalty, and allowing famine to run its course.[29]

But Linkola is best known for his take on Hardin's "lifeboat ethics" analogy to overpopulation. What should people do when a lifeboat is already filled with people and more people are trying to get on board? Linkola took Hardin's argument a step further and said, "Those who hate life will try to load it with more people and sink the lot. Those who love and respect life will take the ship's axe and sever the extra hands that cling to the sides" (p. 130–31).[30]

It's easy to see how Linkola's views of violently defending a lifeboat (Earth) from those clinging to it (overpopulation) could be adapted by the far right and ecofascists. Replace the lifeboat with Western countries, overpopulation in general with overpopulation by immigrants and non-White people, and the need to sever the hand with violence.

Some of the original deep ecologists and anarcho-primitivists from the late 1980s and 1990s also went on some strange political journeys. Derrick Jensen is a prominent activist and writer whose book *A Language Older Than Words* (2000) and ideas were incredibly influential in the Pacific Northwest in the late 1990s and early 2000s.[31] Jensen and the anarcho-primitivist John Zerzan were at the intellectual vanguard of green anarchism that was popular in radical environmental spaces during this time.[32] In 2011, Jensen, along with fellow activists Aric McBay and Lierre Kieth, released their manifesto *Deep Green Resistance* and attempted to found a loose group of the same name. Deep Green Resistance advocated for a vanguard militia of leftists to take down cellphone towers, ports, and other infrastructure to bring down civilization. Leftist environmental activists criticized Deep Green Resistance on multiple grounds. First, Jensen and others in Deep Green Resistance weren't involved in direct action themselves, but rather saw their role as encouraging others and providing a blueprint—leading their critics to call them armchair revolutionaries.[33] Second, Deep Green Resistance claimed to be a radical feminist organization. But they also claimed that the focus of feminist activists on transgender rights came at the expense of the rights of biological females. They argue, for instance, that trans women should not be allowed into female-only spaces like bathrooms, leading critics to accuse them of transphobia.[34] Finally, many of Deep Green's Resistance goals of bringing down industrial civilization and attacking infrastructure to do so are identical to those of their far-right accelerationist counterparts.[35]

***

The idea of ecofascism as a concept had a mixed reception among some of the deep ecologists I talked to. They were also concerned with overpopulation and immigration. For instance, Jim, the conservation activist whom we met in Chapter 2 and who had been a follower of David Foreman, told me his impressions from when he first read Linkola's 2009 book *Can Life Prevail*.[36] He found many of Linkola's arguments "interesting." But he also told me that Linkola's ideas were dangerous since they would be seized upon by critics of conservationism. A full embrace of Linkola would mean deep ecologists would all be labeled ecofascists and "nut jobs that live in a cabin [in the woods]."[37]

Richard, the environmental philosopher and ethicist whom we met in Chapter 2, was sympathetic to the overpopulation and anti-immigration causes, but he had a different view on Linkola. When I broached the idea that many of the overpopulation and immigration concerns advocated by Richard and other deep ecologists like Dave Foreman were being used by far-right activists and ecofascists, Richard disagreed.[38] He told me that he still found Hardin's idea about lifeboat ethics compelling and quite accurate. And he then told me that several years back Linkola's publisher had sent him a copy of the book to review. He said that he "found a lot that [he] agreed with" in Linkola's writings. Richard then said that what he respected most about Linkola was his willingness to confront problems like overpopulation and propose concrete solutions—even extreme ones like reducing the population via violence. He then clarified that he didn't necessarily agree with Linkola's solutions, especially the violent ones, but he admired Linkola's willingness to outline a plan to try to fix things. At the end of our conversation, we came back to Kaczynski, and Richard couldn't help himself. He told me, half laughing, that the reason "Kaczynski hates lefties is because they are a bunch of wussies and don't really care about protecting the environment."

This was the conundrum for deep ecology folks like Jim and Richard. They could dismiss the violence, the Kaczynski adoration, and the extreme accelerationism of ecofascism. But many of the ecofascist ideas about overpopulation, immigration, and environmental degradation were harder to dismiss because they were variants of the arguments that many deep ecologists themselves had made years earlier.

In May 2022, I talked with Nick, a far-right researcher who had been monitoring ecofascism trends in Europe and the United States.[39] The first thing Nick told me was that the ecofascist coalition was not in any way a coherent movement. Nick described the U.S. ecofascists as "a hodgepodge of people who liked Kaczynski and advocated for antisemitism, anarchists, deep green/far right folks, and those who are just into everything extreme." Many of the U.S. ecofascists dreamed of turning the Pacific Northwest into a White nationalist homeland. This wasn't out of step with history, either. Oregon was originally founded as a "Whites only" state and didn't repeal its racial exclusion laws until 1926.[40] But as Nick saw it, the big obstacle to ecofascism becoming a core part of the far-right was that climate denialism was just too embedded in the right wing. Most far-right members could embrace the racism, the accelerationism, and even the concerns about pollution. But climate change was a left-wing Globalist hoax and a bridge too far.[41] In Nick's view, it made it hard for ecofascism to be anything more than a niche movement.

I brought this idea about ecofascism being a niche movement to Max, the antifascist academic who was part of *Earth First! Journal*, in May of 2022. This was shortly after the 2022 Buffalo shooting, in which the shooter Payton Gendron targeted and killed ten people, all of them Black, in a Buffalo supermarket and its parking lot. Gendron's manifesto—like that of many before him—subscribed to the Great Replacement Theory and White Genocide conspiracy theories, blaming Jews and elites. In the manifesto, Gendron he even stated his support for ecofascism. Max had a lot of thoughts on ecofascism.[42] On one hand, he saw the ecofascist impulse as a natural outgrowth of some of the darker tendencies of deep ecology that had been part of Earth First! from the beginning. Max said the idea of wilderness as pristine, untouched, and untainted was a "crappy concept" that was ripe for exploitation by White nationalists—keep wilderness and the nation pure. He also saw the Buffalo shooting, following the 2019 El Paso and Christchurch shootings, as establishing a worrying trend of ecofascist-inspired shootings, and one to watch.

Max and I chatted two years later in 2024, and, by then, his views had evolved.[43] The far-right hadn't really articulated a coherent view of the environment. The small sliver of the far-right that focused on the environment was fixated on the idea of human biodiversity. As a concept, human biodiversity sounds like a bland scientific term. But it's shorthand for those who support eugenics, believe that there are key and important differences between the races, and advocate shutting the borders to keep out non-White races supposedly polluting the nation. Climate change was a fringe issue. Max said that ecofascism, when it was expressed at all, was really a fig leaf for White nationalism and Great Replacement–style theories. It was never the main motivator for racist online nationalists; it was the tenth reason—"oh yeah, in addition to Jews and non-Whites destroying our country's values, they are also destroying the environment." It's not hard to imagine in the future, as climate denialism becomes more untenable, that the right wing make ecofascist-like arguments as justification for shutting the borders. Climate change will just give those in the right wing another reason to dislike immigrants. For now, the depth of climate denialism on the right means that ecofascism remains a fringe, mostly online movement.

***

During this same conversation, Max piqued my curiosity about a different right-wing offshoot that had echoes of environmentalism. He described a new movement that emerged in the early days of the COVID-19 pandemic, following the lockdowns in 2020. Right-wing activists started circulating conspiracies on government plans for a "Great Reset," the term the World Economic Forum gave to policies designed to improve the world economy following the pandemic.[44] To right-wing conspiracists, the pandemic lockdown wasn't designed to combat the spread of COVID-19. Rather, "they" were secretly clearing the way for a global world government takeover. The supposed "they" who were secretly pushing the takeover were a mix of global, wealthy elites, like billionaire philanthropist, George Soros and Bill Gates, and even President Joseph Biden. Great Reset conspiracy supporters were a mix of fitness influencers, homesteaders, anti-vaccine activists, Tucker Carlson, and even Republican Congresswoman Marjorie Taylor Greene. The Great Reset conspiracy theory also grew to encompass the belief that Globalists were going to take away meat, dairy, eggs, and other grocery staples from our diets. From these conspiratorial concerns, the raw milk movement began to grow. At the start, the chief focus of its adherents was on the supposed health wonders of raw (unpasteurized) milk, but it extended to raw meat and even raw eggs.[45] Scientists and public health officials were aghast. Milk in its raw form can be a haven for bacteria and germs. The heating of milk via pasteurization to kill and eliminate disease-causing pathogens is considered one of the major public health innovations of the 20th century.[46]

On the surface, raw milk enthusiasts share similar concerns with environmentalists. Like environmentalists, they are worried about the health effects of modern food production, pollutants, and toxins in their food. They also have a distrust of and disdain for large corporations. But unlike many environmental activists, they either downplay the effects of climate change, or see it as a Globalist conspiracy for the United Nations and other George Soros-backed institutions to take power over people's lives.[47] Raw milk has became a symbol for those who desire self-sufficiency, and want to live in a natural way, away from prying government eyes. It is the newest expression of the right-wing ecology, and it is no longer a fringe movement. Raw milk has gone from a weird hippy, foodie fad to a mainstream Republican talking point. Republican legislators in Iowa, Montana, North Dakota, Alaska, Georgia, and Wyoming have all passed laws since 2020 legalizing the sale of raw milk.[48]

Max described the burgeoning conservative movement's romanticism of the farm and its newfound love for the local farmer's markets as an expression of a granola homestead conservatism. He derisively referred to followers of this movement as "Birkenstock Bonapartes." But Max was on to something: the post-COVID skepticism of expertise had led to this new food-based, largely right-wing movement.

It's important to point out, too, that while some adherents of the militia movement boost raw milk, most raw milk supporters aren't advocating the overthrow of the government. Rather, raw milk has become a symbol of growing populist and far-right skepticism of government authority and scientific expertise.[49]

That antiestablishment impulse isn't exclusive to the right. But in recent years, especially after the COVID-19 lockdowns, it has become a defining feature of the Trumpian right.[50] The core beliefs connecting the antiestablishment right include conspiracy theories about Globalist elites like George Soros, deep distrust of scientists and institutions, and a rejection of government public health policies that are seen as government overreach. In that sense, raw milk fits neatly within this worldview.

To find out more about the raw milk movement, I had a phone conversation with Sue in August of 2024.[51] Many of the folks in the movement described Sue as the godmother of the raw milk movement. Sue is a dairy farmer and longtime influencer in the movement through her website and books, which had become the bible for raw milk supporters. She was super friendly on the phone, saying she had just completed some work on her farm. The first thing that Sue emphasized to me was that her kids grew up on raw milk, and ate liver, eggs, and butter. She said, "They were very high functioning, athletic kids, and they were never sick, and I proved to myself that this was the way to raise children." She believed that raw milk should be a birthright for kids. Then she went on a bit of a tangent, talking about how raw milk prevents facial deformities and would fix the bone structure of children, and reverse the IQ decline. I wasn't quite clear about how that was supposed to happen. But Sue saw unpasteurized milk as a "miracle" drink.

Everything during my conversation with Sue was couched in the health benefit of raw milk. But once we started talking about the recent growth of raw milk adherents, Sue got very excited and political. She said a variety of folks were into raw milk—hippies, Amish, homesteaders. She also told me she personally identified as "conservative."

But one of the most common denominators linking the raw milk advocates was their skepticism toward vaccines. Sue saw vaccine skepticism as the gateway. Once people started to question vaccines, she said, they would begin to question other things, too. Sue told me that after the COVID pandemic and the lockdowns "nobody believes the government anymore."

There was another curious part of my interview with Sue which would be echoed by other raw milk supporters. Sue was very concerned about environmental toxins, especially glyphosate, a common herbicide used on farms. She and others opposed to Big Agriculture claim without evidence that glyphosate causes cancer, or obesity, whereas most worldwide health agencies have stated that it is not dangerous to humans.[52] But while Sue was incredibly concerned about toxins, she was not worried about climate change, believing it was an overblown leftist fear.

Sue then put me in touch with Molly. Molly and I went back and forth a few times before finding a good time to talk on Zoom. She had some "legal issues" related to her raw milk business that she had to take care of before we could chat. We eventually did find a time. Molly was in her late fifties and talked from her kitchen during our Zoom call. She had long, brownish-gray hair, funky glasses, and wouldn't have looked out of place at a local art fair. I asked her how she wanted me to refer to her pseudonymously in my book; she laughed and said, "call me a raw milk trafficker—cause that's what I am!"[53]

Molly said she lived in Central America in the 1980s and was big into health and fitness. Then, when she returned to the United States in the late 1990s, she discovered raw milk. In her old, beat-up car, she delivered raw milk and eggs to customers all over the Southeast and Appalachia. Molly initially delivered the raw milk and eggs for free because she believed in the power of raw milk so much. But she was spending $100 a week out of her own pocket just on ice to keep the raw milk and raw eggs from spoiling during delivery runs. By charging for delivery, she was able to make raw milk her full-time job. Molly said that "since COVID, for the last two years, my business is booming; raw milk is booming."

Molly was also more explicit than Sue about her politics and distrust for the medical community. She was proudly anti-vax and wanted other people to "wake up" about the possibility of "vaccine injury." Molly told me that during the pandemic she was banned from Twitter a couple of times for being so outspoken on vaccines. She said it wasn't surprising: "We are being lied to by Pharma, the CDC, the WHO, and the media [that] gets 70% of their ads from pharmaceutical companies." Molly said that she had zero trust in the medical establishment and had a special disdain for Anthony Fauci, the former director of the National Institute of Allergy and Infectious Diseases (NIAID). She said, "the only way you would get me into a hospital is if I am passed out."

Molly then talked about the political views of her fellow raw milk enthusiasts and customers. She said there are the "crunchy moms" who are now suspicious of vaccines, vegans who used to be pro-Bernie, Amish, and even homesteaders. The common thread was their lack of trust in vaccines and Western medicine. She singled out Robert F. Kennedy (RFK), Jr., the former Democratic presidential candidate who endorsed then–Republican candidate Donald Trump ahead of the 2024 election. RFK Jr. is a big fan of raw milk.[54] Many in the raw milk movement saw RFK Jr. as their main champion due to his willingness to fight against Big Pharma and agribusiness. As Molly told me, "RFK Jr. and Trump ... who would ever put them together?"—but she liked it. "I was going to vote for RFK Jr., and now I'll vote for Trump; hopefully, they can do something ... people are lying to us."

Molly also had strong views on climate change and pollution. She recognized that RFK Jr. was a big believer in climate change, but to her it was a giant "hoax." She didn't believe Earth was warming and icebergs were melting. In her view—and contrary to the science—Earth cools and warms on its own and recent trends have nothing to do with carbon emissions. But she agreed with RFK Jr. on eliminating pollutants, reducing pesticides, and stopping "Exxon from chopping down the rainforest." She wanted a "clean Earth" that was not poisoned by chemicals, and she wanted to eat real food. Getting rid of the toxins from industrial farming, the toxins from vaccines, and the toxins in her food—that was her environmentalism. It didn't matter if it wasn't backed by science because Molly didn't trust the scientists, anyway.

I had a chance to talk to Ryder, a raw milk dairy farmer, a few times.[55] The first time we talked on FaceTime as he was driving back from dropping milk off at a farmer's market in the Mountain West. Ryder was in his early thirties, wearing a baseball cap, and had a laid-back demeanor. He described himself as a fourth-generation dairy farmer and land steward, and an alternative food lunatic. As Ryder cruised along the open road, he told me that his dad was an early adopter of organic farming—"no pesticides and chemicals"—so the idea of raw milk wasn't a stretch for him. When he went to college for ecology and learned more about agriculture, he also became more skeptical of mainstream agricultural practices. Ryder said that a family friend suggested he look into raw milk. He then "did (his) own research" and didn't look back. Following the pandemic, and especially in the past few years, he told me that the consumer demand for his raw milk was "insane," that he "can't even [financially] justify selling cheese and other products, because raw milk sells so fast."

When we talked about the politics, Ryder was a bit more circumspect. Despite the scientific consensus that raw milk does not provide any benefits,[56] he believed in it. Ryder also said his customers came to him for a variety of reasons. As with Molly's customers, there were crunchy moms and organic food hippies. And there were also the homestead/antigovernment types. Ryder identified with environmentalists and sympathized with them. But he described himself as more of a libertarian. He wanted to farm and steward the land naturally, in his own way. In contrast, he described more mainstream environmentalists as authoritarians "who want to boil the environment down to one thing called carbon." His more right-leaning, or more accurately, anti-left political beliefs poked through a bit when he said that the mainstream environmental approach was a "globalist" view of the world that wanted to tell people what to do.

In our follow-up Zoom conversation, Ryder sat on his porch on his farm and opened up a bit more about his politics and how it connected to raw milk. He said he was a big fan of RFK Jr. And to him, raw milk and the ability to sell it were a "gateway drug" to people opening their eyes up to food decisions and even a broader view of society.

After our call, Ryder said if I was interested, he could put me in touch with his friend, Helen, who was "really into the homestead movement" and a big raw milk supporter as well. I contacted Helen, who said she would be happy to chat.

Before Helen and I talked, I looked up her social media profile, and it was prolific. She had a slick website, and her Instagram page looked like it could be from a do-it-yourself home-improvement account, or a how-to-eat-better one, or from any other of the other myriad health and lifestyle influencers. There were posts filled with pop-culture memes about what living off grid was really like versus what you imagined it to be like. There were also the funny but approachable videos of Helen speaking directly to the camera and encouraging her thousands of followers to buy a key product—with a promo code. It was very standard influencer fare. But there were a few posts that hinted at her political leanings and the fact that this was not just a typical lifestyle influencer account. In one of her posts Helen asked why "they" care more about stopping people from taking alternative and unproven cures for COVID, like ivermectin and hydroxychloroquine, than stopping drugs from coming into the country. In another post, Helen encouraged her followers to ignore the "globalists."

Helen was part of the burgeoning homestead movement—a diverse group of individuals who, for a variety of reasons, try to live off the land as much as possible. The movement took off during the early days of the COVID-19 lockdowns. Many homesteaders document their lives, provide tips, and even earn income from their social media channels.[57]

Helen and I talked on Zoom from her off-grid farm in the rural Mountain West.[58] She was in her late twenties or early thirties and had long brown hair, and a mellow, positive vibe that wouldn't have been out of place on a yoga retreat. I could see why she was successful on social media. She didn't come off as a paranoid off-gridder. Her whole vibe was approachable and upbeat.

The first thing I asked Helen was what she meant by "off-grid" homesteading? I was curious, since she did have such a strong social media presence. She told me that she and her husband stumbled into off-grid homesteading by chance. It was 2020, and they were looking for a piece of land to buy near a medium-sized metro area so that they could grow fruits and vegetables and have a small farm that they could leave to their kids—"a legacy" as Helen put it. But given housing prices, it was hard to find something close to a metropolitan area that was affordable. So, they ended up buying a piece of rural property where there weren't any utilities. There wasn't a government road; it was a private road they shared with other landowners. There were no trash or sewage services, nor did they have running water, so they had to figure things out on their own, and that's how she got into the homestead life. I then asked, "what do you do for Internet?" She smiled, and said, "Starlink; thank you, Elon Musk."

Yet, Helen didn't just stumble into this worldview. She grew up in the rural plains of the Midwest, spending summers on her grandparents' farm. When the COVID-19 pandemic started, Helen hated the mask mandates, and "the over-governing" that she saw going on—"it didn't sit right" with her. She wanted less overall government (which she inherently didn't trust), and raw milk fit right into that worldview. In fact, it was through local farmers' markets and co-ops that she met Ryder, and they connected over their love of raw milk and suspicion of industrial agricultural practices.

Helen also told me that the off-grid lifestyle appealed to her and her husband out of fears for what the government could do to them. She mentioned China's "social credit score system" and how she feared that "government overreach" could lead the U.S. government to do something similar here, like shutting off her water, her utilities, or electricity if they ran afoul of the government.

I asked Helen if she really feared that could happen. She said, "yes." She then told me that she and her husband grew all their own fruits and vegetables inside their greenhouse because of "chemtrails." The term "chemtrails" is shorthand for a baseless conspiracy theory. Adherents of the chemtrails conspiracy theory believe that the white streaks of condensation (contrails) behind airplanes are actually secret chemicals sprayed by the government to control the weather or the population.[59] Helen then told me that many homesteaders aren't conspiracy theorists, but she was. This had been the case ever since middle school, when she heard her favorite rappers talking about "the illuminati," and then actually did her own research to find out who the illuminati were. She told me she had been "going down [conspiracy theory] rabbit holes" ever since. Helen had real fears about "the New World Order, the One World government, and George Soros" taking over things. It became clear that Helen's conspiratorial worldview was a key part of her support for homesteading and raw milk. She cared about the environment, but she wasn't totally sold on climate change—"it's hard to wrap my head around that [global warming and that] all of that is man-made." But she also cared about sustainability, and so homesteading and raw milk were a way for her to avoid toxins and do her part to counteract what she felt was the plan of Soros, Big Agriculture, and the New World Order to control the food supply and poison us. Helen ended up by saying she was hopeful that the next four years with President Trump back in office and RFK Jr. by his side they would be able to push back against Big Agriculture and the globalists.

***

One day after I finished my interview with Helen, President-elect Trump announced his intention to make RFK Jr. his nominee to lead the Department of Health and Human Services. Many scientists, public health researchers, and physicians were horrified. RFK Jr.'s views were well outside the mainstream of accepted science.[60] For example, he opposed many routine vaccines and was strongly in favor of alternative medicine. He was a big fan of raw milk. To many in the burgeoning raw milk movement, this announcement was met with jubilation. Their once fringe views on the benefits of raw milk and what it symbolized—a more "natural" way of doing dairy that was a miracle drink—was having a big moment. The irony was that their champion, RFK Jr., was a scion of a famous Democratic family, a big supporter of environmental causes who had even been whispered about possibly being named head of the Environmental Protection Agency under President Obama back in 2008.[61]

This speaks to the scramble of politics that has happened around climate change and the environment. Alarm over toxins in our food, support for farm-to-table, and skepticism toward Big Agriculture were mainstream on the environmental left—and they still are. But through raw milk and skepticism toward the government following the COVID-19 lockdowns, they have emerged as organizing principles for various individuals and groups on the right. Following the 2024 election, Republican commentators pointed to a high voter turnout for President-elect Trump in the Amish parts of Pennsylvania. This followed a state raid on an Amish raw milk farm linked to a disease outbreak.[62] Raw milk raids fit nicely into the narrative of government overreach around health gaining traction in right-wing circles during lockdowns.

The threat of climate change, meanwhile is either downplayed as an overblown liberal talking point or is denied by many on the right. This is not surprising given public opinion on the issue. In 2023, 78% of Democrats considered climate change a major threat, an increase of 17 percentage points since 2009. Only 23% of Republicans considered it a major threat, a 2-percentage point decrease over that same period.[63]

This isn't to say that in the future, when the effects of climate change become even more dramatic, right-wing narratives won't begin to acknowledge the climate crisis more openly. Ecofascism may not always remain on the fringe. But for now, that's where it is.

Today, right-wing environmentalism is best expressed not through climate policy, but through something like raw milk. It taps into fears about food purity, government overreach, and a yearning for a "natural" way of life. It also connects to vaccine skepticism and the broader distrust of experts that has surged in right-wing politics since COVID.

Both raw milk politics and ecofascism function like awkward, distant cousins to the radical environmental movement. They share a faint family resemblance—concerns about pollution, overpopulation, and ecological collapse—but the relationship is strained. And like relatives who show up uninvited to a family gathering, they're rooted in different worldviews, speak a different political language, and ultimately remain outside the movement's ideological home.

8

Soup and Disruption
Searching for Something That Sticks

"There's no puzzle here. Civil disobedience won. Property destruction—also known as 'fucking shit up'—isn't the path forward."

That was the feedback i got from one scholar who studies the radical environmental movement. This scholar pushed back on one of the core questions driving this book: If the climate crisis is getting worse, why haven't more activists turned back to radical tactics?

Their answer was simple. It's because we already know what works. Gandhi, MLK, and Bill McKibben had already cracked the code for social change. Nonviolence is the only strategy that brings real change. The tactics used by the ELF and the more militant Earth First!ers—sabotage, property destruction, and especially arson—weren't just unhelpful. They were harmful. So why would activists revisit them?

But the research shows a more complicated picture than this critique suggests. Yes, the idea that nonviolence works better than ELF-like tactics like sabotage and property destruction has become conventional wisdom—and there's some research to support it.[1] But other studies show the opposite. Some studies find that radical tactics can actually help a movement by shifting public opinion and making more moderate demands seem reasonable.[2] Scholars refer to the influence of radical activists on moderates in a movement as a "radical flank effect." The point is, there's no one-size-fits-all answer when it comes to movement tactics or whether a radical flank is harmful or helpful.

This critique that nonviolent tactics weren't effective or acceptable bugged me. So as part of my research for this book, I decided I needed to know how different groups—activists, young people, and the general public—actually felt about different forms of protest.

I ran three surveys in 2022 and 2023: one with a large, nationally representative sample of U.S. adults; one with a large group of Americans aged 18–29; and one with environmental activists. Initially, it was hard to find a way to survey activists in a systematic way. But eventually, a veteran environmental activist group involved in civil disobedience and direct action agreed to circulate the survey to activists on their listserv.[3] It turned out that the veteran environmental activist group was also eager to know what their own supporters thought about different tactics.

Across all three surveys, I asked the same core questions: How acceptable is it for people to use the following tactics to protest individuals or institutions that are contributing to climate change? Respondents rated each listed tactic on a scale from 0 ("not acceptable at all") to 10 ("always acceptable"). The six tactics ranged from civil disobedience—like tree-sitting or occupying buildings—to more aggressive actions such as vandalizing SUVs or damaging pipelines.

The results, shown in Figure 8.1, were telling. Not surprisingly, activists were the most supportive of protest tactics overall, followed by young people, and then the general public. Activists overwhelmingly backed civil disobedience. But support dropped off sharply when it came to more aggressive tactics. Even among activists, vandalizing SUVs and damaging pipelines were both seen as rarely acceptable. Perhaps even activists weren't ready to use sabotage.

That finding echoed a conversation I had with another scholar who studies social movements, including the environmental movement. She made the case that many activists today view civil disobedience as radical. Blocking roads, shutting the entrances to banks that fund fossil-fuel projects, and throwing soup at paintings—that was as far as activists were willing to go. But more extreme tactics, like sabotage or arson? Those, she said, weren't really under consideration.

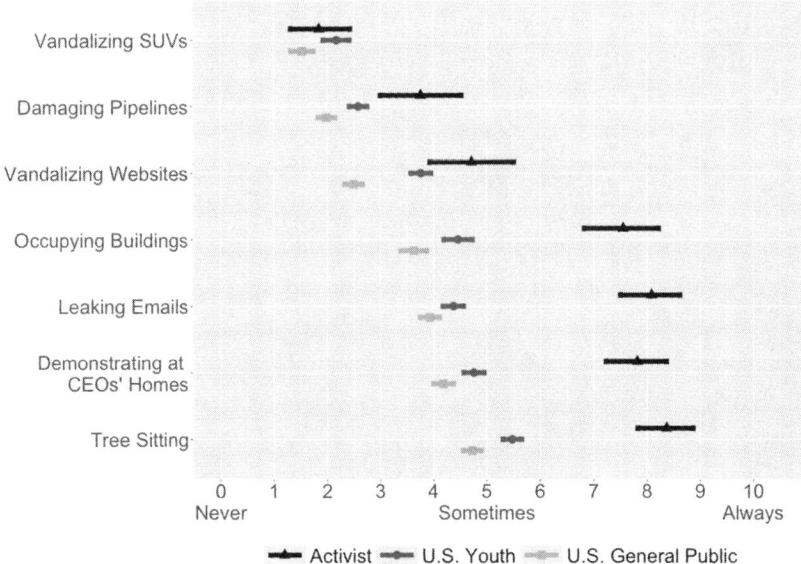

FIGURE 8.1 How acceptable are different tactics? Mean acceptability of different tactics comparing Activist ($N=75$) vs. U.S. Youth ($N=1,086$) vs. U.S. General Public ($N=1,196$) sample. Point estimates are means with 95% confidence intervals.

These critiques troubled me. Had I missed something? Was my central puzzle—that the growing threat from climate change should at least lead some activists to question whether more radical tactics were needed—just wrong? Had radical environmental activists settled the debate on tactics, with civil disobedience being the extent of what they were willing to do?

The short answer is no. These critiques are a misreading of a movement in flux. It's true that activists in recent years had mostly steered away from arson and sabotage and were focused on civil disobedience. But what these critiques miss is that those in the movement are debating and considering more radical tactics. All you had to do was look at what they were reading. In my conversations with environmental activists, two books were constantly brought up. The first was the Malm book, *How to Blow up a Pipeline,* which was discussed about earlier in the book.[4] As the title suggests, Malm explicitly advocates for mass sabotage and property destruction. While many activists had issues with his analysis and interpretation of the ELF's failures, his point that the escalating climate crisis deserved a rethinking of tactics was not that controversial.

The second book was Kim Stanley Robinson's 2020 dystopian science fiction book, *Ministry of the Future*.[5] The book opens with a brutal portrait of a near-future, climate-change-induced heat wave in India causing a massive number of deaths. In the wake of the heat wave, an ecoterrorist group, called the "Children of Kali," forms to take revenge. The Children of Kali use intimidation and violence against wealthy fossil fuel capitalist targets they believe are responsible for preventing action on global warming. Many of the activists I chatted with cited this as a real possibility in the future, and a few even told me that they cheered the Children of Kali on while reading the book.

As we will see in this chapter, activists are constantly experimenting with tactics and are looking for new ways to apply pressure. Just because property destruction and sabotage haven't reemerged doesn't mean activists aren't considering it. They are.

***

While writing this book, I got to know Tim, a direct action organizer, pretty well. I enjoyed talking to him, and we met up for breakfast when he was in D.C. in March of 2024. Tim had a salt-and-pepper beard and a relaxed vibe. He had been loosely involved in protests when he was in college in the early 1990s. Then he went back to grad school, where he jokingly said his "professors" radicalized him.[6] He was active in Texas and in the South during the anti-globalization movement of the late 1990s and early 2000s, when he witnessed the effects of the Green Scare ripple through the movement. What I liked most about talking to Tim was his ability to straddle both worlds. He was active with mainstream environmental groups and understood how the policy process worked. But he also was involved in the more radical side of environmental organizing. He knew the activists, helped strategize campaigns, and was familiar with the history of the movement.

In late October 2024, I shared a link with Tim to a recently published academic paper on the effectiveness of radical environmental tactics.[7] The authors examined the effects of protests that blocked major roadways in the U.K. by the group Just Stop Oil in 2022.

They found that after the road blockade the public became more amenable to mainstream U.K. environmental organizations. In other words, the authors found that more radical tactics can work by making more mainstream environmental groups and policies seem less radical.

When I told Tim about the results, he got very excited and asked me to send him a copy of the paper.[8] I asked him why he was so excited about the article. He told me that one of the main campaigns he had been involved in targeted banks with protests and civil disobedience for their support of fossil fuel companies. He mentioned that certain people within his organization were getting worried that their pressure campaign was ineffective—or, even worse, was backfiring, and bringing negative publicity to the organization. The academic paper, he said, would let him push back against these people, who in his words were "spineless," and provided justification to continue the pressure campaign.

Tim, like many activists, was looking for any tactic or strategy that might give the movement an edge. What was the right way to apply pressure and disrupt the status quo?

***

There was a tension in the global climate movement. In surveys, climate change and the environment were always the third or fourth most important problem, usually behind the economy, immigration, and crime/security.[9] This wasn't just a U.S.-specific problem. It was also true in Europe.[10] Activists needed to capture the public's attention.[11] But to do so, they had to raise the stakes, the spectacle had to be bigger, and so they started turning toward controversial, stunt-like types of protest theater. For instance, activists associated with the group Just Stop Oil threw soup twice on Van Gogh paintings in the U.K., once in 2022 and once in 2024. Speaking of their fellow activists who had recently been sentenced to two years in prison for the attack, one of the soup throwers said, "We will be held accountable for our actions today, and we will face the full force of the law. When will the fossil fuel executives and the politicians they've bought be held accountable for the criminal damage that they are imposing on every living thing?"[12]

In the United States, in February 2024 at the National Archives in Washington, D.C., two activists sprinkled red powder on the encased copy of the U.S. Constitution. In a video the activists posted to social media, they said that they wanted to draw attention to the right of all Americans to a clean environment and life without climate change. Both activists were later sentenced to more than a year in federal prison. Less than a year before his actions at the National Archives, one of the activists, Donald Zepeda, had been part of group that smeared paint on a case protecting a sculpture at the National Gallery of Art in Washington to protest against climate change.[13] In November 2023, the other activist, Jackson Green, had written in red washable paint "Honor them" on the Shaw 54th Regiment Memorial (also at the National Gallery of Art), which honors one of the first Black regiments in the Civil War. Green said that he wanted to honor Black soldiers while also raising awareness about the unequal effects of climate change. He demanded that then President Joseph Biden declare a climate emergency.[14]

Yet, climate activists weren't just targeting prominent museums and cultural sites. In 2023, they blocked the lone, two-lane road into the popular, week-long counterculture festival know as Burning Man, held in the Nevada desert. Activists held signs that read, "Burners of the world, unite!" and "Mother Earth needs our help," while other activists chained themselves together and blockaded the road. The counterculture appeal of Burning Man didn't lead festival goers to be supportive or sympathize with the protest. One festivalgoer said, "They're delusional, it's idiocy.... They think they're going to fix climate change by blocking Burning Man? I don't care what their argument is, they can go fuck themselves."[15]

This tactic of blocking roads is one that climate protesters have increasingly turned to in recent years. For example, in August 2023, activists associated with a climate action group, Declare Emergency, wore yellow vests and blocked roads into Washington, D.C., on a Saturday. Declare Emergency's view was that humans had two to three years to prevent the worst of climate catastrophes, and their website noted: "The science is clear: the use of fossil fuels must end, immediately, if we hope to survive.... We come together and offer resolute non-violent resistance to the fossil fuel madness of the present moment."[16] During the

D.C. road blockage protests, enraged motorists pleaded and screamed at the protesters to move. One woman said, "Get the fuck out of here. We have to go to fucking work . . . we've got kids to feed, bitch!"[17] It was one of several road blockages that the group Declare Emergency carried out in the D.C. region, hoping to goad then President Biden into declaring a climate emergency.

***

It was June 2024, and two Just Stop Oil protesters had just used fire extinguishers to spray-paint Stonehenge, one of the U.K.'s most recognizable prehistoric landmarks, with washable orange paint. The activists wanted the incoming U.K. government of Labour leader Keir Starmer to sign a binding commitment to phase out fossil fuels completely by 2030.[18]

The action at Stonehenge generated intense backlash from both the public and politicians across the spectrum.[19] Even many sympathetic environmentalists were divided on the tactic. An article by an environmental studies professor in *The Atlantic* captured the general sentiment, "Maybe Don't Spray-Paint Stonehenge."[20] The response from Just Stop Oil and other sympathetic activists was that the soup throwing, spray-painting, or other "eco-vandalism" almost never did any actual lasting damage to cultural landmarks. Activists used washable paint, or they smeared something on top of cases protecting the art. In contrast, the threat from climate change was a lasting problem that threatened all of humanity.

Trying to get a sense of how activists in the movement viewed these types of tactics, I reached out to Tim, the direct action organizer, and Cameron, the former veteran-turned-activist.[21] When I asked Tim about the Stonehenge action, he told me he wasn't a fan of the action and did not find it very strategic. He was much happier, he said, "when they do that kind of stuff [targeted vandalism and disruption] at banks and oil companies—the places doing the [actual] evil." Cameron was even more blunt: "Don't care. Over it. The tactic is stale."

A few weeks after the Stonehenge incident, six climate activists invaded the 18th putting green and sprinkled powder during the final round of the 2024 Professional Golf Association (PGA) Traveler's Tour Championship in Connecticut. The activists were from Extinction

Rebellion, and they wore shirts that read, "NO GOLF ON A DEAD PLANET." The activists were eventually arrested, and tournament play resumed. I reached out to Cameron again and asked him, "Still hate this tactic when it targets golfers?" He responded, "No, that's great." He then reflected the very mainstream environmental view that golf was a terrible sport for the environment and climate. He noted that it destroys forests and natural habitats, uses lots of pesticides and fertilizer, and requires a huge amount of water to keep the greens green and fairways manicured.[22] He then added, "Burn all golf courses."

***

I wanted to get the perspective from somebody inside the climate activist groups engaging in these more publicity-driven actions.[23] One of the newer and most prominent groups that was getting a lot of buzz was Climate Defiance. This upstart, U.S.-based group focused on targeting politicians and other decision-makers. Their tactics ranged from the disruptive—invading the field during the Congressional baseball game in June 2024—to the more juvenile—shutting down an event for Exxon CEO Darren Woods and holding signs reading "Eat Shit Darren." They also targeted Democratic West Virginia Senator Joe Manchin over his support for fossil fuels. Climate Defiance's strategy was to be obnoxious, trollish, and theatrical in order to get as many clicks and views on their actions as possible. They were like a Gen-Z, social-media version of Abbie Hoffman and the Yippies from the 1960s counterculture movement. The group even had a list on their website with links to videos and articles of their "Best Actions"—the ones that caused the most uproar.[24]

I chatted on the phone with Aaron, one of the key strategists behind Climate Defiance, in March 2023.[25] He was in his early thirties and had a fast and slightly nasal voice. Aaron told me that when he was in high school, he got "really freaked" about what was happening to the climate. He started volunteering for the Sierra Club, eventually making his way to 350.org when he was in college. While at 350.org, he was involved in some climate disobedience actions, and as he termed it, he caught "the activism bug."

Two particular moments during our conversation really stuck with me. The first was when Aaron started to describe what he and others were hoping to do with Climate Defiance. To him, their goal was to disrupt key political events like a Federal Reserve meeting, the Congressional Baseball Game, or the White House Correspondents' Association Dinner. But it wasn't just to disrupt. Aaron said, "Our goal is to make life miserable for the people who are in charge and have power . . . make their life miserable until they do something." They wanted to ratchet up the pressure and make it so difficult for anti-climate politicians, fossil fuel CEOs, and financiers that they wouldn't be able to show their faces in public.

But Aaron also drew a key distinction. They didn't block traffic, they didn't deface art, and they weren't willing to engage in property destruction. Nor did they stage protests in front of the homes of key stakeholders, although they had given some thought to this approach. There was a second part that was fascinating: Aaron was very careful to not criticize those who did engage in property destruction or more radical tactics. He told me that what he actually found radical was the fact that "people are attending weddings, Taylor Swift concerts, and brunch as the world is on fire and the end nears."

***

In October 2024, I presented some preliminary data from my book to a mixed audience of students, academics, and parents. After the presentation, I got a lot of questions along the lines of, "What do you think are the right tactics or strategies that activist should use?" I would respond with, "There's a big debate about whether radical tactics work, and if so, when." And I would always add that the activists themselves were also trying to figure it out.

I thanked people for coming, and the talk ended. I then started to gather my laptop and charger into my backpack. While I was packing up, I noted a mom and her college-aged son walking toward me. The mom was motioning to her son and was urging him forward.

I asked, "How are you guys? Did you have more questions?"[26]

The mom nudged the son (who I will call Eli) and said, "Tell him." Eli was in his early twenties and had a sheepish grin on his face.

I asked, "Tell me what?" I looped my backpack straps over my shoulders. Sometimes when you give talks in public you get some interesting or bizarre questions, and you need to have your bags ready just in case you need to make a quick exit. But this wasn't one of those times.

Eli told me, "Well, I got arrested a couple of months back."

I responded, "Uggh, I'm sorry; what happened?"

Eli hesitated for a moment. The mom nudged him again and said, "Tell him." I couldn't figure out what was going on. Did the mom want me to help, or did she just want me to listen as she scolded her son? So, I remained quiet. As Eli began to tell his story, I learned that Eli was a college student and had always been politically active, having participated in leftist, environmental, and pro-Palestinian protests. But it was his experience with disruptive climate protests that Eli and his mom wanted to talk to me about. He didn't have much prior experience with civil disobedience–style protests, so he wasn't sure what to expect. But the trainers from the climate activist group, who themselves wouldn't be involved in the disruptive event, told him it wouldn't be too hard. The trainers told Eli he might get arrested, but at most he'd be charged with a misdemeanor, they'd handle bail, and all would be fine. Eli went through with the action.[27] And sure enough, he got arrested with several other activists. But the promised bail and legal representation from the climate activist group never materialized. As a college kid with no income, he eventually had to reach out to his family to help him post bail and was forced to use a public defender. To his great dismay, Eli found that he was facing serious jail time with felony—not misdemeanor—charges. His public defender was ultimately able to plead the charges down to a misdemeanor. But Eli would be on probation for the next year and a half.

Eli told me that he was super jaded by the whole thing. The mom then interjected and angrily exclaimed: "Those fucking activists, they just used my son and tossed him away, with no help and no resources." I told Eli to feel free to reach out to me, and I also mentioned that I could put him in touch with activists who were better organized and provided more effective mutual aid and legal support. Eli and his mom thanked me and walked off.

Afterward I messaged Tim and told him about what had happened to Eli. Tim expressed his frustration. Eli, he said, was just the kind of person the movement needed, but unfortunately, instead of being nurtured and supported by a larger activist community, he was asked to take on risks he wasn't fully aware of and was not being supported. It pissed Tim off, but he acknowledged that it was all too common.

Eli's story raised questions about many of these disruptive actions. They get attention, but to what end? What is the organizing goal or outcome? And where are the networks and subcultures that are going to nurture and support activists? Earth First! had its newsletter and *Earth First! Journal*, but it also had the yearly Round River Rendezvous to meet up with other activists and commiserate. The animal liberation and hardcore straight edge punk scene had bands and zines, but it was also a lifestyle and an ethos. Eugene in the 1990s and early 2000s had a whole radical green anarchist scene that brought tree sitters, anti-globalization anarchists, and Earth First!ers together. If Eli's experience was any indication, the current activist networks weren't nearly as strong.

Part of this weakness in the activist networks stemmed from the fact that activists themselves weren't sure what to do. Should they focus their energy on influencing the policy process, and push for new laws, like the Green New Deal? Should they reject mainstream NGOs and engage in more radical tactics, like property destruction? Should it be a mass movement, or should it be a vanguard movement with a select group of hardcore activists pushing the envelope, or should it be both? Was there still time to even make a difference, with CO_2 emissions still rising? And what should activists do, given the increasing risk of imprisonment they faced in many Republican-led states and the growth of government surveillance?

The issue of repression, especially surveillance, is the elephant in the room. Activists know that the post-9/11 surveillance state is bigger, more aggressive, and harder to outmaneuver than it was in the past. Law enforcement can now pull cellphone tracking data, subpoena communications, and tap into a world saturated with cameras: city-owned, store-owned, and just regular people's doorbells.[28] If you're an activist carrying out sabotage, there are simply more ways to leave your digital footprint.

Social media adds yet another layer. It's a crucial tool for organizing, and many activists bemoan how reliant they've become on it. But it's also a gift to investigators. Nathan, who was active during the ELF era, captured this tension:

> If you brag about doing crimes, or throwing a Molotov cocktail, on social media and wear identifiable clothing, that's going to be a bad idea in general. Social media can be dangerous, [but] social media may not be the problem—you may be stupid. The algorithm is terrible. And I know Facebook is for old people, but I still find it useful [for organizing].[29]

Jesse, the former ELF spokesperson, put it bluntly: "I should also point out that the surveillance state is much larger. It's harder to do the Weather Underground and the ELF. Everybody has a Ring camera [on their door] to monitor their neighbors."[30]

One of the starkest reminders of how much has changed came from Robert, the animal liberation activist. In September 2024, he Zoomed into my class once again to talk about his time in high risk activism and the animal liberation movement.[31] One of my students asked him what advice he would give to younger activists. I expected a response something like: "Don't be afraid to stand up for your beliefs."

Instead, Robert got tactical. "Yeah," he said, "go low tech. Put your phone in a Faraday bag well before you do anything. Bicycle to the target, wear black, and avoid security cameras." Both the students and I were caught off guard a bit by the response, but to Robert this advice was crucial. Surveillance had changed the way law enforcement operated. And it made it harder to carry out the kind of sabotage that previous activists had done.

Other activists also brought up Faraday bags. These are pouches made of material that blocks electronic signals like WiFi, Bluetooth, and GPS. Once a phone goes inside, it essentially goes dark and is shielded from hacking, tracking, and monitoring.[32]

These weren't just paranoid precautions. For activists, they were harsh lessons learned from the Green Scare. And they reflect the cost of operating in a climate where surveillance is omnipresent, and getting caught carries steep consequences.

As we will see in the next chapter, these questions about tactics, repression, and surveillance took on even greater significance in November 2024, with the reelection of Donald Trump.

9

Rise Again?

"Like, I am over helping do anything on [climate at] a national level. We have lost the climate permanently."

Cameron, the former veteran-turned-activist, sent me this message on Wednesday, November 6, 2024, the day after Trump won the U.S. presidential election.[1]

I messaged him back and asked him to elaborate. Cameron told me that he didn't see any path forward on climate activism and that he didn't have any hope in the moment. Many of the activists he knew were depressed and buying guns in advance of what they felt was a coming crackdown. Going forward he would focus on local politics and "batten [down] the hatches," since he felt there was no hope. He added, "America is over. Period. Full stop. No more fighting for it." Cameron ended his message by telling me he would eventually find some hope, "but not right now." His view was that with Trump's reelection, "this country deserves what's coming."

Tim, the direct action organizer, also messaged me on the day after the election. As somebody who was intimately involved with climate NGOs, Tim had difference concerns than Cameron. He pointed to the recent lawsuit filed against Greenpeace over protests that had happened back in 2016 and 2017 and that were related to the Dakota Access

Pipeline. The lawsuit, filed by the pipeline company Energy Transfers, accused Greenpeace of over $300 million in damage for their role in supporting activists who protested the Dakota Access Pipeline. Tim said the strategy behind the lawsuit was clear—bankrupt Greenpeace, one of the most prominent environmental NGOs, and promise to sue into oblivion any other NGO that supported climate activists.[2]

Tim saw the incoming Trump administration as having a thousand different ways they could "turn the screws on" and harass climate activists, particularly going after NGOs like Greenpeace. And he was right to be concerned about the Greenpeace lawsuit. In March 2025, the jury in North Dakota found Greenpeace liable for defamation and coordinating criminal protests. Greenpeace was ordered to pay Energy Transfers over $660 million in damages.[3]

The verdict would be appealed, but the effect on climate NGOs was chilling. It opened the door for polluters and fossil fuel companies to sue NGOs that supported activists who used civil disobedience against polluters. The standard NGO climate activist playbook of disruption, pressure campaigns, and protester support could now expose these very same organizations to legal and financial ruin.

Cameron and Tim had other reasons to be worried. The views of the incoming Trump administration on climate change ran the gamut from downplaying its effects to outright climate denialism.[4] Many in the second Trump administration had close ties to the fossil fuel industry. President Trump and his advisors were united in wanting to increase domestic fossil fuel production, open more public lands to drilling and fracking, and roll back environmental protections and regulations put in place by the Biden administration.

On January 20, 2025, on his first day back in office, President Trump made good on these promises. He issued a flurry of executive orders: withdrawing the United States from the Paris Climate Treaty, opening federal lands to drilling, rolling back restrictions on offshore drilling, and blocking new leases for wind power on federal lands.[5] By March and April, his administration moved to open more than half of the land managed by the U.S. Forest Service to logging. It was not lost on me or other activists that fights over logging and development on federal lands were the reason Earth First! was founded in the first place.

Climate change as a policy problem can likened to a slow-burning wildfire. For Cameron and Tim, the policies that the Biden administration enacted were a small water hose. It wasn't enough to stop the fire, but it was enough to prevent the blaze from burning out of control. Meanwhile Trump and his allies were promising not only to cut the water hose, but also to dump gasoline on the fire as they chanted "drill, baby, drill." To activists it wasn't just bad policy, it was a direct assault on their core beliefs.

But Cameron and Tim had other pressing concerns. Cameron was active with many groups that engaged in nonviolent civil disobedience, as well as a few that also engaged in small-scale sabotage. He also had been involved in clashes with far-right activists in the Pacific Northwest during the 2020 election. Cameron was definitely "not nonviolent" when it came to people he saw as Nazis or fascists. He didn't identify as such, but to Trump supporters, Cameron might as well have been not an organization Antifa.

Cameron felt that the Trump administration would likely target him and his fellow activists as part of their campaign to promote law and order and clamp down on lefty troublemakers. It wasn't even hard to imagine. The outlines of this repression playbook were clear. They had already been used at the state level on Stop Cop City activists in Georgia, as well as at the federal level against animal rights and environmental activists in the early 2000s.[6]

First, arrest everyone remotely connected to a protest where there is sabotage—whether they were involved in the act of sabotage or not. Then charge the activists with domestic terrorism, and label them as being part of a violent extremist organization so that conspiracy charges can be filed even against those not directly involved in the illegal activity. Finally, go after the people supporting the activists (by providing bail funds, or mutual aid) to scare away support networks and crush solidarity.

Tim's concerns were less about fear of arrest and more about the future of the NGO model that he had put much of his activist energy into. He was worried that, like the Greenpeace lawsuit, the Trump Department of Justice would go after NGOs that funded climate activism. If an NGO gave money to any activist who was arrested, the organization would be accused of supporting terrorism. It would face subpoenas, its money would be frozen, its donor list scrutinized and investigated, and then donors would stop donating. Eventually, the model of climate NGOs supporting climate activists that engaged in pressure campaigns to influence policy would be broken.

With a Republican president, House, and Senate, and a conservative-leaning Supreme Court, activists like Tim and Cameron were under no illusions about the levers of power being used against them.

But not all activists were as worried as Tim and Cameron. Adam, the eighty-year-old Pacific Northwest–based anarcho-primitivist whom we met in Chapter 4, had a different view, which aligned with his pessimistic, radical orientation. When we met in Eugene in May 2024, I asked Adam if he was worried about the 2024 election.[7] I saw a smile form on his gray-bearded face. He then said he didn't vote—out of principle—so it didn't matter to him. He saw it as a "choice between Fascist Trump versus Genocide Joe," referencing Joe Biden's support for Israel and Adam's view that the Israelis were engaged in a genocide against the Palestinians in Gaza. And then he said that he almost hoped Trump would win. "That way the mask would be off" the whole capitalist system. Though he would chafe at the comparison, Adam shared the view of accelerationists on the right who viewed the current politics of America as too corrupt to be worth saving. Adam's beliefs stemmed from his anarchist and leftist views that capitalism is inherently contradictory and needed to fall and be replaced. But like others, he saw Trump's victory as bringing about fundamental change.

After the election, I reached out to Adam to see if he still stood by his views on the election. He sent me some of his thoughts, which, honestly, were pretty dark.[8] He referred to American presidential elections as a "racket" that happens every four years. And he reiterated his stance that even though some of the issues he cared about—environmental disasters, Gaza, homelessness, and the threat of AI—had been briefly mentioned during the campaigns, he still was glad he didn't vote. To Adam, Trump's reelection was an inflection point for a civilization that was spiraling into darkness. And he concluded by saying that the capitalist and technology-first American regime was "dying." Yet he hoped that from its ashes a new, better world might emerge. Trump, in his eyes, was an arsonist. But, to Adam, the current regime was so bad that he believed it deserved to be burned until the ground smoldered.

***

A few weeks before the election, I got a chance to talk to Bernard, the Portland-based former Earth First! activist.[9] We had been messaging back and forth. Bernard had been sick again, but he finally felt well enough to talk. I asked him what he thought about the upcoming election. Bernard told me he was worried. He said that many of the leftist activists he knew were "tired and exhausted by the thought of a second Trump administration." He told me that if Trump won, activists would hunker down, and some would be "going to the mountains with a cache and a bunker [of weapons]." Cameron had said something similar to me about activists arming themselves.

It's easy to dismiss Cameron and Bernard's talk of guns as just talk. But there's data to back it up. Since 2020, some of the fastest-growing groups of new gun owners have been Democrats, liberals, and people of color. New gun owners cited feelings of insecurity, threats of political violence, and a desire to protect themselves and their families.[10] So perhaps it's not all bravado.

Bernard then told me an interesting anecdote. A few months before the election in 2024, he had been at a nature summer solstice retreat. It was pretty "woo-woo"—more of a spiritual, get-in-touch-with-nature thing than an activist-focused retreat. Bernard told me that the vibes at the camp were political alienation. Many felt that the left wasn't going to win a war of ideas with the radical right, and that violence was coming. What also stuck with Bernard was the talk of guns. "People I know are definitely buying guns" he told me. He felt the moment reflected the time around the Black Lives Matter protests and election in 2020, when he also saw an increase in his friends and fellow activists buying guns. Bernard said that those "who bought pistols in 2020, are now buying assault rifles. And those who bought assault rifles in 2020 are now doing tactical maneuvers."

After the election, I reached out to Bernard and asked how he was feeling now that Trump had won. He told me he felt the grief of the election loss. But mostly he was frustrated, experiencing a deep sense of pessimism. He felt that many people, even his most politically active and aware friends, "didn't want it to be possible [that Trump would be reelected], so they told themselves it couldn't happen."

A week after the election, I also talked to Cameron.[11] It was not a normal conversation. It was more of a stream-of-consciousness rap session in which he was working through his thoughts. Cameron told me he had been doing a lot of thinking and a lot of talking. He told me he talked to "like, 50 [of his fellow] activists" since the election. He said it was a weird feeling. Because to him and many activists it felt like Trump's election was a "punch in the face."

Cameron then switched gears and became quite pessimistic. He didn't really see many silver linings. He told me that activists "need to take care of each other, and now is a good time to buy a gun." Echoing Bernard's sentiments, he said that "literally over the last week [since the election], ten people [I know] who would never have bought guns and held off until this point, bought guns. It's an indicator that they have no hope."

What concerned Cameron was that the "[climate activists'] strategy for the last twenty years has been to use legal fights to drag out the clock" on fossil fuel and pipeline projects. But Cameron saw this strategy as useless against the coming Trump administration. He predicted that the Trump administration would fast-track every fossil fuel permit, pipeline, or use of public lands. And he had zero faith that the courts would do anything, or even that the Trump administration would listen.

Cameron then paused and hypothetically looked at the world from Trump's perspective. He said, "If I am Trump, I want chaos, and I probably want revenge on particular people—the media, the Democratic Party, and Antifa." Cameron knew that "Antifa" meant people like him and his activist friends. He continued and said if he were Trump, he would tell the Department of Justice to investigate every nonprofit and climate activist organization. And then if anything happened at a rally, he would freeze their accounts and assets. "Greenpeace would go under" and so would many other nonprofits, according to Cameron. It would be fought in the courts, but it "wouldn't matter if it's legal"—to Cameron, the damage would be done.

Cameron ended our chat by saying that he told his fellow leftist activists and organizers over the summer before the election that, if Trump won, "we need to reassess all our priors." The idea was that mass movements and organizing, which follow the 1960s model of pressure and legal tactics and use of the courts, had to change. Cameron saw the model as broken since it was based on analysis from a "different world and a different country"—one that hadn't reelected Trump.

In mid-December 2024, a month after the election, I talked to Alicia, the climate justice activist and organizer whom we first met in Chapter 6. It was a month before Trump was due to be sworn in as president in January 2025.[12] Alicia told me she was still in a state of processing her emotions following Trump's victory. She was especially thinking about the effects on her "trans and [fellow] BIPOC (Black, Indigenous, and People of Color) activists and comrades." Alicia said that she and others had been "preparing" things in case Trump won. She said that she hadn't necessarily wanted Harris to win, either. She viewed the possibility of a Harris victory as "bandage for the problems on the left. Revolution doesn't happen when people are comfortable."

Alicia was also preoccupied with a conversation she had with her younger brother after the election. Her brother had told her that he sympathized with Trump and Trump supporters and that "something had to be done about the border." Alicia didn't know for sure, but she suspected he had voted for Trump, and it enraged her. As the daughter of immigrants, she felt her brother had "betrayed" her family and all immigrants. She then took a moment to process it, and she wasn't as upset; it was her brother, after all. Alicia said that "seeing the number of people of color and young people of color who voted for Trump, my anger is not toward them; it's rather toward the system [that didn't address their needs]."

I also asked Alicia if she was worried about the coming repression. While several of Trump's ideas for targeting left-wing and social justice NGOs did concern her a lot, she also said it was a continuation of previous repressive campaigns at the state level. "The repression that's coming down [with the Trump administration] is not that different from Stop Cop City." Her goal was to use the repression to bring new people into the movement, people who were thinking, "What the fuck just happened [in our country]? I am not OK with this!" Finally, Alicia struck a defiant tone and said matter-of-factly, "They can't repress us all."

The repression that Alicia mentioned was on the mind of a lot of activists. In March 2025, Cameron told me that he knew of several environmental NGOs that had been notified that their communications via Google might be subpoenaed for lawsuits or investigations. Also, several activists he knew across the country had federal law enforcement knock on their doors since Trump's inauguration. As Cameron told me, "It's just shaking the trees. But it scares people."[13]

***

One concern loomed especially large: surveillance. Activists were increasingly worried about how the Trump administration might weaponize advanced surveillance tools against social movements.

That's how I ended up on a Signal call in early 2025 with Reed, a self-described movement tech security specialist.[14] Reed had a warm but slightly jittery energy. It made sense, given that his job was to think through all the ways governments could surveil activists and disrupt organizing. From early on he was drawn to leftist causes and was an early adopter of PGP (Pretty Good Privacy) encryption, a tool that ensures that emails and messages are both secure and authentic. Reed told me that he had always been suspicious of what the U.S. government was doing with surveillance, going back to efforts in the 1960s and 1970s to disrupt civil rights activists. But it was the 2013 Snowden disclosures—in which Edward Snowden, an intelligence contractor, leaked to journalists classified documents about broad government surveillance of U.S. and domestic communications—that opened his eyes: "The scale and scope of the government's ability to monitor activists [post-9/11] was just massive."

Reed had already been teaching courses on information security. But after the Snowden disclosures, he doubled down on helping activists stay secure. And now, in 2025, his concerns had only grown. He worried that the Trump administration would apply AI and machine learning patterns "to figure out innocuous shit," and then use theses digital breadcrumbs to arrest even careful activists. But Reed emphasized that the Trump administration didn't need to pass new laws or design new surveillance-gathering programs. "The only thing that stopped it [the really terrible abuse of surveillance] were norms. We built an East German Stasi wet dream of surveillance, and a system that is enabling authoritarianism, and now we have an authoritarian [in Trump]."

He ended our call with a point that stuck with me. Referencing how the ELF was ultimately undone by informants, Reed said:

> Fundamentally, it comes down to security culture. We need better deep community ties and support for any opsec or infosec [operational security or informational security]. We need to build trust and build stronger communities. Infiltrators are classically shitty people—they sow division.

In other words, if the government infiltrates the movement, it won't be because of surveillance tech. It'll be because activists let them in.

***

In the 150-plus interviews that I conducted with more than 110 activists and experts while researching this book, I would usually end my interviews with one question. It's the question that motivated me to write this book in the first place. *Given the threat from climate change, why haven't we seen the emergence of more radical tactics from the environmental movement?* The answers to this question were surprising and contradictory. In more than half of my interviews, people were pessimistic about the future of the movement. They cited denialism and apathy from potential supporters, apathy and a lack of strategic vision within the movement itself, and general despondence that any radical action taken would make a difference. Others cited prison sentences and law enforcement repression as crippling the movement. But at the same time, more than half the people I interviewed believed that more radical tactics were coming. There was duality to the way people thought of the movement. The movement wasn't doing enough, couldn't do enough, but at the same time was on the precipice of major radical action.

Two former Earth First!ers believed the movement was at a crossroads. Jim, the soft-spoken former acolyte of Dave Foreman, told me that in his view, "things wax and wane" with radical movements.[15] But Jim also saw it as a problem that everything within the current activist vein was viewed through the lens of racial politics. He saw that as self-defeating. Yet, Jim said he understood why people felt so strongly when they watched cops murder someone, as when they viewed the killing of George Floyd in 2020. "Emotional suffering is visceral," he said. Jim contrasted this emotional suffering, something that he felt was necessary to galvanize people to a cause, with the current messaging of climate justice activists. The visceral grievance and outrage just weren't there. Calls by climate activists to dismantle capitalism and the fossil fuel infrastructure don't have the same resonance as people being murdered. Jim also felt that just enough technological progress had been made to distract people. "We have solar panels, wind energy, and you can drive a Tesla." Jim called it a "Green Nirvana" but felt it was a "mirage just attractive enough to mute the Greta Thunberg–types and prevent people from getting radicalized." The promise of technical solutions to a fundamental social problem of climate change reduced the sense of urgency among activists.

Mark, one of the early core members of Earth First!, whom we first met in Chapter 2, had a slightly different view.[16] Mark had been part of various leftist movements in the 1960s and 1970s before finding his way to Earth First!. When I asked him why more radical tactics had not yet emerged, he first expressed his disdain for many of the current climate-focused, big NGOs. He called them a "mutual admiration society." Mark told me the problem was that activists and the public had heard that "the indicators are all going in the wrong direction" and "we have ten years to make changes [with carbon emissions]," or we are in big trouble. And yet, ten years have passed, and the tactics haven't really changed, and now activists are talking about methane emissions instead of carbon. It was confusing to the average person.

In Mark's view, activists need to back up their rhetoric with action, but they also must provide people with hope. When he was involved in the civil rights movement in the 1960s as a young teen, he and other activists in the movement "hoped that their children would live better lives." He contrasted that with the pessimism of climate activists: "there's no hope in the movement," and all that people are being told is to buy electric cars. But along with that hope, Mark wanted the movement to have an edge and be willing to use muscle to achieve its climate goals. He said, "I am not advocating violence, but we need to have the pitchforks ready. We can inflict a certain amount of chaos into society." For Mark it was an open question whether younger activists had that radical willingness to throw down.

Jim and Mark had different views on problems within the movement, but both agreed that the movement needed harder, more radical tactics. The election of Trump only heightened this feeling of a movement at a crossroads.

***

Across the environmental movement and among both veteran organizers and younger climate activists, a key question looms: *what now?*[17]

The academic literature on social movements captures this dilemma well. On one hand, both the political opportunity and the resources needed for mobilization are increasingly constrained.[18] Conventional policy channels for environmental advocacy are closing fast. Under the Trump administration, the Environmental Protection Agency and federal courts will be at best, indifferent—and at worst, openly hostile—to environmental regulation. Federal law enforcement under a Trump administration has signaled that it will treat leftist activists, including environmental activists, as domestic terrorists.[19] At the same time, the NGOs, legal aid networks, and protest funding mechanisms are all under siege. The Greenpeace–Energy Transfer lawsuit in North Dakota and the legal targeting of Stop Cop City bail fund activists in Georgia are harbingers of a broader crackdown.[20] So both the political opportunities and the resources needed to mobilize and sustain environmental activism are under tremendous pressure.

And yet, the grievances and moral outrage felt by environmental activists are likely to intensify. Rising temperatures, more extreme heat waves, worsening droughts and floods, and increasing sea-level rise mean that the impacts of climate change are becoming more visible and more dire. At the same time, the Trump administration has pledged to open federal lands to fossil fuel exploration and logging, ramp up domestic oil production, and roll back the transition to electric vehicles. For many activists, these aren't just anti-environmental policies. They represent a betrayal of future generations and an abandonment of climate science in favor of fossil fuel profits and reactionary politics.

Social movement scholars show that when sacred values are flagrantly violated, it can be a powerful force for action.[21] For environmental activists, protection of the environment and climate isn't just a political position, but also a core, sacred value. When that value is betrayed or attacked, it can drive people into activism and push activists toward more confrontational or escalatory tactics even in the face of repression.

So, what happens next? That's the question activists are asking themselves and each other. As a social scientist, I'm cautious about making predictions. Political violence is rare. Radical shifts in activist tactics are also hard to predict. Your prediction can be right given the information available to you at any given time, but it can still turn out to be wrong.

So, I am not going to make a hard prediction about what will happen to the radical environmental movement. But I think it's helpful to think about four possible ways the movement might evolve, depending on how activists respond to repression, shifts in federal policy, and the climate crisis:

1) Situation Normal: Status Quo
2) Deescalation and Demobilization
3) Escalation and Radicalization
4) Pro-Democracy Fusion

Situation Normal: Status Quo

In this scenario, activists weather some repressive moves by the Trump administration, but they continue pressing forward. They focus on blocking new drilling and timber projects on public lands and new proposed pipelines, and they engage in low-level civil disobedience—tree-sits, lockdowns, and disruptions—while also filing lawsuits against the administration. Some activists are arrested, but the crackdown isn't as severe as anticipated. Many NGOs continue to raise money, and support activists and legal challenges against the Trump administration's environmental policies.

Some small legal victories have been achieved that provide enough hope to activists who can ride out the administration and defend existing environmental gains. Climate activists are also keeping up the pressure on corporations and financial institutions to cut emissions and divest from fossil fuel companies. Activists are increasingly involved in local politics and state-level policy processes, particularly in Democratic-led states where they think they can make a difference.

The overall structure of activism is unchanged. NGOs provide funding for civil disobedience and legal challenges to fossil fuel expansion. Violence and sabotage by activists are frowned upon and rare. Youth climate activists who began with groups like Fridays for the Future and the Sunrise Movement are now involved in mainstream climate NGOs. Some are even running for political office themselves. Climate politics is increasingly a key part of the Democratic Party. Policies centered on climate change, adaptation, and support for electric vehicles have again become core tenets of the party, as it seeks to build on Biden's pro-climate, pro-union, and pro-domestic green manufacturing coalition.

This future is entirely plausible. And the best prediction of the future is generally the past. But there are reasons to question the stability of this status quo. Even before Trump was inaugurated, cracks appeared. In early January 2025, the six largest U.S. banks—JP Morgan, Citigroup, Bank of America, Morgan Stanley, Wells Fargo, and Goldman Sachs—withdrew from a voluntary alliance meant to align banking and investment choices with net-zero emissions by 2050 (the Net Zero Banking Alliance).[22] It was a signal that the private sector feared the Trump administration more than climate activists.

The new administration wasted little time in enacting their anti-climate and pro-fossil fuel agenda. Within the first couple of months, it aggressively rolled back environmental rules and regulations, and sought to fast-track fossil fuel projects—leaving activists with fewer ways to influence policy.[23] As the Greenpeace lawsuit showed, nonviolent civil disobedience will be met with heavy financial and legal consequences. The Trump administration has also made it clear that it intends to target leftist activist networks.

All of this makes the status quo hard to sustain. What happens when activists can't rely on their standard playbook of protest, pressure, lawsuits, and procedural delays? In the next three sections we will explore three different paths forward: Deescalation and Demobilization, Escalation and Radicalization, and Pro-Democracy Fusion.

Deescalation and Demobilization

Initially, the Trump administration decides to make examples of a few activists. Those who blocked entrances to corporate offices, demonstrated outside the homes of CEOs, or disrupted shareholder meetings are singled out. Anybody with a past involvement in left-wing protests has been branded as Antifa. The activists are hit with serious charges like material support for terrorism, and many are being overcharged on purpose. Some even may be charged as part of a vast criminal conspiracy, even if the link is tenuous—all the better to link activists with a shadowy network of leftwing activists and tie them to George Soros, Antifa, or other leftist boogeyman. People only tangentially related to the defendants are being subpoenaed and forced to appear before federal grand juries. Environmental NGOs with even the faintest connections to environmental groups that use civil disobedience are having their finances turned upside down by federal investigators. Their donors are facing the same treatment. The NGOs are being financially crippled.

This scenario isn't hard to imagine. As in the case of Stop Cop City in Georgia, the overcharging and arresting of anyone remotely connected to the movement is intentional. While some of the charges may be thrown out on appeal, this shock-and-awe approach does what it's intended to do. It has a devastating effect on the ability of the radical environmental movement to organize and coordinate protests. Many activists begin to believe they are under surveillance (even if they are not). Like during the Green Scare, the use of informants stokes paranoia within the movement, and many start to wonder which of their fellow activists may be cooperating with the federal government. And so activists turn on each other.

Seeing their fellow activists face repression and heavy jail time for what many view as minor acts of civil disobedience has a chilling effect on the movement. Some see the environmental cause as a lost one and not worth the risk of heavy jail time for the potential to make a marginal impact. As in the wake of Operation Backfire and the Green Scare in the early 2000s, some activists burn out while others shift into other leftist causes where they feel they can make a bigger difference.

There's no longer a coherent national climate justice movement, only pockets of local and state activism. Their impact is modest. Given the pessimism and concern of many activists I talked to, this isn't a far-fetched path. It's a very real possibility.

But it's not the only one. There are two other paths.

Escalation and Radicalization

Imagine that the Trump administration starts targeting activists as discussed in the previous Deescalation and Demobilization scenario. Activists face intense jail time for relatively minor acts of civil disobedience. NGOs are gutted. Finances are frozen. Donors fear the federal scrutiny. But instead of demobilizing, there's a growing subset of people within the radical environmental movement who see playing by the rules as a fool's errand. If prison is inevitable, why not take more decisive action against the people responsible for those driving climate collapse?

The environmental crisis worsens. Yet the EPA and the Trump administration are rolling back environmental rules, pumping more oil, and nobody is doing anything about it. Individual activists and small groups start targeting fossil fuel and chemical company CEOs with violence.

The mainstream NGOs that would have usually socialized and pushed activists against violent tactics are a shell of their former selves and don't carry the same heft. A mostly online movement of activists actively cheers on these sporadic acts of violence. Leftist politicians don't openly endorse the tactics, but they stop short of outright condemnation. Some even say they understand the sentiment, given the stakes.

This movement, with its disdain for corporations and its openness to radical leftist politics, echoes the ELF in some ways. But there are notable differences. The movement is much more online. It is also radically anti-Big Tech and targets technology companies that are viewed as contributing to climate change. And at its core, this new, radical environmental movement does not disavow violence. It believes there are villains who are poisoning the planet and need to pay for it.

This idea of environmentalists going after corporate CEOs may feel like dystopian fiction. But on December 4, 2024, Brian Thompson, the CEO of UnitedHealthcare, was gunned down in broad daylight in New York City. The alleged perpetrator in the Thompson murder, Luigi Mangione, is a fan of Ted Kaczynski, the Unabomber. Writings found on Mangione further suggest he held deep-seated anger toward corporate America and health insurance CEOs. Mangione wrote: "Frankly, these parasites (CEOs) had it coming."[24] Much was made of the fact that some Americans openly cheered on the shooter's action, recounting stories of their friends or family–or they, themselves, having been denied coverage by health care companies during illness.[25]

After the murder, several activists I had previously interviewed reached out to me.[26] The fact that people didn't just straight-out condemn the violence was a lightbulb moment for many of them. Tim, the direct action organizer, messaged me on Signal: "Pretty crazy week for political violence." I asked him if he was referring to the UnitedHealthcare CEO shooting, and he answered "yes"; it was all people were talking about in his world. Tim wrote that the anger of ordinary people toward UnitedHealthcare was "mind-blowing." He messaged me:

> It's ER nurses and people who've lost family due to claim denials [who sympathize with the shooter]. If they catch him alive the shooter is going to be celebrated as a folk hero. I have a friend whose wife is a doctor, who messaged me "woohoo!" when she heard about the shooting.

Tim admitted he was concerned about some blowback on activists, and groups like his, which confront CEOs in public. But, overall, he was heartened that at least part of the public was OK with going after parts of corporate America that, in Tim's view, were clearly bad actors.

Bernard, the Portland-based former Earth First!er, also reached out and told me that he thought what happened with the Thompson shooting was "great."

It was not necessarily great strategically, he clarified, but it was great because it expanded the "limited range of strategies that are most psychologically amenable." If a major American CEO could be gunned down on the streets, it meant that more tactics were on the table, and, to Bernard and others, this was a good thing. Bernard also told me that he himself was currently engaged in paramilitary training, less from a desire to deploy the methods, but to expand his views on what was possible.

Cameron, the veteran-turned-activist, was even blunter:

> I'm really annoyed that the media is so fucking out of touch [with the surprise over the reaction of the public to the killing]. You know how many people we murder [in this country] and no one says shit. This guy [the UnitedHealthcare CEO] was a piece of shit. And most normal people see that.

I shared with Cameron an article that argued that Mangione, the shooter, fit with Eric Hobsbawm's theory of social banditry.[27] Hobsbawm, a Marxist historian, came up with the idea of a social bandit as an individual who lives outside the law, but whom the populace still supports because he is perceived to fight against elites or an unjust system, like Pancho Villa.[28] In other words, social bandits may be criminals, but to their supporters they are carrying out a type of vigilante justice that is otherwise unavailable to ordinary citizens.

Cameron agreed and said, "Everyone wants a measure of justice, and they see none in our society. So, when Robin Hood comes along [in the guise of Mangione], it brings a little joy."

Pro-Democracy Fusion

There's another possible path.

Imagine the Trump administration goes broader in its repression—targeting immigrants, academics, international students, LGBT activists, progressives, environmentalists, voting rights advocates, and antifascists. Protests are restricted, NGOs are investigated, surveillance increases. Anything that smells remotely of left-wing causes comes under scrutiny.

But instead of splintering, activists fuse together. Environmental activists see their struggle as part of a larger struggle for democracy. The climate crisis doesn't disappear, but it takes a back seat among the immediate threats to democracy. Radical environmental activists join forces with other civil society actors like racial justice advocates, academics, and labor and immigrant activists in a broad-based movement against Trump. They use mass protests, targeted disruption, and occasional sabotage. They recognize that to fight for the climate, they first have to fight for democracy.

There's evidence that this shift was already taking hold early in the first few months of Trump's term. In March 2025, Tim, the direct action organizer, messaged me after a strategy meeting with several climate NGOs and activists. They were wrestling with a core question: "Is democracy a precondition for doing climate work?" His answer: "We decided we will do both." So, the climate and democracy shared a linked fate.

One notable case in point was the "Tesla Takedown" movement. Elon Musk, the wealthiest person in the world and CEO of the Tesla car company, assumed a prominent role in Trump's second term. He began purging government agencies through the Department of Government Efficiency (DOGE). Despite its name, DOGE isn't an official government department, but rather an initiative designed to reduce government spending. Through his control of DOGE and rhetoric around the massive reorganizations of the federal government, Musk became a symbol of billionaire influence in the second Trump administration and attracted a large amount of criticism. There were reports that Musk was directing DOGE to use AI tools to spy on federal workers for signs of dissent against him and Trump.[29] In response, the decentralized Tesla Takedwon movement formed. It held regular protests outside of Tesla stores and across the United States and even internationally.[30] There were incidents of vandalism of Tesla showrooms and charging stations, including use of Molotov cocktails, and even gunfire.[31] The Trump Department of Justice launched a task force to look into the spate of vandalism, calling those who engaged in such property destruction "domestic terrorists."[32] It wasn't lost on Tim—or on me—that more than twenty years earlier, ELF activists had made torching SUVs a signature tactic.[33]

Alicia, the climate change organizer and activist, messaged me around the same time as the Tesla Takedown movement was taking off.[34] "Billionaires [like Elon Musk] are the problem." She told me that climate couldn't be the sole focus of activists anymore. They had to stand up to President Trump and Musk, and that democracy couldn't be ignored.

To Alicia, the right-wing, fascist Trump government was the main problem. She wasn't scared, but she told me that, "For activism in a state of fascism [Trump's America], it has to go underground." She viewed Musk as the enemy and wanted people who supported Musk or drove his cars to pay a price. "There should be more [Tesla vandalism]. I want us to overwhelm the system."

She added: "And if you are going to do it [vandalism], don't get caught."

***

A realization I came to while doing research for this book was that I wasn't the only one searching for answers. Activists were searching, too. Caroline was a climate justice and environmental organizer whom I had talked to several times. By day, she monitored forests for illegal logging, and on the side she was involved in leftist and anarchist environmental organizing. We grabbed coffee when I was in the Pacific Northwest in May 2024. Caroline had long brown hair, hipster glasses, wore a baseball cap, and was in her mid-late 20s. She had an easy-going demeanor and talked about all the different campaigns she had been involved in. But when Caroline and I spoke in November 2024, a week after Trump had been elected, she was despondent.[35] She conveyed to me that the "million-dollar question" which many of her activist friends were asking themselves was: were they going to be "repressed" or "radicalized?" Caroline didn't know the answer. She stated that activists "are looking for a better way to do things, or how to win." In a moment of candor, she said that "I don't know what I am doing." As an activist, Caroline was always experimenting and looking for new things. But Trump's reelection felt like uncharted territory. She asked if I had any answers. I told her I didn't, but I sent her some citations from political science and sociology on social movements that I hoped she might find useful.

Throughout the book we've heard several times from Cameron and Tim. I first connected with them to better understand the radical environmental movement. But over time, we became friends. We would share news articles on recent actions by activists, and thoughts on politics ahead of the 2024 presidential election. Both Cameron and Tim were also interested in academic research on social movements and political violence. I would pass along research that I thought they might find interesting—whether it was on the politics of Trumpism, attitudes toward environmentalism, or support for political violence. I figured they found the research interesting, both because of their own natural intellectual curiosity and because they hoped the it might help them in their own activism and eventually help the movement succeed.

Many of the activists I interviewed asked me whether I thought the movement would radicalize. I answered that I believed there was a good chance that more radical tactics were coming. I had talked to enough activists who were losing faith in the efficacy of nonviolent civil disobedience. And I'd seen the skies in Washington, D.C. choked by wildfires, and I felt the scorching hot summer temperatures—and that was just a small taste of the effects of climate change. As the climate crisis deepens, and the space for protest narrows, activists are asking themselves what tactics they are willing to use and what they are willing to risk.

But it's not just a question of whether activists will escalate their tactics, but rather what type of movement and subculture will nurture and support them going forward? In earlier waves, the radical environmental movement had Earth First!, and then the hardcore punk and straight edge scene and animal rights. For a time, Eugene, Oregon was the epicenter of the movement. What will serve as the new incubator? And will climate remain the central cause, or will it just become one issue in a broader movement?

***

A conversation that stuck with me was the first one I had with Bernard, the Portland-based Earth First!er that took place in October 2022.[36] We had tried to connect a few times before then, but Bernard's health had not been good, and he had been feeling weak. Finally, we talked, and at the end of the interview I asked him for his thoughts on the future of the movement. He spoke to me in a quiet, soft voice. He said that it sometimes felt nihilistic to be an environmental activist during a period of ecological collapse. He was quite pessimistic about the future of the movement: "I don't know what's happening, but I know we will die trying—and it wouldn't surprise me at all. People have always thought that, given objective external conditions, eventually people will conclude that 'the environmentalists were right—civilizational collapse is upon us!' And I don't think this is necessarily going to happen . . . the limit does not exist." Bernard paused for a moment and continued. "People can generate alternate narratives, all the way down to the last tree that gets incinerated." It's a brutal description, but in my research and travels I'd seen people justify enough crazy beliefs to not totally dismiss Bernard's apocalyptic view.

Two years later, I came to see Bernard as a metaphor for the movement. Bernard was still here, and though frustrated, he was not as nihilistic. He was pessimistic about what was going to happen under Trump. His tattooed and scarred body betrayed his past battles with addiction and his hard life as an activist. And he couldn't count on his health. It could give out on him at a moment's notice and lay him up for weeks. Yet at the same time, soft-spoken Bernard was undergoing paramilitary training and still willing to fight for an uncertain future.

METHODS APPENDIX

A.1 Database of Eco Direct Actions (1995–2022)

A.1.1 Construction of Database of Eco Direct Actions

The dataset was constructed to collect all publicly known instances of eco direct actions of environmentally or animal-motivated civil disobedience (e.g., tree-sits, lockdowns, road blockages, disruptions), sabotage and vandalism (e.g., freeing animals, smashing windows, spray painting graffiti, sabotaging equipment), and violence (e.g., arson, bombings, shootings) from 1995 to 2022 in the United States. To collect this data, I turned to a variety of sources.

- Previous collections including the Terrorism and Extremist Violence in the United States (TEVUS) Database and the Global Terrorism Database (GTD)
- Journalist Will Potter's efforts to document eco direct actions for his book *Green Is the New Red*
- Animal rights activist Peter Young's efforts to document Animal Liberation Front (ALF) actions from 1975 to 2022 in his book *Animal Liberation Front: Complete Diary of Actions*
- ProQuest News Aggregator to search using terms ("green scare" OR ecoterrorism OR ecoterror) OR (eco OR "climate activist" OR "climate protester" OR "radical environmental" OR "environmental activist" OR "environmental protestor" OR "anti pipeline") AND (graffiti OR sabotage OR monkeywrenching OR vandalism OR blockade OR arson OR "civil disobedience" OR

"tree spiking" OR "tree sit" OR lockdown OR "property destruction" OR disrupt OR "block traffic" OR "strike" OR "sit in")
- Social media and website posts from Earth First! and other Animal Liberation Front Press Office, confirmed by other newspapers

Each event in the dataset represents a discrete event. Some events contained more than one tactic, such as vandalism and arson, and in that case, the intensity of the event was determined by the more intense tactic (e.g., arson in that case). The unit of time is at the month level, so for a tree-sit that lasted eleven months, there would be eleven entries in the dataset. Motivations for reach action—animal, environmental, or both—were ascertained by the (1) target of the action, (2) perpetrators, and (3) any additional information (such as graffiti or communiqués).

A.1.2 Yearly Eco Direct Actions

Table A.1 Yearly counts of eco direct actions, 1995–2022

Year	Number of Actions
1995	51
1996	90
1997	87
1998	58
1999	77
2000	72
2001	75
2002	51
2003	103
2004	52
2005	62
2006	22
2007	36
2008	30
2009	30
2010	48
2011	54
2012	56

Year	Number of Actions
2013	37
2014	5
2015	10
2016	18
2017	25
2018	16
2019	49
2020	25
2021	20
2022	72

A.1.3 Normalized Counts of Eco Direct Actions

One concern is that the media doesn't cover all actions in a similar way. Reporting bias is inherent in the study of conflict and protest.[1] The media has incentives to report when activists use extreme or intense tactics such as arson or vandalism, compared to peaceful civil disobedience.[2] These extreme actions are most likely to be investigated and prosecuted, and to garner additional coverage. Yet activists also seek out civil disobedience actions that are likely to attract media attention and coverage.[3] To address the possibility of systematic undercounts, particularly in the civil disobedience data, I have standardized the data and transformed it so that the maximum yearly counts are 1 and minimum are 0 across all event types. The results are shown in Figure A.1. They show that as the amount of vandalism and sabotage declined post-2004, civil disobedience became an increasingly prominent tactic post-2010.

A.2 In-Depth Qualitative Interviews

From November 2021 through December 2024, I conducted more than 150 semistructured interviews with 112 individuals. The majority of the interviews were with current and former activists (65% of interviews). The rest were researchers and academics who were also engaged in activism (19%), pure academia (8%), law enforcement (5%), and journalism (3%); they were familiar with the past and current iteration of the radical environmental movement. Gaining trust within clandestine activist networks is hard. To start with, I reached out to public-facing activists and researchers who were familiar with the radical environmental movement. I explained that I was an academic researcher interested in talking to people familiar and active either presently or in the past in the radical environmental movement. These initial connections were crucial because for many of the activist interviews I had to be vouched for by other activists I previously

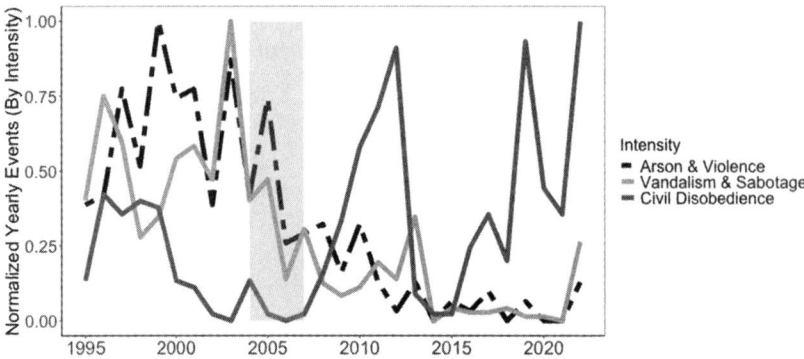

FIGURE A.1 Normalized yearly counts of disaggregated eco direct actions (1995–2022). Vertical shaded region signifies the key years of Operation Backfire, 2004–2006.

interviewed. For activists—the bulk of my interview sample—my main goal in sampling was to try to get as much breadth across two strata:

1) *Level of engagement in radical tactics*: I wanted to interview activists who were involved in some of the most radical and intense actions (property destruction and sabotage) as well as those who did some sabotage and mostly engaged in civil disobedience.
2) *Period of activity:* I wanted to interview activists who were present at the beginning of Earth First!, active during the 1990s with the ELF/ALF, as well as during and after Operation Backfire in the early 2000s, as well as current activists.

The interviews lasted forty-five minutes to two and half hours, with the average lasting just under an hour. Most of the interviews were conducted via phone, Zoom, or Signal, and a few were in person. The interviews received Institutional Review Board (IRB) approval from American University #IRB-2022-224 and #IRB-2024-242.

Given the sensitive nature of the project, especially for current and former activists who spent time in prison, or face the risk of repression or prison, I took steps to minimize risk to all participants:

1) All the interviews were done as "not for attribution"—interviewees could choose how they wanted to be pseudonymously identified (e.g., "former ecoactivist").
2) Notes were taken during the interviews, but none of the interviews were recorded.
3) For activists, none of the questions I asked were directly about actions people had participated in. Rather, the questions focused on their views on strategy and tactics writ large. I didn't want to directly ask about any potential clandestine or illegal activity, but rather I focused on their thoughts on how

their activity fit into the movement, why it declined, and what the future of these tactics might be.

All of the people interviewed are identified by pseudonyms and their preferred self-described identity (e.g., "a longtime direct action organizer"). Again, for reasons of sensitivity and concerns given the topics and experiences of some of the interviews, nothing was recorded. I took notes that I later transcribed. Transcriptions of the interviews were then coded within NVivo software to capture similar themes that emerged across interviews to the key questions.[4]

All the interviews started off with a consent script stating that I was an academic researcher interested in the past and future of the radical environmental movement. I told interviewees that I wasn't recording anything; that all the interviews were done on background (their names wouldn't be used); that they could ignore any questions or stop the interview at any time; and that I wasn't directly interested in their individual participation in any illegal or clandestine actions, but my focus rather was their thoughts and strategies on tactics.

The interviews were semistructured to allow for the emergence of key themes. I asked interviewees three sets of broad questions. I would then ask follow-up questions and probes to get a richer understanding of how the person being interviewed made sense of these questions.

1) For activists, what was their pathway into the movement? Were they specifically radicalized around environmental issues, or were they involved in other movements (antiwar, social justice, or animal rights)? What were the key moments in their own journey into the movement, or did they recall any specific instances of political awakening?
2) Why did the radical environmental movement collapse in the early 2000s? Was it because of faulty tactics, law enforcement, other movements taking primacy, etc.? Why did arson and sabotage become so prevalent during this period? And what were their thoughts on the effectiveness of groups like the ELF? How did Operation Backfire affect the movement, and how did it change (if at all) their own views on activism?
3) Given the threat from climate change, what did the future of radical tactics and the radical environmental movement writ large look like? Did they see the climate justice movement becoming more radicalized? How did they think the increasing weather events—droughts, floods, heatwaves, wildfires, which are exacerbated by climate change—will shape future activism?

A.3 Demographics and Procedures for Surveys and Interviews

A.3.1 U.S. General Population Survey

This survey was conducted via the Lucid Online Survey platform in June and July 2022, and it used three standard screener questions to weed out inattentive respondents. The survey found that 59% passed the most intense screener; fifty observations were dropped from the final analysis for speeding through the survey (taking it in three minutes or less); and 89.9% passed the attention check that was done pretreatment.

$N=1,196$

Age

- 18–29 21.1%
- 30–44 31.2%
- 45–59 23.9%
- 60+ 23.8%

Partisanship

- 43.8% Republican, or Republican leaning
- 56.2% Democratic, or Democratic-leaning

Gender

- 46.2% Male

Race

- 77.9% Non-Hispanic White

Education

- 40.0% Have graduated college or have a graduate degree

A.3.2 U.S. 18- to 29-Year-Old Survey

The survey was conducted via the Lucid Online Survey platform in April 2023. It was designed to approximate the 18- to 29-year-old U.S. population. It used three standard screener questions to weed out inattentive respondents. In all, 51% passed the most intense screener; eleven observations were dropped from the final analysis for speeding through the survey (taking it in 3 minutes or less); and 84.3% passed the attention check that was done pretreatment.

$N=1,086$

Age

- 12.5% 18–20 years old
- 23.3% 21–23 years old
- 27.8% 24–26 years old
- 26.2% 27–29 years old

Partisanship

- 37.8% Republican, or Republican leaning
- 62.2% Democratic, or Democratic leaning

Gender

- 49.2% Male

Race

- 59.8% Non-Hispanic White

Education

- 24.2% Have graduated college or have a graduate degree

A.3.3 U.S. Activist Survey

I worked with a veteran U.S. environmental direct action group to develop a survey and ask questions to their activist supporters regarding support for different tactics and thoughts on the movement. The survey was filled out in September and October 2022. They emailed an anonymous link out to the members on their listserv. The email invitation and demographics are below.

EMAIL INVITATION

We are conducting a survey of our fellow activists and supporters. The purpose of our survey is as follows:

- We want to find out a little bit more about who you are.
- We want to find out more about what drives your interest in the environment.
- We want to see how you feel about different protest activities and tactics.
- We want to get your broader thoughts on the movement.

We are working with Professor Zeitzoff at American University to help conduct this research.

The survey should take 8–10 minutes of your time

- The survey is completely anonymous. All answers are completely anonymous.

- You don't have to participate, or answer any questions you don't want to. We will generate a report, and you will be able to see how other members of the XXXX network feel about these things.

Demographics

$N=75$

Age

- 4% 18–29 years old
- 1.3% 30–39 years old
- 12% 40–49 years old
- 9.3% 50–59 years old
- 24% 60–69 years old
- 36% 70–79 years old
- 13.3% 80 plus years old

Gender

- 37.3% Male

Race

- 86.7% White

Education

- 87.1% Have graduated college or have a graduate degree

Protest Participation

- 66.7% Had participated in an environmental protest in the past year
- 26.7% Had engaged in civil disobedience such as a sit-in, blocking traffic, or lockdown in the past year

A.3.4. Survey Measures

Climate Change Threat (Five Items, Five-Point Agree-Disagree)

Climate change is the long-term change in average weather patterns, including increased global temperatures known as global warming.

Global warming started in the 1850s and continues through the present.

Below are some statements about global warming.
Please tell us how much you agree or disagree with each statement.

1. Human activity, especially burning fossil fuels, is the main cause of global warming.
2. Global warming will lead to more extreme heatwaves, droughts and floods, and stronger hurricanes.
3. Global warming will threaten the future of humanity.
4. The threat of global warming is overblown. (**Reverse coded**)
5. I am worried about global warming.

Support for Eco Tactics (17 Items, 11 Points: 0-Never Acceptable to 10-Always Acceptable)

In the Lucid General Public and Youth survey, respondents rated ten random tactics drawn from the full seventeen. In the Activist survey, only seven tactics were marked with **.

Now we are going to ask you about several different tactics groups and individuals have used to protest against people and policies that contribute to climate change and global warming.

Please tell us how often you feel each tactic is acceptable on a scale from 0 to 10, where 0 is never acceptable, 5 is sometimes acceptable, and 10 is always acceptable.

1. How acceptable is holding protest signs?
2. How acceptable is occupying buildings of companies that are big polluters?**
3. How acceptable is vandalizing websites of companies that are big polluters?**
4. How acceptable is sabotaging equipment for logging or oil companies?
5. How acceptable is damaging oil pipelines?**
6. How acceptable is marching while carrying weapons?
7. How acceptable is sitting in trees to prevent them from being cut down?**
8. How acceptable is using harsh words on social media?
9. How acceptable is holding public rallies?

10. How acceptable is vandalizing SUVs or other vehicles that consume a lot of gas?**
11. How acceptable is publicly confronting executives of companies that are big polluters?
12. How acceptable is threatening executives of companies that are big polluters?
13. How acceptable is leaking emails of companies that are big polluters?**
14. How acceptable is setting fire to buildings and equipment of companies that are big polluters?
15. How acceptable is blocking traffic?
16. How acceptable is demonstrating outside the homes of executives of companies that are big polluters?**
17. How acceptable is kidnapping executives of companies that are big polluters?

**Asked across all three surveys.

BIBLIOGRAPHY

Abbey, Edward. *The Monkey Wrench Gang*. 1st edition. Lippincott Williams & Wilkins, 1975.

Albertson, Bethany, and Shana Kushner Gadarian. *Anxious Politics: Democratic Citizenship in a Threatening World*. Cambridge University Press, 2015.

Alinsky, Saul. *Rules for Radicals: A Pragmatic Primer for Realistic Radicals*. Random House, 1971.

Atran, Scott, and Jeremy Ginges. "Devoted Actors and the Moral Foundations of Intractable Intergroup Conflict." In Decety, Jean, and Thalia Wheatley, eds. *The Moral Brain: A Multidisciplinary Perspective*, 69–85. Boston Review, 2015. https://doi.org/10.7551/mitpress/9988.001.0001.

Bari, Judi. *Timber Wars*. Common Courage Press, 1994.

Barnett, Brett A. "20 Years Later: A Look Back at the Unabomber Manifesto." *Perspectives on Terrorism* 9, no. 6 (2015): 60–71.

Beers, Diane L. *For the Prevention of Cruelty: The History and Legacy of Animal Rights Activism in the United States*. Ohio University Press, 2006.

Belgioioso, Margherita. "Going Underground: Resort to Terrorism in Mass Mobilization Dissident Campaigns." *Journal of Peace Research* 55, no. 5 (September 1, 2018): 641–55. https://doi.org/10.1177/0022343318764795.

Best, Steven, and Anthony J. Nocella. *Terrorists Or Freedom Fighters?: Reflections on the Liberation of Animals*. Lantern Books, 2004.

Blattman, Christopher, and Edward Miguel. "Civil War." *Journal of Economic Literature* 48, no. 1 (March 2010): 3–57. https://doi.org/10.1257/jel.48.1.3.

Blum, Rachel M. *How the Tea Party Captured the GOP: Insurgent Factions in American Politics*. University of Chicago Press, 2020.

Bookchin, Murray. *Our Synthetic Environment*. Knopf, 1962.

Boyle, Michael P., Douglas M. McLeod, and Cory L. Armstrong. "Adherence to the Protest Paradigm: The Influence of Protest Goals and Tactics on News

Coverage in U.S. and International Newspapers." *The International Journal of Press/Politics* 17, no. 2 (April 1, 2012): 127–44. https://doi.org/10.1177/1940161211433837.

Brown, Joseph M. "Civil Disobedience, Sabotage, and Violence in US Environmental Activism." *The Oxford Handbook of Comparative Environmental Politics*, August 11, 2021. https://doi.org/10.1093/oxfordhb/9780197515037.013.34.

Brown, Joseph M. "Notes to the Underground: Credit Claiming and Organizing in the Earth Liberation Front." *Terrorism and Political Violence* 32, no. 2 (February 17, 2020): 237–56. https://doi.org/10.1080/09546553.2017.1364637.

Brown, Joseph M. "Stop Cop City!—Understanding the Strategic Choices of Protest Movements." *Terrorism and Political Violence* Forthcoming (2025). https://doi.org/10.1080/09546553.2025.2489740.

Bueno De Mesquita, Ethan. "Terrorist Factions." *Quarterly Journal of Political Science* 3, no. 4 (December 31, 2008): 399–418. https://doi.org/10.1561/100.00008006.

Busby, Joshua. *States and Nature: The Effects of Climate Change on Security*. Cambridge University Press, 2022.

Campion, Kristy. "Defining Ecofascism: Historical Foundations and Contemporary Interpretations in the Extreme Right." *Terrorism and Political Violence* 35, no. 4 (May 19, 2023): 926–44. https://doi.org/10.1080/09546553.2021.1987895.

Carson, Jennifer Varriale, Laura Dugan, and Sue-Ming Yang. "A Comprehensive Application of Rational Choice Theory: How Costs Imposed by, and Benefits Derived from, the U.S. Federal Government Affect Incidents Perpetrated by the Radical Eco-Movement." *Journal of Quantitative Criminology* 36, no. 3 (September 1, 2020): 701–24. https://doi.org/10.1007/s10940-019-09427-8.

Carson, Jennifer Varriale, Gary LaFree, and Laura Dugan. "Terrorist and Non-Terrorist Criminal Attacks by Radical Environmental and Animal Rights Groups in the United States, 1970–2007." *Terrorism and Political Violence* 24, no. 2 (April 1, 2012): 295–319. https://doi.org/10.1080/09546553.2011.639416.

Carson, Rachel. *Silent Spring*. Houghton Mifflin Harcourt, 1962.

Cederman, Lars-Erik, Andreas Wimmer, and Brian Min. "Why Do Ethnic Groups Rebel? New Data and Analysis." *World Politics* 62, no. 1 (January 2010): 87–119. https://doi.org/10.1017/S0043887109990219.

Chamberlain, Mia Cathryn Randøy, and Ole Jacob Madsen. "Rebels With a Cause: Public Attitudes on Radical Protest Actions A Review of Empirical Evidence of Radical Flank Effects." *Human Arenas*, March 20, 2025. https://doi.org/10.1007/s42087-025-00485-y.

Chase, Alston. *A Mind for Murder: The Education of the Unabomber and the Origins of Modern Terrorism*. W. W. Norton, 2004.

Chenoweth, Erica. "The Role of Violence in Nonviolent Resistance." *Annual Review of Political Science* 26, no. 1 (2023): 55–77. https://doi.org/10.1146/annurev-polisci-051421-124128.

Chenoweth, Erica, and Maria J. Stephan. *Why Civil Resistance Works: The Strategic Logic of Nonviolent Conflict*. Columbia University Press, 2011.

Cobb, Charles E. *This Nonviolent Stuff'll Get You Killed: How Guns Made the Civil Rights Movement Possible*. Basic Books, 2014.

Coleman, Kate. *The Secret Wars of Judi Bari: A Car Bomb, the Fight for the Redwoods and the End of Earth First!* San Francisco: Encounter Books, 2005.

Davenport, Christian. *How Social Movements Die*. Cambridge University Press, 2015.

Davenport, Christian. *Media Bias, Perspective, and State Repression: The Black Panther Party*. Cambridge University Press, 2009.

Davenport, Christian, and Benjamin Appel. *The Death and Life of State Repression: Understanding Onset, Escalation, Termination, and Recurrence*. Oxford University Press, 2022.

Doherty, Eamon P. *Digital Forensics for Handheld Devices*. CRC Press, 2012.

Donaghey, Jim. "The 'Punk Anarchisms' of Class War and CrimethInc." *Journal of Political Ideologies* 25, no. 2 (May 3, 2020): 113–38. https://doi.org/10.1080/13569317.2020.1750761.

Dunlap, Alexander. "'I Don't Want Your Progress! It Tries to Kill . . . Me!' Decolonial Encounters and the Anarchist Critique of Civilization." *Globalizations* 0, no. 0 (n.d.): 1–27. https://doi.org/10.1080/14747731.2022.2073657.

Earl, Jennifer. "Tanks, Tear Gas, and Taxes: Toward a Theory of Movement Repression." *Sociological Theory* 21, no. 1 (2003): 44–68. https://doi.org/10.1111/1467-9558.00175.

Ehrlich, Paul R. *The Population Bomb*. Ballantine Books, 1968.

Ergas, Christina, Laura McKinney, and Shannon Elizabeth Bell. "Intersectionality and the Environment." In *Handbook of Environmental Sociology*, edited by Beth Schaefer Caniglia, Andrew Jorgenson, Stephanie A. Malin, Lori Peek, David N. Pellow, and Xiaorui Huang, 15–34. Springer International Publishing, 2021. https://doi.org/10.1007/978-3-030-77712-8_2.

Estes, Nick. *Our History Is the Future: Standing Rock Versus the Dakota Access Pipeline, and the Long Tradition of Indigenous Resistance*. Verso Books, 2019.

Feinberg, Matthew, Robb Willer, and Chloe Kovacheff. "The Activist's Dilemma: Extreme Protest Actions Reduce Popular Support for Social Movements." *Journal of Personality and Social Psychology* 119 (2020): 1086–1111. https://doi.org/10.1037/pspi0000230.

Feldstein, Steven. *The Rise of Digital Repression: How Technology Is Reshaping Power, Politics, and Resistance*. Oxford University Press, 2021.

Fisher, Dana R., and Sohana Nasrin. "Shifting Coalitions within the Youth Climate Movement in the US." *Politics and Governance* 9, no. 2 (April 28, 2021): 112–23. https://doi.org/10.17645/pag.v9i2.3801.

Fleming, Sean. "Searching for Ecoterrorism: The Crucial Case of the Unabomber." *American Political Science Review* 118, no. 4 (November 2024): 1986–99. https://doi.org/10.1017/S000305542300148X.

Foreman, Dave. *Confessions of an Eco-Warrior*. 1st edition. New York: Harmony, 1991.

Foreman, Dave. *Man Swarm and the Killing of Wildlife*. Raven's Eye Press, 2011.

Foreman, Dave, and Bill Haywood. *Ecodefense: A Field Guide to Monkeywrenching*. 3rd edition. Abbzug Press, 1993.

Gilbert, Danielle. "The Logic of Kidnapping in Civil War: Evidence from Colombia." *American Political Science Review* 116, no. 4 (November 2022): 1226–41. https://doi.org/10.1017/S0003055422000041.

Gillham, Patrick F. "Securitizing America: Strategic Incapacitation and the Policing of Protest Since the 11 September 2001 Terrorist Attacks." *Sociology Compass* 5, no. 7 (2011): 636–52. https://doi.org/10.1111/j.1751-9020.2011.00394.x.

Gore, Al. *An Inconvenient Truth: The Crisis of Global Warming*. Revised edition. Viking Books for Young Readers, 2007.

Grant, Madison. *The Passing of the Great Race: Or, The Racial Basis of European History*. C. Scribner, 1916.

Grubbs, Jennifer D. *Ecoliberation: Reimagining Resistance and the Green Scare*. McGill-Queen's Press—MQUP, 2021.

Gurr, Ted Robert. *Why Men Rebel*. Princeton University Press, 1970.

Hadden, Jennifer, and Sidney Tarrow. "Spillover or Spillout? The Global Justice Movement in the United States After 9/11." *Mobilization: An International Quarterly* 12, no. 4 (January 11, 2008): 359–76. https://doi.org/10.17813/maiq.12.4.t221742122771400.

Haenfler, Ross. "Rethinking Subcultural Resistance: Core Values of the Straight Edge Movement." *Journal of Contemporary Ethnography* 33, no. 4 (August 1, 2004): 406–36. https://doi.org/10.1177/0891241603259809.

Haenfler, Ross. *Straight Edge: Clean-Living Youth, Hardcore Punk, and Social Change*. Rutgers University Press, 2006.

Haines, Herbert H. *Black Radicals and Civil Rights Mainstream*. University of Tennessee Press, 2002.

Hardin, Garrett. "The Tragedy of the Commons." *Science* 162, no. 3859 (December 13, 1968): 1243–48. https://doi.org/10.1126/science.162.3859.1243.

Hirsch-Hoefler, Sivan, and Cas Mudde. "'Ecoterrorism': Terrorist Threat or Political Ploy?" *Studies in Conflict & Terrorism* 37, no. 7 (July 3, 2014): 586–603. https://doi.org/10.1080/1057610X.2014.913121.

Hobsbawm, Eric J. *Primitive Rebels: Studies in Archaic Forms of Social Movement in the 19th and 20th Centuries*. Manchester University Press, 1959.

Hofstadter, Richard. *The Paranoid Style in American Politics*. Knopf Doubleday Publishing Group, 1965.

Hughes, Brian, Dave Jones, and Amarnath Amarasingam. "Ecofascism: An Examination of the Far-Right/Ecology Nexus in the Online Space." *Terrorism and Political Violence* 34, no. 5 (July 4, 2022): 997–1023. https://doi.org/10.1080/09546553.2022.2069932.

Hultgren, John. *Border Walls Gone Green: Nature and Anti-Immigrant Politics in America*. University of Minnesota Press, 2015.

Jasper, James M. *The Art of Moral Protest: Culture, Biography, and Creativity in Social Movements*. University of Chicago Press, 2008.

Jensen, Derrick. *A Language Older Than Words*. Chelsea Green Publishing, 2000. https://www.goodreads.com/book/show/60970.

Justino, Patricia. "Poverty and Violent Conflict: A Micro-Level Perspective on the Causes and Duration of Warfare." *Journal of Peace Research* 46, no. 3 (May 1, 2009): 315–33. https://doi.org/10.1177/0022343309102655.

Kaczynski, David. *Every Last Tie: The Story of the Unabomber and His Family*. Duke University Press, 2015.

Kennedy, Alec Tyson, Cary Funk, and Kennedy Brian. "What the Data Says about Americans' Views of Climate Change." *Pew Research Center* (blog), August 9, 2023. https://www.pewresearch.org/short-reads/2023/08/09/what-the-data-says-about-americans-views-of-climate-change/.

Klein, Naomi. *This Changes Everything: Capitalism vs. The Climate*. 1st edition. Riverside: Simon & Schuster, 2013.

Kline, Benjamin. *First Along the River: A Brief History of the U.S. Environmental Movement*. Rowman & Littlefield, 1997.

LaDuke, Winona. *To Be A Water Protector: The Rise of the Wiindigoo Slayers*. Fernwood Publishing, 2020.

Lee, Francis L. F. "Triggering the Protest Paradigm: Examining Factors Affecting News Coverage of Protests." *International Journal of Communication* 8, no. 0 (August 14, 2014): 22.

Lee, Taeku. *Mobilizing Public Opinion: Black Insurgency and Racial Attitudes in the Civil Rights Era*. University of Chicago Press, 2002.

Linkola, Pentti. *Can Life Prevail?* 1st edition. Arktos Media Ltd., 2009.

Loadenthal, Michael. "The Earth Liberation Front: A Movement Analysis." *Radical Criminology*, no. 2 (September 21, 2013): 15–46.

Loadenthal, Michael. "Eco-Terrorism? Countering Dominant Narratives of Securitisation: A Critical, Quantitative History of the Earth Liberation Front (1996–2009)." *Perspectives on Terrorism* 8, no. 3 (2014): 16–50.

Loadenthal, Michael. "Feral Fascists and Deep Green Guerrillas: Infrastructural Attack and Accelerationist Terror." *Critical Studies on*

Terrorism 15, no. 3 (2022): 169–208. https://doi.org/10.1080/17539153.2022.2031129

Loadenthal, Michael. "'The Green Scare' & 'Eco-Terrorism': The Development of US Counter-Terrorism Strategy Targeting Direct Action Activists." *The Terrorization of Dissent: Corporate Repression, Legal Corruption and the Animal Enterprise Terrorism Act*, January 1, 2013.

Mahajan, Ilica. "Here's How Cops Are Using High-Tech Tools to Monitor Protesters." The Marshall Project, November 12, 2024. https://www.themarshallproject.org/2024/11/12/protest-surveillance-technologies.

Malm, Andreas. *How to Blow Up a Pipeline: Learning to Fight in a World on Fire*. Verso Books, 2021.

Manes, Christopher. *Green Rage: Radical Environmentalism and the Unmaking of Civilization*. Reprint edition. Back Bay Books, 1991.

Mann, Michael E. *Our Fragile Moment: How Lessons from Earth's Past Can Help Us Survive the Climate Crisis*. PublicAffairs, 2023.

Martiskainen, Mari, Stephen Axon, Benjamin K. Sovacool, Siddharth Sareen, Dylan Furszyfer Del Rio, and Kayleigh Axon. "Contextualizing Climate Justice Activism: Knowledge, Emotions, Motivations, and Actions among Climate Strikers in Six Cities." *Global Environmental Change* 65 (November 1, 2020): 102180. https://doi.org/10.1016/j.gloenvcha.2020.102180.

Mattson, Kevin. *We're Not Here to Entertain: Punk Rock, Ronald Reagan, and the Real Culture War of 1980s America*. Oxford University Press, 2020.

McAdam, Doug. *Political Process and the Development of Black Insurgency, 1930–1970*. University of Chicago Press, 1999.

McAdam, Doug. "Social Movement Theory and the Prospects for Climate Change Activism in the United States." *Annual Review of Political Science* 20, no. 1 (2017): 189–208. https://doi.org/10.1146/annurev-polisci-052615-025801.

McAdam, Doug, John D. McCarthy, and Mayer N. Zald. *Comparative Perspectives on Social Movements: Political Opportunities, Mobilizing Structures, and Cultural Framings*. Cambridge University Press, 1996.

McCarthy, John D., and Mayer N. Zald. "Resource Mobilization and Social Movements: A Partial Theory." *American Journal of Sociology* 82, no. 6 (May 1977): 1212–41. https://doi.org/10.1086/226464.

McCollum, Rod, and Undark. "Do Video Doorbells Really Prevent Crime?" *Scientific American*. Accessed April 10, 2025. https://www.scientificamerican.com/article/do-video-doorbells-really-prevent-crime/.

McKibben, Bill. *The End of Nature*. Random House, 1989.

Menton, Mary, and Philippe Le Billon. *Environmental Defenders: Deadly Struggles for Life and Territory*. Routledge, 2021.

Meyer, David S., and Debra C. Minkoff. "Conceptualizing Political Opportunity*." *Social Forces* 82, no. 4 (June 1, 2004): 1457–92. https://doi.org/10.1353/sof.2004.0082.

Miller-Idriss, Cynthia. *Hate in the Homeland: The New Global Far Right*. Princeton University Press, 2022.

Moore, Sam, and Alex Roberts. *The Rise of Ecofascism: Climate Change and the Far Right*. 1st edition. Polity, 2022.

Morozov, Evgeny. *The Net Delusion: The Dark Side of Internet Freedom*. PublicAffairs, 2012.

Mosley, Layna. *Interview Research in Political Science*. Cornell University Press, 2013.

Nadeem, Reem. "2. Top Problems Facing the U.S." *Pew Research Center* (blog), May 23, 2024. https://www.pewresearch.org/politics/2024/05/23/top-problems-facing-the-u-s/.

Nagtzaam, Gerry. *From Environmental Action to Ecoterrorism?: Towards a Process Theory of Environmental and Animal Rights Oriented Political Violence*. Edward Elgar Publishing, 2017.

Neas, Sally, Ann Ward, and Benjamin Bowman. "Young People's Climate Activism: A Review of the Literature." *Frontiers in Political Science* 4 (August 4, 2022). https://doi.org/10.3389/fpos.2022.940876.

Normandin, Sebastian, and Sean A. Valles. "How a Network of Conservationists and Population Control Activists Created the Contemporary US Anti-Immigration Movement." *Endeavour* 39, no. 2 (June 1, 2015): 95–105. https://doi.org/10.1016/j.endeavour.2015.05.001.

Nunes, Teresa. "Zines in Three Contemporary Grassroots' Movements in Brazil and the United States—ProQuest." Purder University Dissertation, 2006. https://www.proquest.com/openview/66b26d37f8ff64242afbd3668edda04e/1?pq-origsite=gscholar&cbl=18750&diss=y&casa_token=UnfNA5Oi7_8AAAAA:Xvo-dkFoo8iXyCnlxsTBfaIyOHwVjQYHOYg8Cx_54botuD9AKFdHK4ni8tD5INC1skRmnb_Iqg.

Oliver, J. Eric, and Wendy M. Rahn. "Rise of the Trumpenvolk: Populism in the 2016 Election." *The ANNALS of the American Academy of Political and Social Science* 667, no. 1 (September 1, 2016): 189–206. https://doi.org/10.1177/0002716216662639.

Ostarek, Markus, Brent Simpson, Cathy Rogers, and James Ozden. "Radical Climate Protests Linked to Increases in Public Support for Moderate Organizations." *Nature Sustainability* 7, no. 12 (December 2024): 1626–32. https://doi.org/10.1038/s41893-024-01444-1.

Parkin, Scott. "Why 2021 Needs More Direct Action." *Green and Red Media* (blog), January 19, 2021. https://medium.com/green-and-red-media/why-2021-needs-more-direct-action-3a2f6dfa3014.

Pearlman, Wendy. "Emotions and the Microfoundations of the Arab Uprisings." *Perspectives on Politics* 11, no. 2 (June 2013): 387–409. https://doi.org/10.1017/S1537592713001072.

Pellow, David Naguib. *Total Liberation: The Power and Promise of Animal Rights and the Radical Earth Movement.* University of Minnesota Press, 2014.

Pellow, David Naguib. *What Is Critical Environmental Justice?* John Wiley, 2017.

Peterka-Benton, Daniela, and Bond Benton. "Online Radicalization Case Study of a Mass Shooting: The Payton Gendron Manifesto." *Journal for Deradicalization*, no. 35 (June 30, 2023): 1–32.

Petras, George, and Jennifer Borresen. "From Mona Lisa to The Scream: Climate Protesters Deface Art in Europe – and Now the US." USA TODAY. Accessed May 21, 2025. https://www.usatoday.com/in-depth/graphics/2022/11/30/climate-activists-attack-paintings-mona-lisa-scream/10699588002/.

Pike, Sarah M. M. *For the Wild: Ritual and Commitment in Radical Eco-Activism.* 1st Edition. University of California Press, 2017.

Porta, Donatella della. *Clandestine Political Violence.* Cambridge University Press, 2013.

Potter, Will. *Green Is the New Red: An Insider's Account of a Social Movement under Siege.* 1st Edition. City Lights Publishers, 2011.

Rathbun, Brian C., Joshua D. Kertzer, and Mark Paradis. "Homo Diplomaticus: Mixed-Method Evidence of Variation in Strategic Rationality." *International Organization* 71, no. S1 (April 2017): S33–60. https://doi.org/10.1017/S0020818316000412.

Robinson, Kim Stanley. *The Ministry for the Future.* Orbit, 2020.

Roselle, Mike, and Josh Mahan. *Tree Spiker: From Earth First! To Lowbagging: My Struggles in Radical Environmental Action.* 1st edition. St. Martin's Press, 2009.

Rudd, Mark. *Underground: My Life with SDS and the Weathermen.* Illustrated edition. William Morrow Paperbacks, 2010.

Sageman, Marc. *Understanding Terror Networks.* University of Pennsylvania Press, 2004.

Scacco, Alexandra. "Who Riots? Explaining Individual Participation in Ethnic Violence." Ph.D. dissertation, Columbia University, 2010. https://www.proquest.com/docview/205442831/abstract/29053A197BD244B9PQ/1.

Scarce, Rik. *Eco-Warriors: Understanding the Radical Environmental Movement,* Updated Edition. Routledge, 2016.

Schock, Kurt. *Unarmed Insurrections: People Power Movements in Nondemocracies.* University of Minnesota Press, 2005.

Seitz, Steffen. "Conspiracy and Social Movements." *Michigan Law Review* 124 (2025), 1-53.

Shantz, Jeffrey A., and Barry D. Adam. "Ecology and Class: The Green Syndicalism of IWW/Earth First Local 1." *International Journal of Sociology and Social Policy* 19, no. 7/8 (January 1, 1999): 43–72. https://doi.org/10.1108/01443339910788857.

Simi, Pete, and Robert Futrell. *American Swastika: Inside the White Power Movement's Hidden Spaces of Hate*. Rowman & Littlefield, 2010.

Simpson, Brent, Robb Willer, and Matthew Feinberg. "Radical Flanks of Social Movements Can Increase Support for Moderate Factions." *PNAS Nexus* 1, no. 3 (July 1, 2022): pgac110. https://doi.org/10.1093/pnasnexus/pgac110.

Singer, Peter. *Animal Liberation: The Definitive Classic of the Animal Movement*. Reissue Edition. Harper Perennial Modern Classics, 1975.

Sola, Justin L., and Tara D. Warner. "Firearms, Families, and Financial Distress: Economic Instability and Increased Gun Desire." *Social Science Quarterly* 105, no. 6 (2024): 2017–33. https://doi.org/10.1111/ssqu.13462.

Sovacool, Benjamin K., and Alexander Dunlap. "Anarchy, War, or Revolt? Radical Perspectives for Climate Protection, Insurgency and Civil Disobedience in a Low-Carbon Era." *Energy Research & Social Science* 86 (April 1, 2022): 102416. https://doi.org/10.1016/j.erss.2021.102416.

Spadaro, Paola. "Climate Change, Environmental Terrorism, Eco-Terrorism and Emerging Threats." *Journal of Strategic Security* 13, no. 4 (January 1, 2020). https://doi.org/10.5038/1944-0472.13.4.1863.

Spiro, Jonathan Peter. *Defending the Master Race: Conservation, Eugenics, and the Legacy of Madison Grant*. UPNE, 2009.

Staudenmeier, Peter. *Ecology Contested: Environmental Politics between Left and Right*. New Compass Press, 2022.

Tarrow, Sidney. "Social Movements in Contentious Politics: A Review Article." *American Political Science Review* 90, no. 4 (December 1996): 874–83. https://doi.org/10.2307/2945851.

Taylor, Bron. "Earth and Nature-Based Spirituality (Part I): From Deep Ecology to Radical Environmentalism." *Religion* 31, no. 2 (April 1, 2001): 175–93. https://doi.org/10.1006/reli.2000.0256.

Tetlock, Philip E. "Thinking the Unthinkable: Sacred Values and Taboo Cognitions." *Trends in Cognitive Sciences* 7, no. 7 (July 1, 2003): 320–24. https://doi.org/10.1016/S1364-6613(03)00135-9.

Thackeray, Stephen J., Sharon A. Robinson, Pete Smith, Rhea Bruno, Miko U. F. Kirschbaum, Carl Bernacchi, Maria Byrne, et al. "Civil Disobedience Movements Such as School Strike for the Climate Are Raising Public Awareness of the Climate Change Emergency." *Global Change Biology* 26, no. 3 (March 1, 2020): 1042–44. https://doi.org/10.1111/gcb.14978.

Thaler, Kai M. "Mixed Methods Research in the Study of Political and Social Violence and Conflict." *Journal of Mixed Methods Research* 11, no. 1 (January 1, 2017): 59–76. https://doi.org/10.1177/1558689815585196.

Thompson, A. K. *Black Bloc, White Riot: Anti-Globalization and the Genealogy of Dissent*. AK Press, 2010.

Thomson, Jennifer. "Surviving the 1970s: The Case of Friends of the Earth." *Environmental History* 22, no. 2 (April 2017): 235–56. https://doi.org/10.1093/envhis/emw100.

Tilly, Charles, and Sidney G. Tarrow. *Contentious Politics*. Oxford University Press, 2015.

Tyson, Alec, Brian Kennedy, and Cary Funk. "Gen Z, Millennials Stand Out for Climate Change Activism, Social Media Engagement with Issue." *Pew Research Center Science & Society* (blog), May 26, 2021. https://www.pewresearch.org/science/2021/05/26/gen-z-millennials-stand-out-for-climate-change-activism-social-media-engagement-with-issue/.

Tyson, Alec, Cary Funk, and Brian Kennedy. "What the Data Says about Americans' Views of Climate Change." *Pew Research Center* (blog), 2023. https://www.pewresearch.org/short-reads/2023/08/09/what-the-data-says-about-americans-views-of-climate-change/.

Uscinski, Joseph E., Adam M. Enders, Casey Klofstad, Michelle Seelig, John Funchion, Caleb Everett, Stefan Wuchty, Kamal Premaratne, and Manohar Murthi. "Why Do People Believe COVID-19 Conspiracy Theories?" *Harvard Kennedy School Misinformation Review* 1, no. 3 (April 28, 2020). https://doi.org/10.37016/mr-2020-015.

Uscinski, Joseph E., Adam M. Enders, Michelle I. Seelig, Casey A. Klofstad, John R. Funchion, Caleb Everett, Stefan Wuchty, Kamal Premaratne, and Manohar N. Murthi. "American Politics in Two Dimensions: Partisan and Ideological Identities versus Anti-Establishment Orientations." *American Journal of Political Science* 65, no. 4 (2021): 877–95. https://doi.org/10.1111/ajps.12616.

Uscinski, Joseph E., and Joseph M. Parent. *American Conspiracy Theories*. Oxford University Press, 2014.

Valek, Rebecca, Julie A. Ward, Vanya Jones, and Cassandra K. Crifasi. "Political Violence, Racial Violence, and New Gun Ownership: Results from the 2023 National Survey of Gun Policy." *Injury Epidemiology* 11 (September 6, 2024): 48. https://doi.org/10.1186/s40621-024-00527-z.

Vanderheiden, Steve. "Eco-Terrorism or Justified Resistance? Radical Environmentalism and the 'War on Terror.'" *Politics & Society* 33, no. 3 (September 1, 2005): 425–47. https://doi.org/10.1177/0032329205278462.

Wasow, Omar. "Agenda Seeding: How 1960s Black Protests Moved Elites, Public Opinion and Voting." *American Political Science Review* 114, no. 3 (August 2020): 638–59. https://doi.org/10.1017/S000305542000009X.

Weidmann, Nils B. "A Closer Look at Reporting Bias in Conflict Event Data." *American Journal of Political Science* 60, no. 1 (2016): 206–18. https://doi.org/10.1111/ajps.12196.

Wheeler, Jim. "Madison Grant and the Dark Side of the Conservation Movement." *The Public Historian* 45, no. 3 (August 1, 2023): 75–82. https://doi.org/10.1525/tph.2023.45.3.75.

Woodhouse, Keith Makoto. *The Ecocentrists: A History of Radical Environmentalism*. Columbia University Press, 2018.

Yamane, David, Jesse DeDeyne, and Alonso Octavio Aravena Méndez. "Who Are the Liberal Gun Owners?" *Sociological Inquiry* 91, no. 2 (2021): 483–98. https://doi.org/10.1111/soin.12406.

Zakin, Susan. *Coyotes and Town Dogs: Earth First! and the Environmental Movement*. Penguin Books, 1995.

Zell, Craig. "Protest Tactics and Motivations Surrounding Mountaintop Removal Mining in West Virginia." Graduate Theses, Dissertations, and Problem Reports, January 1, 2015. https://doi.org/10.339/etd.7028.

Zerzan, John. *Future Primitive and Other Essays*. The Anarchist Library, 1994.

NOTES

Preface

1. Oregon Department of Transportation, "2020 Labor Day Wildfires Hazard Tree and Debris Removal Operations," July 2022, https://wildfire-auth.oregon.gov/Documents/DMTF%20After%20Action%20Report.pdf.
2. Krissy Ewald, "Environmental Activists Protest BLM Timber Sale," *KLCC*, July 2023, https://www.klcc.org/npr-science-environment/2023-07-05/environmental-activists-protest-blm-timber-sale.
3. Interview #EA-N99-0524.
4. See Rachel McDonald, "Bedrock Fire East of Eugene Surpasses 10,000 Acres," *KLCC*, August 2023, https://www.klcc.org/disasters-accidents/2023-08-01/bedrock-fire-east-of-eugene-surpasses-10-000-acres, and U.S. Department of Agriculture, "Bedrock Emergency Fire Closure," June 2023, https://www.fs.usda.gov/Internet/FSE_DOCUMENTS/fseprd1125705.pdf.
5. Kera Abraham, "Flames of Dissent PT. III: Eco-Anarchy Imploding," *Eugene Weekly*, November 2006, https://eugeneweekly.com/2006/11/22/eugene-weekly-11-22-06-2 and Kim Murphy, "Logging Protesters Sit to Conquer," *The Los Angeles Times*, September 2001, https://www.latimes.com/archives/la-xpm-2001-sep-26-mn-50074-story.html.
6. "Climate Change and Wildfire in Idaho, Oregon, and Washington," USDA Climate Hub, https://www.climatehubs.usda.gov/hubs/northwest/topic/climate-change-and-wildfire-idaho-oregon-and-washington, accessed May 20, 2025.
7. John E. Lewis, "Senate Committee on Environment and Public Works," Congressional Testimony, May 2005, https://archives.fbi.gov/archives/news/testimony/addressing-the-threat-of-animal-rights-extremism-and-eco-terrorism. Also Vanessa Grigoriadis, "The Rise and Fall of the

Eco-Radical Underground," *Rolling Stone*, June 2011, https://www.rollingstone.com/culture/culture-news/the-rise-and-fall-of-the-eco-radical-underground-245345.

8. "WMO Confirms 2024 as Warmest Year on Record at about 1.55°C Above Pre-Industrial Level," World Meteorological Association, January 2025, https://wmo.int/news/media-centre/wmo-confirms-2024-warmest-year-record-about-155degc-above-pre-industrial-level.

Chapter 1

1. Interviews #EA-N73-0223 and ##EA-N73FU3-0524
2. Interview #EA-N17-0222.
3. Dani Burlison, "Headwaters Forest Reserve and the Battle that Saved It," *Earth Island Journal*, February 2019, https://www.earthisland.org/journal/index.php/articles/entry/headwaters-forest-reserve-humboldt-california.
4. Kate Coleman, *The Secret Wars of Judi Bari: A Car Bomb, the Fight for the Redwoods and the End of Earth First!* (Encounter Books, 2005); Judi Bari, *Timber Wars* (Common Courage Press, 1994).
5. Dana R. Fisher and Sohana Nasrin, "Shifting Coalitions within the Youth Climate Movement in the US," *Politics and Governance* 9, no. 2 (April 28, 2021): 112–23, https://doi.org/10.17645/pag.v9i2.3801; Alec Tyson, Brian Kennedy, and Cary Funk, "Gen Z, Millennials Stand Out for Climate Change Activism, Social Media Engagement with Issue," *Pew Research Center Science & Society* (blog), May 26, 2021, https://www.pewresearch.org/science/2021/05/26/gen-z-millennials-stand-out-for-climate-change-activism-social-media-engagement-with-issue.
6. George Petras and Jennifer Borresen, "From Mona Lisa to the Scream: Climate Protesters Deface Art in Europe—and Now the US," *USA TODAY*, accessed May 21, 2025, https://www.usatoday.com/in-depth/graphics/2022/11/30/climate-activists-attack-paintings-mona-lisa-scream/10699588002.
7. See Will Potter, *Green Is the New Red: An Insider's Account of a Social Movement Under Siege*, 1st ed. (City Lights Publishers, 2011).
8. David Wallace-Wells, "The Uninhabitable Earth," *New York Magazine*, July 2017, https://nymag.com/intelligencer/2017/07/climate-change-earth-too-hot-for-humans.html.
9. Laura Paddison, "'The Climate Time-bomb Is Ticking': The World Is Running out of Time to Avoid Catastrophe, New UN Report Warns," CNN, March 2023, https://www.cnn.com/2023/03/20/world/ipcc-synthesis-report-climate-intl/index.html.
10. Ajit Niranjin, "This Article Is More Than 10 Months Old Temperatures 1.5C Above Pre-Industrial Era Average for 12 Months, Data Shows," *The Guardian*, July 2024, https://www.theguardian.com/environment/article/

2024/jul/08/temperatures-1-point-5c-above-pre-industrial-era-average-for-12-months-data-shows.

11. Mann was a critic of Wallace-Wells and others who argue that the Earth would be "uninhabitable" by the end of the century, calling such framing doomist and also leading to inaction. See Chris Mooney, "Scientists Challenge Magazine Story about 'Uninhabitable Earth,'" *The Washington Post*, July 2017, https://www.washingtonpost.com/news/energy-environment/wp/2017/07/12/scientists-challenge-magazine-story-about-uninhabitable-earth.

12. Michael E. Mann, *Our Fragile Moment: How Lessons from Earth's Past Can Help Us Survive the Climate Crisis* (PublicAffairs, 2023).

13. Brianna Sacks, "California's 2020 Smoke Storm Was Horrific. What Did the State Learn?," *The Washington Post*, June 2023, https://www.washingtonpost.com/climate-environment/2023/06/10/smoke-pollution-crisis-california.

14. Ian Livingston, "PM Update: Smoke Bringing Some of World's Worst Air to D.C. Region," *The Washington Post*, July 2023, https://www.washingtonpost.com/weather/2023/07/17/dc-wildfire-smoke-pollution-forecast.

15. Alejandra Borunda, "Some of Canada's Wildfires Likely Made Worse by Human-Driven Climate Change," *National Public Radio*, https://www.npr.org/2023/08/22/1195154996/some-of-canadas-wildfires-likely-made-worse-by-human-driven-climate-change.

16. Tammy Webber and Linley Sanders, "After Summer's Extreme Weather, More Americans See Climate Change As a Culprit, AP-NORC Poll Shows," Associated Press, September 2023, https://apnews.com/article/climate-change-poll-opinions-attitudes-extreme-weather-993c392ee57d023ca55600431a39a4be.

17. Alec Tyson, Cary Funk, and Brian Kennedy, "What the Data Says about Americans' Views of Climate Change," *Pew Research Center* (blog), August 9, 2023, https://www.pewresearch.org/short-reads/2023/08/09/what-the-data-says-about-americans-views-of-climate-change.

18. Bethany Albertson and Shana Kushner Gadarian, *Anxious Politics: Democratic Citizenship in a Threatening World* (Cambridge University Press, 2015).

19. Samuel Webb, "Tyre Extinguishers Go Global As Climate Activists Vow to Make Owning Suvs 'Impossible' around World," *The Independent*, March 2022, https://www.independent.co.uk/climate-change/news/tyre-extinguishers-suv-global-b2043124.html.

20. "Activists End German Coal Mine Blockade," *DW*, June 2019, https://www.dw.com/en/germany-climate-activists-end-coal-blockade-in-garzweiler/a-49321479.

21. "France: Several Police and Protesters Injured in Clash over Planned Reservoir," *The Guardian*, March 2023, https://www.theguardian.com/

world/2023/mar/25/france-several-police-and-protesters-injured-in-clash-over-planned-reservoir.
22. Mary Menton and Philippe Le Billon, *Environmental Defenders: Deadly Struggles for Life and Territory* (Routledge, 2021).
23. Benjamin Kline, *First Along the River: A Brief History of the U.S. Environmental Movement* (Rowman & Littlefield, 1997).
24. Madison Grant, *The Passing of the Great Race: Or, The Racial Basis of European History* (C. Scribner, 1916).
25. Peter Staudenmaier documents the many linkages between the Nazi fascist ideology and the 19th-and 20th-century German romantic and environmental movement. "Blood and soil"—the national slogan represented a marriage of the of the pseudoscience of eugenics and the purity of the Nordic race, with the purity of 19th-century German romanticism about nature and the countryside, and the filth of urban decay—much of which was due to the malign Jewish influence. See Peter Staudenmaier, "Fascist Ecology: The 'Green Wing' of the Nazi Party and Its Historical Antecedents," *Pomegranate: The International Journal of Pagan Studies* 15, Winter (2001): 4–022. (2011) and Jim Wheeler, "Madison Grant and the Dark Side of the Conservation Movement," *The Public Historian* 45, no. 3 (August 1, 2023): 75–82, https://doi.org/10.1525/tph.2023.45.3.75.
26. Jonathan Peter. Spiro, *Defending the Master Race: Conservation, Eugenics, and the Legacy of Madison Grant* (UPNE, 2009), p. 57
27. Jedediah Purdy, "Environmentalism's Racist History," *The New Yorker*, August 2015, https://www.newyorker.com/news/news-desk/environmentalisms-racist-history.
28. Jonathan Peter Spiro, *Defending the Master Race: Conservation, Eugenics, and the Legacy of Madison Grant* (UPNE, 2009).
29. Purdy, "Environmentalism's Racist History."
30. Paul R. Ehrlich, *The Population Bomb* (Ballantine Books, 1968).
31. Brittney Bush Bollay, "The Overpopulation Myth and Its Dangerous Connotations," *Sierra Club*, January 2020, https://www.sierraclub.org/washington/blog/2020/01/overpopulation-myth-and-its-dangerous-connotations.
32. Rachel Carson, *Silent Spring* (Houghton Mifflin Harcourt, 1962).
33. Lorraine Boissoneault, "The Cuyahoga River Caught Fire at Least a Dozen Times, but No One Cared Until 1969," *Smithsonian Magazine*, June 2019, https://www.smithsonianmag.com/history/cuyahoga-river-caught-fire-least-dozen-times-no-one-cared-until-1969-180972444.
34. Keith Makoto Woodhouse, *The Ecocentrists: A History of Radical Environmentalism* (Columbia University Press, 2018), p. 30–35.
35. Woodhouse, *The Ecocentrists*, p. 50.
36. Steven V. Roberts, "The Better Earth," *The New York Times*, March 1970, https://www.nytimes.com/1970/03/29/archives/the-better-earth-a-report-on-ecology-action-a-brash-activist.html.

37. Susan Zakin, *Coyotes and Town Dogs: Earth First! And the Environmental Movement* (Penguin Books, 1995), p. 8.
38. Rik Scarce, *Eco-Warriors: Understanding the Radical Environmental Movement, Updated Edition* (Routledge, 2016); Woodhouse, *The Ecocentrists*.
39. Christopher Manes, *Green Rage: Radical Environmentalism and the Unmaking of Civilization*, Reprint edition (Back Bay Books, 1991); Woodhouse, *The Ecocentrists*; Scarce, *Eco-Warriors*; Sarah M. M. Pike, *For the Wild: Ritual and Commitment in Radical Eco-Activism*, 1st ed. (University of California Press, 2017); Bron Taylor, "Earth and Nature-Based Spirituality (Part I): From Deep Ecology to Radical Environmentalism," *Religion* 31, no. 2 (April 1, 2001): 175–93, https://doi.org/10.1006/reli.2000.0256.
40. David Naguib Pellow, *Total Liberation: The Power and Promise of Animal Rights and the Radical Earth Movement* (University of Minnesota Press, 2014); Naomi Klein, *This Changes Everything: Capitalism vs. The Climate*, 1st ed. (Simon & Schuster, 2013); Mari Martiskainen et al., "Contextualizing Climate Justice Activism: Knowledge, Emotions, Motivations, and Actions among Climate Strikers in Six Cities," *Global Environmental Change* 65 (November 1, 2020): 102180, https://doi.org/10.1016/j.gloenvcha.2020.102180.
41. It's true that at times radical activists have made common cause with mainstream organizations like the Sierra Club, such as in their opposition to mountain top mining in West Virginia. Craig Zell, "Protest Tactics and Motivations Surrounding Mountaintop Removal Mining in West Virginia," *Graduate Theses, Dissertations, and Problem Reports*, January 1, 2015, https://doi.org/10.33915/etd.7028.
42. Woodhouse, *The Ecocentrists*, 124.
43. Danielle Gilbert, "The Logic of Kidnapping in Civil War: Evidence from Colombia," *American Political Science Review* 116, no. 4 (November 2022): 1226–41, https://doi.org/10.1017/S0003055422000041; Kai M. Thaler, "Mixed Methods Research in the Study of Political and Social Violence and Conflict," *Journal of Mixed Methods Research* 11, no. 1 (January 1, 2017): 59–76, https://doi.org/10.1177/1558689815585196; Brian C. Rathbun, Joshua D. Kertzer, and Mark Paradis, "Homo Diplomaticus: Mixed-Method Evidence of Variation in Strategic Rationality," *International Organization* 71, no. S1 (April 2017): S33–60, https://doi.org/10.1017/S0020818316000412.
44. Interview #EA-N51-0622.
45. See Panagioti Tsolkas, an Earth First! organizer on direct action: "Generally accepted on the list (of direct actions) are endless varieties of blockades, occupations, and sabotage of all shapes and forms (what we refer to as *monkeywrenching*); though things like mass marches, home demos, banner hangs, costly administrative petitions, and *pro-se* legal challenges (or *paperwrenching*), political pranks and miscellaneous

deviltry also often make the cut—depending on who you're talking to." Panagioti Tsolkas, "Direct Action: What It Is and Why We Use It—A Brief Introduction from an Earth First! Organizer," *Earth Island Journal*, November 2013, https://www.earthisland.org/journal/index.php/articles/entry/direct_action_what_it_is_and_why_we_use_it/## See also Scott Parkin, "Why 2021 Needs More Direct Action," *Green and Red Media* (blog), January 19, 2021, https://medium.com/green-and-red-media/why-2021-needs-more-direct-action-3a2f6dfa3014.

46. Jennifer Varriale Carson, Gary LaFree, and Laura Dugan, "Terrorist and Non-Terrorist Criminal Attacks by Radical Environmental and Animal Rights Groups in the United States, 1970–2007," *Terrorism and Political Violence* 24, no. 2 (April 1, 2012): 295–319, https://doi.org/10.1080/09546553.2011.639416; Paola Spadaro, "Climate Change, Environmental Terrorism, Eco-Terrorism and Emerging Threats," *Journal of Strategic Security* 13, no. 4 (January 1, 2020), https://doi.org/10.5038/1944-0472.13.4.1863.
47. Interview # EA-N80-0223.
48. See the Appendix for more information on the interviews.
49. Michael Loadenthal, "'The Green Scare'& 'Eco-Terrorism': The Development of US Counter-Terrorism Strategy Targeting Direct Action Activists," *The Terrorization of Dissent: Corporate Repression, Legal Corruption and the Animal Enterprise Terrorism Act*, January 1, 2013; Potter, *Green Is the New Red*.
50. Zakin, *Coyotes and Town Dogs*; Manes, *Green Rage*; Woodhouse, *The Ecocentrists*; Scarce, *Eco-Warriors*.
51. Gerry Nagtzaam, *From Environmental Action to Ecoterrorism?: Towards a Process Theory of Environmental and Animal Rights Oriented Political Violence* (Edward Elgar Publishing, 2017); Joseph M. Brown, "Notes to the Underground: Credit Claiming and Organizing in the Earth Liberation Front," *Terrorism and Political Violence* 32, no. 2 (February 17, 2020): 237–56, https://doi.org/10.1080/09546553.2017.1364637; Michael Loadenthal, "Eco-Terrorism? Countering Dominant Narratives of Securitisation: A Critical, Quantitative History of the Earth Liberation Front (1996–2009)," *Perspectives on Terrorism* 8, no. 3 (2014): 16–50.
52. "The Sunday Read: The 'Valve Turners,'" *The Daily: New York Times Podcast*, January 2021, and D. Schlosberg and L. B. Collins, "From Environmental to Climate Justice: Climate Change and the Discourse of Environmental Justice," *WIREs Clim Change* 5 (2014): 359–74, https://doi.org/10.1002/wcc.275. Keerti Gopal, "Like 'Em or Not, Climate Defiance Is Determined to Get in Your Face," *Mother Jones*, February 2024, https://www.motherjones.com/politics/2024/02/climate-defiance-fossil-fuel-protests-radical-extinction-rebellion.
53. Ted Robert Gurr, *Why Men Rebel* (Princeton University Press, 1970); Christopher Blattman and Edward Miguel, "Civil War," *Journal of*

Economic Literature 48, no. 1 (March 2010): 3–57, https://doi.org/10.1257/jel.48.1.3; Patricia Justino, "Poverty and Violent Conflict: A Micro-Level Perspective on the Causes and Duration of Warfare," *Journal of Peace Research* 46, no. 3 (May 1, 2009): 315–33, https://doi.org/10.1177/0022343309102655; Lars-Erik Cederman, Andreas Wimmer, and Brian Min, "Why Do Ethnic Groups Rebel? New Data and Analysis," *World Politics* 62, no. 1 (January 2010): 87–119, https://doi.org/10.1017/S0043887109990219.

54. Marc Sageman, *Understanding Terror Networks* (University of Pennsylvania Press, 2004); Alexandra Scacco, "Who Riots? Explaining Individual Participation in Ethnic Violence" (PhD dissertation, Columbia University, 2010), https://www.proquest.com/docview/205442831/abstract/29053A197BD244B9PQ/1; Ross Haenfler, "Rethinking Subcultural Resistance: Core Values of the Straight Edge Movement," *Journal of Contemporary Ethnography* 33, no. 4 (August 1, 2004): 406–36, https://doi.org/10.1177/0891241603259809; Cynthia Miller-Idriss, *Hate in the Homeland: The New Global Far Right* (Princeton University Press, 2022); Pete Simi and Robert Futrell, *American Swastika: Inside the White Power Movement's Hidden Spaces of Hate* (Rowman & Littlefield, 2010).

55. David S. Meyer and Debra C. Minkoff, "Conceptualizing Political Opportunity*," *Social Forces* 82, no. 4 (June 1, 2004): 1457–92, https://doi.org/10.1353/sof.2004.0082; Sidney Tarrow, "Social Movements in Contentious Politics: A Review Article," *American Political Science Review* 90, no. 4 (December 1996): 874–83, https://doi.org/10.2307/2945851; Doug McAdam, "Social Movement Theory and the Prospects for Climate Change Activism in the United States," *Annual Review of Political Science* 20, no. 1 (2017): 189–208, https://doi.org/10.1146/annurev-polisci-052615-025801.

56. Christian Davenport, *How Social Movements Die* (Cambridge University Press, 2015); Christian Davenport and Benjamin Appel, *The Death and Life of State Repression: Understanding Onset, Escalation, Termination, and Recurrence* (Oxford University Press, 2022); Jennifer Earl, "Tanks, Tear Gas, and Taxes: Toward a Theory of Movement Repression," *Sociological Theory* 21, no. 1 (2003): 44–68, https://doi.org/10.1111/1467-9558.00175.

57. Erica Chenoweth, "The Role of Violence in Nonviolent Resistance," *Annual Review of Political Science* 26, no. 1 (2023): 55–77, https://doi.org/10.1146/annurev-polisci-051421-124128; Erica Chenoweth and Maria J. Stephan, *Why Civil Resistance Works: The Strategic Logic of Nonviolent Conflict* (Columbia University Press, 2011); Kurt Schock, *Unarmed Insurrections: People Power Movements in Nondemocracies* (University of Minnesota Press, 2005); Saul Alinsky, *Rules for Radicals: A Pragmatic Primer for Realistic Radicals* (Random House, 1971); Brent Simpson, Robb Willer, and Matthew Feinberg, "Radical Flanks of Social

Movements Can Increase Support for Moderate Factions," *PNAS Nexus* 1, no. 3 (July 1, 2022): 110, https://doi.org/10.1093/pnasnexus/pgac110; Matthew Feinberg, Robb Willer, and Chloe Kovacheff, "The Activist's Dilemma: Extreme Protest Actions Reduce Popular Support for Social Movements," *Journal of Personality and Social Psychology* 119 (2020): 1086–1111, https://doi.org/10.1037/pspi0000230; Charles E. Cobb, *This Nonviolent Stuff'll Get You Killed: How Guns Made the Civil Rights Movement Possible* (Basic Books, 2014); Donatella della Porta, *Clandestine Political Violence* (Cambridge University Press, 2013); Margherita Belgioioso, "Going Underground: Resort to Terrorism in Mass Mobilization Dissident Campaigns," *Journal of Peace Research* 55, no. 5 (September 1, 2018): 641–55, https://doi.org/10.1177/0022343318764795; Brown, "Notes to the Underground."

58. Jean Chemnick and E&E News, "How Gutting the EPA's Research Team Could Impact Clean Air and Water Rules," *Scientific American*, March 2024, https://www.scientificamerican.com/article/trumps-epa-plans-to-gut-research-what-that-means-for-clean-air-and-water. The White House, "Immediate Expansion of American Timber Production," March 2025, *Presidential Executive Order*, https://www.whitehouse.gov/presidential-actions/2025/03/immediate-expansion-of-american-timber-production.

59. Stan Cox, "Anti-Protest Laws Won't Silence Climate Activists," *The Nation*, November 2024, https://www.thenation.com/article/environment/anti-protest-laws-climate-activists.

60. Steven Feldstein, *The Rise of Digital Repression: How Technology Is Reshaping Power, Politics, and Resistance* (Oxford University Press, 2021).

Chapter 2

1. Interview #EA-N82-0323.
2. Edward Abbey, *The Monkey Wrench Gang*, 1st ed. (Lippincott Williams & Wilkins, 1975).
3. Scarce, *Eco-Warriors*, p. 58-59.
4. Scarce, p. 56-57.
5. Nagtzaam, *From Environmental Action to Ecoterrorism?*
6. The initial RARE II was later challenged successfully in court, and larger areas were added for preservation in the 1980s as part of the National Wilderness Preservation System. Neil Kagan, "Blazing a Path to Wilderness: A Case Study of Impact Litigation Through the Lens of Legislative History," *Michigan Journal of Environmental and Administrative Law*, no. 11.1 (2021): 87, https://doi.org/10.36640/mjeal.11.1.blazing.
7. There's a dispute about the origin of the term. Some see it as a lampoon of a character in an old 1942 movie, *The Forest Rangers*, while others argue that it stands for the acronym: "forest rape endlessly done, done in endless

succession." See footnote 68 in Jeff Lalande, "The 'Forest Ranger' in Popular Culture: 1910–2000," *Forest History Today* (2003): 28.

8. Jennifer Thomson, "Surviving the 1970s: The Case of Friends of the Earth," *Environmental History* 22, no. 2 (April 2017): 235–56, https://doi.org/10.1093/envhis/emw100.

9. Ann Japenga, "Earth First! A Voice Vying for the Wilderness: Group Says Radical," *Los Angeles Times*, September 5, 1985; ProQuest Historical Newspapers: Los Angeles Times, p. E1, https://www.latimes.com/archives/la-xpm-1985-09-05-vw-24905-story.html.

10. Mike Roselle and Josh Mahan, *Tree Spiker: From Earth First! to Lowbagging: My Struggles in Radical Environmental Action* (St. Martin's Press, 2009), 113–26.

11. Dan Whipple, "Blue Planet: Ecoterrorism Redefined," September 2002, *UPI Science News*, https://www.upi.com/Science_News/2002/09/13/Blue-Planet-Ecoterrorism-redefined/80991031944222.

12. Zakin, *Coyotes and Town Dogs*, 248–60.

13. Bron Taylor, "The Earth First! Journal as a Gateway to Movement History," *Environment and Society*, https://www.environmentandsociety.org/exhibitions/radical-environmentalisms-print-history/earth-first-journal-gateway-movement-history.

14. Interview #EA-N79-0323.

15. Woodhouse, *The Ecocentrists*, p. 273–74.

16. Interview #EA-N82-0323.

17. Interview #EA-N79-0323.

18. Dave Foreman, *Man Swarm and the Killing of Wildlife* (Raven's Eye Press, 2011). In *Man Swarm* Foreman argued that overpopulation was the number one threat to the planet, and core threat to animals and wilderness. One of the main arguments in *Man Swarm* that garnered heavy criticism was his belief that America had to restrict or halt immigration. To Forman, more immigrants meant more people and more people in particular living the resource-heavy American lifestyle that would destroy wilderness. See also Ian Angus, "Dave Foreman's Man Swarm: Defending Wildlife by Attacking Immigrants," *Climate and Capitalism*, April 2012, https://climateandcapitalism.com/2012/04/25/dave-foreman-defending-wildlife-by-attacking-immigrants.

19. Many critics disagree with concerns about overpopulation and see it as a mistaken return of the Malthusian argument that population would soon exceed the food/resource supply, whereas technological improvements and even markets have mechanisms for regulating scarce resources. See Giorgos Kallis, *Limits: Why Malthus Was Wrong and Why Environmentalists Should Care* (Stanford University Press, 2019) and Charles C. Mann, *The Wizard and the Prophet: Two Remarkable Scientists and Their Dueling Visions to Shape Tomorrow's World* (Knopf, 2018).

20. Interview #AA-N70-0223.

21. Sebastian Normandin and Sean A. Valles, "How a Network of Conservationists and Population Control Activists Created the Contemporary US Anti-Immigration Movement," *Endeavour* 39, no. 2 (June 1, 2015): 95–105, https://doi.org/10.1016/j.endeavour.2015.05.001.
22. John Hultgren, *Border Walls Gone Green: Nature and Anti-Immigrant Politics in America* (University of Minnesota Press, 2015), p. 70-72. And Jason L. Riley, "The End of an Anti-Immigration Environmentalist," July 2019, *The Wall Street Journal*, https://www.wsj.com/articles/the-end-of-an-anti-immigration-environmentalist-11563921859.
23. Mark Potok, "The Creepy Racist Network Behind Trump Aide Stephen Miller," *The Daily Beast*, November 2019, https://www.thedailybeast.com/the-creepy-racist-network-behind-trump-aide-stephen-miller and Carly Goodman, "John Tanton Has Died. He Made America Less Open to Immigrants—and More Open to Trump," *The Washington Post*, July 2019, https://www.washingtonpost.com/outlook/2019/07/18/john-tanton-has-died-how-he-made-america-less-open-immigrants-more-open-trump.
24. Goodman, "John Tanton Has Died."
25. "John Tanton," *Southern Poverty Law Center: Extremist Files*, https://web.archive.org/web/20250305225138/https://www.splcenter.org/resources/extremist-files/john-tanton.
26. Interview #AA-N38-0522.
27. Interview #AA-N13-0222.
28. Interview #AA-N1-0122.
29. Interview #EA-N61-1022.
30. Interview #EA-N79-0323.
31. Sports Illustrated Staff, "Protector or Provocateur? Dave Foreman," May 1991, *Sports Illustrated*, https://vault.si.com/vault/1991/05/27/protector-or-provocateur-dave-foreman-cofounder-of-the-radical-group-earth-first-faces-trial-for-conspiracy-also-at-issue-to-what-extremes-may-environmentalists-protests-go.
32. Bron Taylor, "The Earth First! Journal as a Gateway to Movement History."
33. Dave Foreman and Bill Haywood, *Ecodefense: A Field Guide to Monkeywrenching*, 3rd ed. (Abbzug Press, 1993). The book has gone through three editions and has over 150 ratings on Goodreads, https://www.goodreads.com/book/show/992984.Ecodefense.
34. Dave Foreman, *Confessions of an Eco-Warrior*, 1st ed. (Harmony, 1991).
35. Foreman, *Confessions of an Eco-Warrior*, p. 118.
36. Foreman, *Confessions of an Eco-Warrior*, p. 175.
37. Janet Biehl, "Murray Bookchin Biography—Anarchy Archives." Accessed April 30, 2025, http://dwardmac.pitzer.edu/Anarchist_Archives/bookchin/bio1.html.
38. Murray Bookchin, *Our Synthetic Environment* (Knopf, 1962).

39. Murray Bookchin, "Ecology and Revolutionary Thought," *Anarchy*, 1965, https://theanarchistlibrary.org/library/lewis-herber-murray-bookchin-ecology-and-revolutionary-thought.
40. Woodhouse, *The Ecocentrists*, p. 192-93.
41. Douglas Martin, "Murray Bookchin, 85, Writer, Activist and Ecology Theorist, Dies," *The New York Times*, August 2006, https://www.nytimes.com/2006/08/07/us/07bookchin.html.
42. Murray Bookchin and Dave Foreman, *Defending the Earth: A Debate* (Black Rose Books, 1991), https://theanarchistlibrary.org/library/murray-bookchin-and-dave-foreman-defending-the-earth-a-debate.
43. Bron Taylor, "The Earth First! Journal as a Gateway to Movement History." Also, Bron Taylor, "The Religion and Politics of Earth First!," *The Ecologist* 21, no. 6 (1991): 258–66.
44. Timothy Ingalsbee, "Earth First! Activism: Ecological Postmodern Praxis in Radical Environmentalist Identities," *Sociological Perspectives* 39, no. 2 (1996): 263–76. *JSTOR*, https://doi.org/10.2307/1389312, accessed June 17, 2024.
45. Zachary Fryer-Biggs and Malcolm Cecil-Cockwell, "The Radicals: How Extreme Environmentalists Are Made," *The Atlantic* (February 2012), https://www.theatlantic.com/national/archive/2012/02/the-radicals-how-extreme-environmentalists-are-made/252768.
46. Interview #EA-N82-0323.
47. Interview #EA-N20-0322.
48. Jeffrey A. Shantz and Barry D. Adam, "Ecology and Class: The Green Syndicalism of IWW/Earth First Local 1," *International Journal of Sociology and Social Policy* 19, no. 7/8 (January 1, 1999): 43–72, https://doi.org/10.1108/01443339910788857.
49. See Steve Ongerth, *Redwood Uprising: The Story of Judi Bari and Earth First!* Self-published, 2010, Chapter 37; Evelyn Nieves, "Truth Is Still Elusive in 1990 Pipe Bombing," *The New York Times*, June 2002, https://www.nytimes.com/2002/06/16/us/truth-is-still-elusive-in-1990-pipe-bombing.html. Journalist Kate Coleman in her book *The Secret Wars of Judi Bari: A Car Bomb, the Fight for the Redwoods and the End of Earth—First!* (Encounter, 2005) argues that Judi Bari's ex-husband was the most likely suspect in the bombing. But again there is no conclusive proof either way.
50. Interview #EA-N41-0522.
51. Woodhouse, *The Ecocentrists*, p. 175.
52. Nicholas Kristof, "Forest Sabotage Is Urged by Some," *The New York Times*, January 1986, https://www.nytimes.com/1986/01/22/us/forest-sabotage-is-urged-by-some.html.
53. Larry Stammer, "Environment Radicals Target of Probe into Lumber Mill Accident," *The Los Angeles Times*, May 1987, https://www.latimes.com/archives/la-xpm-1987-05-15-mn-5213-story.html.

54. Ron Huber, "Earth First's First Treesitting Civil Disobedience Action (1985)," *Penobscot Bay Watch*, 2018, https://www.penbay.org/ronhuber/treesit_first1985.html.
55. Woodhouse, *The Ecocentrists*; Foreman, *Confessions of an Eco-Warrior*, p. 139.
56. Bari, *Timber Wars*.
57. Zakin, *Coyotes and Town Dogs*. And also Kelpie Wilson, "Redwood Summer: Anatomy of an Action," *Fifth Estate* (#335), Winter 1990–1991, https://www.fifthestate.org/archive/335-winter-1990-91/redwood-summer.
58. Lydia Bailey, "Earth First! Protests the Destruction of Redwood Forests (Redwood Summer), United States, 1990," February 2013, https://nvdatabase.swarthmore.edu/content/earth-first-protests-destruction-redwood-forests-redwood-summer-united-states-1990. See also Mark Stein, "Redwood Summer: It Was Guerrilla Warfare," *The Los Angeles Times*, September 1990, https://www.latimes.com/archives/la-xpm-1990-09-02-mn-2050-story.html.
59. "Founder of Earth First Quits Group," *Tampa Bay Times*, August 1990, https://www.tampabay.com/archive/1990/08/21/founder-of-earth-first-quits-group.
60. See Foreman acknowledge this critique: Foreman, *Confessions of an Eco-Warrior*, p. 137–38.
61. "Earth First Co-Founder Splits with Radical Group," *The Lewiston Tribune*, August 1990, https://www.lmtribune.com/northwest/earth-first-co-founder-splits-with-radical-group-1b489ecc.
62. Martha F. Lee, *Earth First!: Environmental Apocalypse* (Syracuse University Press, 1995), https://theanarchistlibrary.org/library/martha-f-lee-earth-first-environmental-apocalypse.
63. James Sidener, "Earth First! Divided by Second Thoughts," *Arizona Republic*, January 1990, A1–A4.
64. Sidener, "Earth First! Divided by Second Thoughts."
65. Elizabeth Manning, "Activist Who Survived a Bombing Leaves a Legacy," *High Country News*, March 1997, https://www.hcn.org/issues/issue-107/activist-who-survived-bomb-leaves-a-legacy.
66. Interview #AO-N25-0422.
67. Interview #AA-N13-0222.
68. Rustin and Shuttlesworth were notable U.S. civil rights activists who helped found the Southern Christian Leadership Conference, which preached nonviolent pressure campaign tactics. "Southern Christian Leadership Conference (SCLC)," The Stanford University Martin Luther King Jr. Research and Education Institute, https://kinginstitute.stanford.edu/southern-christian-leadership-conference-sclc.
69. This was the trajectory of the militant far-left U.S. group, the Weather Underground, which splintered from Students for a Democratic Society in

the late 1960s. And the militant pro-unification group the Republican Provisional Irish Republican Army (PIRA) split from the Original Irish Republican Army also in the late 1960s. See Mark Rudd, *Underground: My Life with SDS and the Weathermen*, Illustrated edition (William Morrow Paperbacks, 2010); Ethan Bueno De Mesquita, "Terrorist Factions," *Quarterly Journal of Political Science* 3, no. 4 (December 31, 2008): 399–418, https://doi.org/10.1561/100.00008006.

70. Rachel M. Blum, *How the Tea Party Captured the GOP: Insurgent Factions in American Politics* (University of Chicago Press, 2020).
71. Pellow, *Total Liberation*.

Chapter 3

1. Interview # EA-N80FU3-02240924.
2. Jennifer D. Grubbs, *Ecoliberation: Reimagining Resistance and the Green Scare* (McGill-Queen's Press [MQUP], 2021); Michael Loadenthal, "The Earth Liberation Front: A Movement Analysis," *Radical Criminology*, no. 2 (September 21, 2013): 15–46; Joseph M. Brown, "Civil Disobedience, Sabotage, and Violence in US Environmental Activism," *The Oxford Handbook of Comparative Environmental Politics*, August 11, 2021, https://doi.org/10.1093/oxfordhb/9780197515037.013.34; Nagtzaam, *From Environmental Action to Ecoterrorism?*
3. Interview # EA-N80-0223 and Michael Loadenthal, "The Earth Liberation Front."
4. Nagtzaam, *From Environmental Action to Ecoterrorism?* p. 46–50.
5. Mittens XVX, "Interview: Animal Liberation, Punk & Direct Action: An Interview with ALF Founder Ronnie Lee:," *DIY Conspiracy*, May 2023, https://diyconspiracy.net/ronnie-lee-interview.
6. Diane L. Beers, *For the Prevention of Cruelty: The History and Legacy of Animal Rights Activism in the United States* (Ohio University Press, 2006).
7. Nagtzaam, *From Environmental Action to Ecoterrorism?* p. 51.
8. Steven Best and Anthony J. Nocella, *Terrorists or Freedom Fighters?: Reflections on the Liberation of Animals* (Lantern Books, 2004), p. 8.
9. Peter Singer, *Animal Liberation: The Definitive Classic of the Animal Movement*, Reissue edition (Harper Perennial Modern Classics, 1975).
10. Pellow, *Total Liberation*, p. 51.
11. Nagtzaam, *From Environmental Action to Ecoterrorism?*, p. 53.
12. Interview #EA-N83-0323.
13. "Greenpeace Attempts to Make Captain Paul Watson 'Disappear,'" 2011, https://web.archive.org/web/20110304220727/http://www.seashepherd.org/who-we-are/paul-watson-and-greenpeace.html.
14. Pellow, *Total Liberation*. p. 50.
15. In 2022, a rupture occurred within the Sea Shepherd Conservation Society, with some chapters staying loyal to Watson and calling themselves Sea Shepherds Origins to distinguish themselves from the other chapters

that they feel had strayed from the central mission. Nick Kilvert, "He's Walked the Plank, but Ousted Sea Shepherd Captain Paul Watson Says He's Building a 'Navy,'" *ABC News*, November 2022, https://www.abc.net.au/news/science/2022-11-27/sea-shepherd-paul-watson-exiled-building-navy/101570694.

16. Khatchadourian Raffi, "Neptune's Navy," *The New Yorker*, November 2007, https://www.newyorker.com/magazine/2007/11/05/neptunes-navy.
17. Paul Waston, "Greenpeace Denounces Sea Shepherd Society. Paul Watson Replies . . .," *Rewilding Earth*, April 2007, https://rewilding.org/greenpeace-denounces-sea-shepherd-society-paul-watson-replies.
18. Rick Lyman, "Iceland Adventure 'Easy' for Whaling 'Terrorists,'" *The Ledger*, November 1986.
19. #EA-N8-0222.
20. Martin Bright, "Inside the Labs Where Lives Hang Heavy in the Balance," *The Guardian*, January 2001, https://www.theguardian.com/uk/2001/jan/21/martinbright.theobserver.
21. Catherine E. Smith, "Radical Animal Rights Activists Set the Stage for a First Amendment Showdown over Harassment on the Internet," *SPLC Intelligence Report*, July 2005. https://www.splcenter.org/fighting-hate/intelligence-report/2005/threatscom.
22. Natasha Lennard, "How the Prosecution of Animal Rights Activists as Terrorists Foretold Today's Criminalization of Dissent," *The Intercept*, December 2019, https://theintercept.com/2019/12/12/animal-people-documentary-shac-protest-terrorism.
23. Kim Severson, "For Animal Rights Activists, a Bona Fide Hit," *The New York Times*, March 2008, https://www.nytimes.com/2008/03/12/travel/12iht-15animal.10995177.html.
24. Pellow, *Total Liberation*, p. 3.
25. Benjamin K. Sovacool and Alexander Dunlap, "Anarchy, War, or Revolt? Radical Perspectives for Climate Protection, Insurgency and Civil Disobedience in a Low-Carbon Era," *Energy Research & Social Science* 86 (April 1, 2022): 102416, https://doi.org/10.1016/j.erss.2021.102416.
26. Grubbs, *Ecoliberation*, p. 4.
27. Mittens XVX, "Interview: Animal Liberation," *DIY Conspiracy*, 2023, https://diyconspiracy.net/ronnie-lee-interview.
28. Ross Haenfler, *Straight Edge: Clean-Living Youth, Hardcore Punk, and Social Change* (Rutgers University Press, 2006).
29. Kevin Mattson, *We're Not Here to Entertain: Punk Rock, Ronald Reagan, and the Real Culture War of 1980s America* (Oxford University Press, 2020), p. 34–36.
30. The "hardline" subculture was a smaller, but influential, offshoot of the vegan straight edge scene supported by Vegan Reich's lead singer, Sean Muttaqi. Hardline was a more extreme version of vegan straight edge, and its adherents supported deep ecology and militant veganism. It was

pro-animal liberation, anti-abortion, and anti-homosexuality. The latter two stances led many leftist vegan straight edges to critique them and call them "ecofascists" (Eeyore 2022).
31. Teresa Nunes, "Zines in Three Contemporary Grassroots' Movements in Brazil and the United States—ProQuest," Purdue University Doctoral Dissertation, 2006.
32. "METAL MUSICIANS FOR ANIMAL RIGHTS, VEGANISM AND THE ENVIRONMENT," *Metaloda*, January 2025, https://metaloda.com/metal-musicians-for-animal-rights-veganism-and-the-environment.
33. Interview #EA-N80-0223.
34. "The Militant Vegan Animal Liberation Zine Collection, 1993-1995," Firestorm, https://firestorm.coop/products/21214-the-militant-vegan.html and *Destroy Babylon* https://archive.org/details/destroy_babylon_3/page/n11/mode/2up.
35. Interview #EA-N23-0322.
36. Interview #EA-N75-0223.
37. Interview #AA-N13-0222.
38. Black bloc is a tactic used by activists who wear black clothing and face coverings to make it hard for police and others to identify individual activists, and the black garb also protects them from pepper spray. See A. K. Thompson, *Black Bloc, White Riot: Anti-Globalization and the Genealogy of Dissent* (AK Press, 2010).
39. Interview #EA-N71-0223.
40. Interview #EA-N60-0522.
41. Interview #EA-N80FU2-0624.
42. Ryan Downey, "Earth Crisis Biography," *Allmusic*, https://www.allmusic.com/artist/earth-crisis-mn0000160870#biography; "Vegan Reich," *Discogs*, https://www.discogs.com/artist/319751-Vegan-Reich.
43. Interview #EA-N8-0222.
44. Interview #EA-N83-0323.

Chapter 4

1. Interview #EA-N68FU2-0524.
2. Interview #EA-N68-0223.
3. Camilla Mortensen, "The Big Chill: Will the Terror Label Stifle Activism?," *Eugene Weekly*, June 2007, https://eugeneweekly.com/2007/06/14/eugene-weekly-6-14-07-2; and Potter, *Green Is the New Red*.
4. Interview #EA-N68-0223.
5. Shannon Finnell, "Whistory: For Everything There Is a Season—Especially in the Whiteaker," *Eugene Weekly*, August 2012, https://eugeneweekly.com/2012/08/02/whistory.
6. Brenton Gicker and John Zerzan, "Anarchy in Eugene: A Sleepy College Town Explodes," Summer 1999, *Fifth Estate* #353, https://www.fifthestate.org/archive/353-summer-1999/anarchy-in-eugene.

7. Kera Abraham, "Flames of Dissent PT. II: Eco-Anarchy Rising," *Eugene Weekly*, November 2006, https://eugeneweekly.com/2006/11/09/eugene-weekly-eco-anarchy-rising-part-11-09-06.
8. Interview #EA-N68-0223.
9. Kenneth B. Noble, "Lobbyist Is Killed in Letter Bombing Tied to 15 Others," *The New York Times*, April 1995, https://www.nytimes.com/1995/04/25/us/lobbyist-is-killed-in-letter-bombing-tied-to-15-others.html.
10. "The Unabomber," *FBI Famous Cases*, https://www.fbi.gov/history/famous-cases/unabomber.
11. "Text of Unabomber's Letter Received by N.Y. Times April 26, 1995," https://www.upcounsel.com/lectl-text-of-unabombers-letter-received-by-NY-times-april-26-1995.
12. Theodore John Kaczynski, *Industrial Society and Its Future*, 1995, https://www.washingtonpost.com/wp-srv/national/longterm/unabomber/manifesto.text.htm.
13. Brett A. Barnett, "20 Years Later: A Look Back at the Unabomber Manifesto," *Perspectives on Terrorism* 9, no. 6 (2015): 60–71; Sean Fleming, "Searching for Ecoterrorism: The Crucial Case of the Unabomber," *American Political Science Review* 118, no. 4 (November 2024): 1986–99, https://doi.org/10.1017/S000305542300148X.
14. Fleming, "Searching for Ecoterrorism."
15. David Kaczynski, *Every Last Tie: The Story of the Unabomber and His Family* (Duke University Press, 2015).
16. Alston Chase, A Mind for Murder: The Education of the Unabomber and the Origins of Modern Terrorism (W. W. Norton & Company, 2004).
17. William Glaberson, "Kaczynski Can't Drop Lawyers or Block a Mental Illness Defense," *The New York Times*, January 1998, https://www.nytimes.com/1998/01/08/us/kaczynski-can-t-drop-lawyers-or-block-a-mental-illness-defense.html.
18. William Booth, "Kaczynski Pleads Guilty," *The Washington Post*, January 1998, https://www.washingtonpost.com/wp-srv/national/longterm/unabomber/bkgrdstories.plead0123.htm.
19. Michael R. Sisak, Mike Balsamo, and Jake Offenhartz, "'Unabomber' Ted Kaczynski Died by Suicide in Prison Medical Center, AP Sources Say," Associated Press, June 2023, https://apnews.com/article/ted-kaczynski-unabomber-1197f597364b36e56bdbcaca9837bdc4.
20. Susan Headden, "Return of the 'Unabomber,'" *US News and World Report*, May 1995, https://www.usnews.com/cmsmedia/78/5c/329da2f14faaa3322ba022e2718f/unabomber.PDF.
21. Earth First! Journal, "ABC Trash Journalism—Unabomber and Earth First!? ?," *Albion Monitor/News*, April 1996, http://albionmonitor.com/4-15-96/efresponse.html.

22. Peter Staudenmeier, *Ecology Contested: Environmental Politics between Left and Right* (New Compass Press, 2022), footnote 45.
23. John Zerzan, "Green Anarchy: An Introduction," *An Archive of Green Anarchy Magazine 2001–2008*, June 2012, https://greenanarchy.anarchyplanet.org/2012/06/05/introduction-by-john-zerzan.
24. Zerzan, "Green Anarchy: An Introduction," June 2012.
25. John Zerzan, *Future Primitive and Other Essays* (The Anarchist Library, 1994).
26. Kenneth B. Noble, "Prominent Anarchist Finds Unsought Ally in Serial Bomber," *The New York Times*, May 1995, https://www.nytimes.com/1995/05/07/us/prominent-anarchist-finds-unsought-ally-in-serial-bomber.html.
27. John Zerzan, "Whose Unabomber?," *Green Anarchist* #40-41, March 1996, https://theanarchistlibrary.org/library/john-zerzan-whose-unabomber.
28. Panagioti Tsolkas, "Re-visiting Uncle Ted: A look at Technological Slavery: The Collected Writings of Theodore J. Kaczynski a.k.a. 'The Unabomber,'" *Earth First Journal*, May 2011, https://earthfirstnews.wordpress.com/wp-content/uploads/2011/05/revisiting-uncle-ted-kaczynski-writings-of-unabomber-fc-earth-first-journal.pdf.
29. Interview #AA-N37-0522.
30. Jim Donaghey, "The 'Punk Anarchisms' of Class War and CrimethInc.," *Journal of Political Ideologies* 25, no. 2 (May 3, 2020): 113–38, https://doi.org/10.1080/13569317.2020.1750761.
31. See Theodore John Kaczynski, Patrick Barriot, and David Skrbina, *The Road to Revolution* (Xenia, 2008), https://azinelibrary.org/trash/The.Road_.to_.Revolution—Ted.Kaczynski.pdf and Tsolkas, Panagioti. "Re-visiting Uncle Ted," May 2011.
32. "Terror on Trial: Life in Supermax's 'Bombers Row,'" CNN, December 2007, https://www.cnn.com/2007/US/law/12/17/court.archive.mcveigh4/index.html.
33. Theodore Kaczynski, "Comments on Timothy McVeigh," Letter sent to Lou Michel and Dan Herbeck, April 2000, https://theanarchistlibrary.org/library/ted-kaczynski-ted-kaczynski-s-comments-on-timothy-mcveigh.
34. Interview # EA-N54-0822.
35. Interview #AA-N37-0522.
36. Charles Homans, "The Strange, Post-Partisan Popularity of the Unabomber," *The New York Times*, March 2025, https://www.nytimes.com/2025/03/22/magazine/unabomber-ted-kaczynski-luigi-mangione.html.
37. Interview # EA-N68FU-0623.
38. Jeff Barnard, "Two Plead Guilty in 1998 ELF Ski Resort Fire," *The Seattle Times*, December 2006, https://www.seattletimes.com/seattle-news/two-plead-guilty-in-1998-elf-ski-resort-fire.

39. Randy Wyrick, "Eco-terrorists Set Fire to Vail Mountain 20 Years Ago, and the Response Showed How Mutual Aid Could Benefit Mountain Communities," *The Denver Post*, October 2018, https://www.denverpost.com/2018/10/27/vail-mountain-arson-looking-back.
40. Associated Press, "Group Says It Set Vail Fires on Behalf of Lynx," *Desert News*, October 1998, https://www.deseret.com/1998/10/22/19408164/group-says-it-set-vail-fires-on-behalf-of-lynx.
41. Matthew Wolfe, "The Rise and Fall of America's Environmentalist Underground," *The New York Times*, May 2022, https://www.nytimes.com/2022/05/26/magazine/earth-liberation-front-joseph-mahmoud-dibee.html.
42. Rachel McDonald, "Remembering Warner Creek 20 Years Later," *Jefferson Public Radio*, August 2015, https://www.ijpr.org/2015-08-14/remembering-warner-creek-20-years-later.
43. Vanessa Grigoriadis, "The Rise and Fall of the Eco-Radical Underground," *Rolling Stone*, June 2011, and Rachel McDonald, "Remembering Warner Creek 20 Years Later," August 2015.
44. Nagtzaam, *From Environmental Action to Ecoterrorism?* p. 167–68.
45. Brown, "Notes to the Underground"; Loadenthal, "The Earth Liberation Front."
46. Steven M. Chermak et al., "An Overview of Bombing and Arson Attacks by Environmental and Animal Rights Extremists in the United States, 1995–2010," *Final Report to the Resilient Systems Division, Science and Technology Directorate*, U.S. Department of Homeland Security (College Park, MD: START) (2013). https://www.dhs.gov/sites/default/files/publications/OPSR_TP_TEVUS_Bombing-Arson-Attacks_Environmental-Animal%20Rights-Extremists_1309-508.pdf.
47. Robert Sullivan, "The Face of Eco-Terrorism," *The New York Times*, December 1988, https://www.nytimes.com/1998/12/20/magazine/the-face-of-eco-terrorism.html.
48. Bryan Denson, "The Case of the Eco-Terrorists and the Book Deal," *The New York Times*, February 2023, https://www.nytimes.com/2023/02/06/special-series/craig-rosebraugh-earth-liberation-front.html.
49. "Eco-terrorism in the West: A Who's Who of the Convicted, the Arrested, the Missing," *The Oregonian*, August 2018, https://www.oregonlive.com/news/erry-2018/08/3cc02205f06447/ecoterrorism-in-the-west-a-who.html.
50. Brooke Gladstone, "How Radical Climate Activists Became a Domestic Terror Threat in the U.S.," *WNYC*, September 2012, https://www.wnycstudios.org/podcasts/otm/segments/how-radical-climate-activists-became-domestic-terror-threat-us-on-the-media?tab=transcript.
51. William McCall, "Radical Environmentalists Go Out with Whimper," *NBC News*, July 2007, https://www.nbcnews.com/id/wbna19914154.

52. McKenzie Funk, "Firestarter," *Outside*, August 2007, https://www.outsideonline.com/outdoor-adventure/environment/firestarter.
53. Vanessa Grigoriadis, "The Rise and Fall of the Eco-Radical Underground," June 2011.
54. Grigoriadis, 2011.
55. David Moberg, "How the Battle in Seattle Changed Everything," *In These Times*, November 2020, https://inthesetimes.com/article/seattle-world-trade-organization-labor-protests-wto-trade.
56. Gene Johnson, "Impact of WTO Protests in Seattle Still Felt 2 Decades Later," Associated Press, November 2019, https://apnews.com/article/239fb5aca78345f0807fa4c9c505db9a.
57. ACLU of Washington, "ACLU Report Says Response to Seattle WTO Protests Was Flawed, Out of Control," American Civil Liberties Union, July 2000, https://www.aclu.org/press-releases/aclu-report-says-response-seattle-wto-protests-was-flawed-out-control.
58. "If a Tree Falls: A Story of the Earth Liberation Front (Documentary Film)," *The Paley Center for Media*, 2010, https://www.paleycenter.org/collection/item/?q=meet&p=98&item=107229.
59. James Croxton and Nadya Malinowska, "Eugene Rising, Part IV: Welcome to the Anarchist Capital of the World," *Double Sided Media*, February 2021, https://doublesidedmedia.com/2021/02/18/eugene-rising-part-iv.
60. Debra Gwartney, "Anarchists' Rally Erupts into Riot in Eugene," *The Oregonian*, June 1999, https://web.archive.org/web/20011031030946/http://www.oregonlive.com:80/news/99/06/st061905.html.
61. Interview #EA-N47-0622.
62. Tullis Tracy, "Is Briana Waters a terrorist?," *Salon*, March 2008, https://www.salon.com/2008/03/27/briana_waters/.
63. Interview #EA-N99-0524.
64. Alleen Brown, "The Green Scare How a Movement That Never Killed Anyone Became the FBI's No. 1 Domestic Terrorism Threat," *The Intercept*, March 2019, https://theintercept.com/2019/03/23/ecoterrorism-fbi-animal-rights.
65. Interview #EA-N73-0223.
66. Interview #LE-N3-0222.
67. Tony Davis, "Forest Service Building Is Torched by Night Raiders," *High Country News*, December 1996, https://www.hcn.org/issues/issue-95/forest-service-building-is-torched-by-night-raiders.
68. Tony Davis, "Last Line of Defense Civil Disobedience and Protest Slowdown 'Lawless Logging,'" *High Country News*, September 1996, https://www.hcn.org/issues/issue-89/last-line-of-defense.
69. Interview #LE-N105-0222.
70. Interview # EA-N56-0122.
71. #EA-N60-0522.

72. Herbert H. Haines, *Black Radicals and Civil Rights Mainstream* (University of Tennessee Press, 2002).
73. Rudd, *Underground*.
74. Interview #EA-N57-0722.
75. Interview #AA-N26-0422.
76. Andreas Malm, *How to Blow Up a Pipeline: Learning to Fight in a World on Fire* (Verso Books, 2021).
77. Malm, *How to Blow Up a Pipeline*, p. 151–52.
78. Interview ##EA-N47-0622.
79. Interview #EA-N60-0522.
80. Eric Devericks, "E.L.F. Members Are Terrorists," *The Seattle Times*, March 2008, https://web.archive.org/web/20130826131035/http://blog.seattletimes.nwsource.com/antagonisticink/2008/03/elf_members_are_terrorists.html and Rachel Rosnick "THE 'NEW' COINTELPRO?: NOT SO FAST . . .," University of Pittsburgh, MA Thesis, 2010.
81. Eric Devericks, "E.L.F. Members Are Terrorists," March 2008.
82. Steve Vanderheiden, "Eco-Terrorism or Justified Resistance? Radical Environmentalism and the 'War on Terror,'" *Politics & Society* 33, no. 3 (September 1, 2005): 425–47, https://doi.org/10.1177/0032329205278462.
83. Interview #EA-N71-0223.
84. Interview #AO-N15-0222.
85. Potter, *Green Is the New Red*; Sivan Hirsch-Hoefler and Cas Mudde, "'Ecoterrorism': Terrorist Threat or Political Ploy?," *Studies in Conflict & Terrorism* 37, no. 7 (July 3, 2014): 586–603, https://doi.org/10.1080/1057610X.2014.913121.

Chapter 5

1. Interview # EA-N100-0422.
2. Interview #EA-N100FU-0524.
3. Interview # EA-N73FU2-0324.
4. Interview #EA-N99-0524.
5. Interview #EA-N42-0522.
6. Potter, *Green Is the New Red*.
7. James F. Jarboe, "Domestic Terrorism Section Chief, Counterterrorism Division Federal Bureau of Investigation Testimony," U.S. House Resources Committee, Subcommittee on Forests and Forest Health Washington, DC, February 2002, https://archives.fbi.gov/archives/news/testimony/the-threat-of-eco-terrorism.
8. Jarboe, "Domestic Terrorism Section Chief."
9. "Eco-Terrorism and Lawlessness on the National Forests," Oversight Hearing Before the Subcommittee on Forests and Forest Health of the Committee on Resources U.S. House of Representatives, February 2002,

228　NOTES

https://www.govinfo.gov/content/pkg/CHRG-107hhrg77615/html/CHRG-107hhrg77615.htm.

10. Hal Bernton, "An Activist Turned Informant," *The Seattle Times*, May 2006, https://archive.seattletimes.com/archive/?date=20060507&slug=ecoarrests07m.
11. Kera Abraham, "Flames of Dissent PT. IV: THE BUST: The Local Spark That Ignited an Eco-Sabotage Boom—and Bust," *Eugene Weekly*, December 2006, https://eugeneweekly.com/2006/12/07/flames-of-dissent-2.
12. Matthew Wolfe, "The Rise and Fall of America's Environmentalist Underground," *The New York Times*, May 2022.
13. Wolfe, "The Rise and Fall of America's Environmentalist Underground."
14. "Operation Backfire: Searching for Two Final Fugitives," *FBI Portland Field Office News*, August 2018, https://www.fbi.gov/contact-us/field-offices/portland/news/operation-backfire.
15. "Eleven Defendants Indicted on Domestic Terrorism Charges: Group Allegedly Responsible for Series of Arsons in Western States, Acting on Behalf of Extremist Movements," U.S. Department of Justice Press, January 2006. Release https://www.justice.gov/archive/opa/pr/2006/January/06_crm_030.html.
16. John Vida, "The Green Scare," *The Guardian*, April 2008, https://www.theguardian.com/environment/2008/apr/03/greenbuilding.ethicalliving.
17. Kera Abraham, "Flames of Dissent PT. III: Eco-Anarchy Imploding," *Eugene Weekly*, November 2006; Spadaro, "Climate Change, Environmental Terrorism, Eco-Terrorism and Emerging Threats"; Carson, Dugan, and Yang, "A Comprehensive Application of Rational Choice Theory."
18. "Most Wanted: Josephine Sunshine Overaker," *FBI Most Wanted: Domestic Terrorism*. https://www.fbi.gov/wanted/dt/josephine-sunshine-overaker.
19. See Figure 1 from the Preface and Spadaro, "Climate Change, Environmental Terrorism, Eco-Terrorism and Emerging Threats"; Jennifer Varriale Carson, Laura Dugan, and Sue-Ming Yang, "A Comprehensive Application of Rational Choice Theory: How Costs Imposed by, and Benefits Derived from, the U.S. Federal Government Affect Incidents Perpetrated by the Radical Eco-Movement," *Journal of Quantitative Criminology* 36, no. 3 (September 1, 2020): 701–24, https://doi.org/10.1007/s10940-019-09427-8. Several other works focus on the legal cases of Operation Backfire. The documentary *If a Tree Falls*, Mathew Wolfe's investigative piece for *The New York Times*, https://www.nytimes.com/2022/05/26/magazine/earth-liberation-front-joseph-mahmoud-dibee.html, and Potter, *Green Is the New Red*.
20. Interview #LE-N3-0222.
21. Hal Bernton, "An Activist Turned Informant," *The Seattle Times*, May 2006.

22. Interview # LE-N105-0222.
23. Interview #EA-N99-0524.
24. Interview #EA-N41-0522.
25. Interview #EA-N47-0622.
26. Jennifer Hadden and Sidney Tarrow, "Spillover or Spillout? The Global Justice Movement in the United States after 9/11," *Mobilization: An International Quarterly* 12, no. 4 (January 11, 2008): 359–76, https://doi.org/10.17813/maiq.12.4.t221742122771400.
27. Interview #EA-N56-0122.
28. "Michigan State University Eco-Terrorist Sentenced in Arson Case," U.S. Attorney's Office, Western District of Michigan, February 2009, https://archives.fbi.gov/archives/detroit/press-releases/2009/de020509.htm.
29. Interview #EA-N60-0522,
30. Natasha Lennard, "How the Prosecution of Animal Rights Activists as Terrorists Foretold Today's Criminalization of Dissent," *The Intercept*, December 2019, https://theintercept.com/2019/12/12/animal-people-documentary-shac-protest-terrorism.
31. "Three Militant Animal Rights Activists Sentenced to Between Four and Six Years in Prison," United States Department of Justice U.S. Attorney, District of New Jersey, September 2006, https://www.justice.gov/archive/usao/nj/Press/files/pdffiles/Older/shac0912rel.pdf.
32. Loadenthal, "'The Green Scare'& 'Eco-Terrorism.'"
33. Interview #EA-N23-0322.
34. Interview #EA-N14-0222.
35. Interview # EA-N75-0223.
36. Interview #EA-N80-0223.
37. Panagioti Tsolkas, "No System But the Ecosystem: Earth first! and Anarchism," *Anarchist Studies. org* (2015), https://anarchiststudies.org/no-system-but-the-ecosystem-earth-first-and-anarchism-by-panagioti-tsolkas-1.
38. Bryan Denson, "The Case of the Eco-Terrorists and the Book Deal," *The New York Times*, February 2023.
39. Denson, "The Case of the Eco-Terrorists."

Chapter 6

1. Interview EA-N61-1022.
2. Interview # EA-N61FU2-0524.
3. Pike, *For the Wild*.
4. "Earth First!," *The Radical Environmental Journal* 23, no. 4 (2003), https://archive.org/details/001_20221116_20221116_2033/page/64/mode/2up?q=%22carson+mccann%22.
5. Corydon Ireland, "McKibben's Movement: 350.org," *The Harvard Gazette*, October 2009, https://news.harvard.edu/gazette/story/2009/10/mckibben-brings-350-home.

6. Nick Estes, *Our History Is the Future: Standing Rock Versus the Dakota Access Pipeline, and the Long Tradition of Indigenous Resistance* (Verso Books, 2019).
7. Blak Nicholson, "Companies Decry 'Valve Turners' Who Shut Down Pipelines," Associated Press, March 2019, https://apnews.com/article/0fe28195510141eea0e407687fd49ce5.
8. Mike Jordan, "The US Activists Holed Up in Treehouses to Block $90m 'Cop City,'" *The Guardian*, June 2022, https://www.theguardian.com/environment/2022/jun/16/us-activists-protest-atlanta-cop-city-training-forest; and Joseph M. Brown, "Stop Cop City!—Understanding the Strategic Choices of Protest Movements," *Terrorism and Political Violence*, Forthcoming (2025), https://doi.org/10.1080/09546553.2025.2489740.
9. Ryan Fatica, "Atlanta Fights to Save Its Forests," *Unicorn Riot*, May 2022, https://unicornriot.ninja/2022/atlanta-fights-to-save-its-forest.
10. Luke Mogelson, "Revisiting Portland's Summer of Rage," *The New Yorker*, June 2023, https://www.newyorker.com/culture/photo-booth/revisiting-portlands-summer-of-rage.
11. Tessa Stuart, "Jane's Revenge: Biden's Justice Department Uses Abortion Access Law to Indict Pro-Choice Vandals," *Rolling Stone*, January 2023, https://www.rollingstone.com/politics/politics-news/janes-revenge-biden-prosecution-abortion-1234669486.
12. Matthew C. Nisbet, "How Bill McKibben Changed Environmental Politics and Took on the Oil Patch," *Policy Options Politiques*, May 2013, https://policyoptions.irpp.org/magazines/arctic-visions/how-bill-mckibben-changed-environmental-politics-and-took-on-the-oil-patch.
13. Bill McKibben, *The End of Nature* (Random House, 1989).
14. "Bill McKibben Talk Marks the 30th Anniversary of 'The End of Nature,'" *Middlebury News*, April 2019, https://www.middlebury.edu/announcements/news/2019/04/bill-mckibben-talk-marks-30th-anniversary-end-nature.
15. Matthew C. Nisbet, "How Bill McKibben Changed Environmental Politics and Took on the Oil Patch," *Policy Options*, May 2013. https://policyoptions.irpp.org/magazines/arctic-visions/how-bill-mckibben-changed-environmental-politics-and-took-on-the-oil-patch/.
16. Matthew C. Nisbet, "Nature's Prophet: Bill McKibben as Journalist, Public Intellectual and Activist," *Joan Shorenstein Center on the Press, Politics and Public Policy Discussion Paper Series*, March 2013, https://dash.harvard.edu/bitstream/handle/1/37376523/2013_D78.pdf?sequence=1&isAllowed=y.
17. "The 350.org Climate Change Worldwide Protest," *The Guardian*, October 2009, https://www.theguardian.com/environment/gallery/2009/oct/27/350-campaign-climate-change-protest.
18. Interview #EA-N51FU4-0924.

19. Talia Buford, "RFK Jr., Hannah Arrested at W.H.," *Politico*, February 2013, https://www.politico.com/story/2013/02/rfk-jr-daryl-hannah-among-48-arrested-at-kxl-protest-087609.
20. Bill McKibben, "White House Tar Sands Sit-in Ends with Surge of Support," *HuffPost*, September 2011, https://www.huffpost.com/entry/white-house-tar-sands-sit_b_947965.
21. "Developer Officially Cancels Keystone XL Pipeline Project Blocked by Biden," *Reuters*, June 2021, https://www.reuters.com/business/energy/tc-energy-terminates-keystone-xl-pipeline-project-2021-06-09.
22. Interview #EA-N65-1122.
23. Interview #EA-N63-1022.
24. Michael Sainato, "Protesters against Line 3 Tar Sands Pipeline Face Arrests and Rubber Bullets," *The Guardian*, August 2021, https://www.theguardian.com/environment/2021/aug/10/protesters-line-3-minnesota-oil-gas-pipeline.
25. Rebecca Hersher, "Key Moments in the Dakota Access Pipeline Fight," National Public Radio, February 2017, https://www.npr.org/sections/thetwo-way/2017/02/22/514988040/key-moments-in-the-dakota-access-pipeline-fight.
26. Estes, *Our History Is the Future*; Rebecca Solnit, "Standing Rock Protests: This Is Only the Beginning," *The Guardian*, September 2016, https://www.theguardian.com/us-news/2016/sep/12/north-dakota-standing-rock-protests-civil-rights.
27. Several members of the Standing Rock tribe addressed the U.N. Human Rights Council in September 2016. Daniel A. Medina, "Standing Rock Sioux Takes Pipeline Fight to UN Human Rights Council in Geneva," NBC News, September 2016, https://www.nbcnews.com/storyline/dakota-pipeline-protests/standing-rock-sioux-takes-pipeline-fight-un-human-rights-council-n651381.
28. "Actress Shailene Woodley Arrested during Pipeline Protest," BBC News, October 2016, https://www.bbc.com/news/world-us-canada-37614797.
29. Rebecca Hersher, "Key Moments in the Dakota Access Pipeline Fight," National Public Radio, February 2017.
30. But the Standing Rock Sioux Tribe did win a victory in 2020 that was affirmed by the U.S. Supreme Court on appeal in 2022. The courts said that there needed to be a greater environmental impact study on the pipeline's effects on the tribe's water. Nina Lakhani, "US Supreme Court Rejects Dakota Access Pipeline Appeal," *The Guardian*, February 2022, https://www.theguardian.com/us-news/2022/feb/22/us-supreme-court-dakota-access-pipeline.
31. Interview #EA-N51FU4-0924.
32. Winona LaDuke, *To Be a Water Protector: The Rise of the Wiindigoo Slayers* (Fernwood Publishing, 2020).

33. Lucien Bruggeman, Devin Dwyer, and Stephanie Ebbs, "Climate Activist's Fight Against 'Terrorism' Sentence Could Impact the Future of Protests," ABC News, April 2022, https://abcnews.go.com/US/climate-activists-fight-terrorism-sentence-impact-future-protests/story?id=84345514.
34. Dar Danielson, "Two Women Take Credit for Vandalism along the Dakota Access Pipeline," *Radio Iowa*, July 2017, https://www.radioiowa.com/2017/07/24/two-woman-take-credit-for-vandalism-along-the-dakota-access-pipeline-audio.
35. Julia Shipley, "The Long Legal Saga of DAPL Arsonist Ruby Montoya Is Coming to an End," *Grist*, September 2022, https://grist.org/protest/ruby-montoya-dakota-access-pipeline.
36. Michelle Nijhuis, "'I'm Just More Afraid of Climate Change Than I Am of Prison," *The New York Times*, February 2018, https://www.nytimes.com/2018/02/13/magazine/afraid-climate-change-prison-valve-turners-global-warming.html.
37. Nina Lakhani, "Revealed: Rightwing US Lobbyists Help Craft Slew of Anti-Protest Fossil Fuel Bills." *The Guardian*, September 2022, https://www.theguardian.com/us-news/2022/sep/14/rightwing-lobbyists-at-heart-of-anti-protest-bills-in-republican-states.
38. Interview # EA-N10-0222.
39. Klein, *This Changes Everything*.
40. Interview ##EA-N66-1222.
41. "Ralph Nader Fast Facts," CNN, March 2013, https://www.cnn.com/2013/03/08/us/ralph-nader-fast-facts/index.html.
42. Naomi Klein, *This Changes Everything: Capitalism vs. The Climate*, 1st ed. (Simon & Schuster, 2013). Nina Lakhani and Hilary Beaumont, "'Fear and Intimidation': How Peaceful Anti-Pipeline Protesters Were Hit with Criminal and Civil Charges," *The Guardian*, September 2024, https://www.theguardian.com/us-news/2024/sep/27/mountain-valley-pipeline-protest.
43. Ariana Skibell, "Why Is Biden Backing Manchin's Pet Pipeline?" *Politico*, April 2023, https://www.politico.com/newsletters/power-switch/2023/04/25/why-is-biden-backing-manchins-pet-pipeline-00082767.
44. Nina Lakhani, "US Anti-pipeline Activists Say Charges against Them 'Meant to Intimidate,'" *The Guardian*, February 2025, https://www.theguardian.com/environment/2025/feb/25/mountain-valley-pipeline-activists.
45. Interview #EA-N98-0324.
46. Mike Ludwig, "Appalachian Pipeline Blockade Ends with Arrests After 932 Days," *Truthout*, April 2021, https://truthout.org/audio/yellow-finch-blockade-of-mountain-valley-pipeline-ends-after-932-days.
47. Jeff Williamson, "Elected Official Arrested after Attaching Himself to an MVP Truck in Giles County," *WSLS*, April 2021, https://www.wsls.com/news/local/2021/04/30/elected-official-arrested-after-attaching-himself-

to-an-mvp-truck-in-giles-county/ And Cody Bloomfield, "Despite Repression, Activists Continue to Shut Down Mountain Valley Pipeline," *Truthout*, March 2024, https://truthout.org/articles/despite-repression-activists-continue-to-shut-down-mountain-valley-pipeline.

48. Ben Martin, "How the Youth Climate Movement Has Evolved from School Strikes to Systemic Change," Green Economy Coalition, March 2023, https://www.greeneconomycoalition.org/news-and-resources/from-school-strikes-to-systemic-change-how-the-youth-climate-movement-has-evolved.

49. Sandra Laville and Jonathan Watts, "Across the Globe, Millions Join Biggest Climate Protest Ever," *The Guardian*, September 2019, https://www.theguardian.com/environment/2019/sep/21/across-the-globe-millions-join-biggest-climate-protest-ever.

50. Lisa Friedman, "What Is the Green New Deal? A Climate Proposal, Explained," *The New York Times*, February 2019, https://www.nytimes.com/2019/02/21/climate/green-new-deal-questions-answers.html.

51. Alexandria Ocasio-Cortez, (@RepAOC). Post on X/Twitter, April 2023, https://x.com/RepAOC/status/1649108769433845777.

52. Fisher and Nasrin, "Shifting Coalitions within the Youth Climate Movement in the US"; Sally Neas, Ann Ward, and Benjamin Bowman, "Young People's Climate Activism: A Review of the Literature," *Frontiers in Political Science* 4 (August 4, 2022), https://doi.org/10.3389/fpos.2022.940876.

53. "Join the Movement: Become a Sunrise Member," https://www.sunrisemovement.org/become-a-member.

54. Dana R. Fisher and Quinn Renaghan, "Understanding the Growing Radical Flank of the Climate Movement As the World Burns," Brookings, July 2023, https://www.brookings.edu/articles/understanding-the-growing-radical-flank-of-the-climate-movement-as-the-world-burns.

55. Ruairí Arrieta-Kenna, "The Sunrise Movement Actually Changed the Democratic Conversation. So What Do You Do for a Sequel?," *Politico*, June 2019, https://www.politico.com/magazine/story/2019/06/16/sunrise-movement-boot-camp-227109.

56. Ann Banard, "Climate Change Protests: With Fake Blood, Extinction Rebellion Hits N.Y.," *The New York Times*, October 2019, https://www.nytimes.com/2019/10/07/nyregion/extinction-rebellion-nyc-protest.html.

57. Louise Boyle, "Arrests Made after XR Blocks Printers for US Newspapers Including NYT on Earth Day," *The Independent*, April 2022, https://www.the-independent.com/climate-change/news/xr-protest-earth-day-fossil-fuels-dc-b2063321.html.

58. Peter Kalmus, "Climate Scientists Are Desperate: We're Crying, Begging and Getting Arrested," *The Guardian*, April 2022, https://www.

theguardian.com/commentisfree/2022/apr/06/climate-scientists-are-desperate-were-crying-begging-and-getting-arrested.
59. Interview #EA-N62-1022.
60. Chenoweth, "The Role of Violence in Nonviolent Resistance"; Chenoweth and Stephan, *Why Civil Resistance Works*.
61. Interview #EA-N46-0622.
62. Wen Stephenson, "The Grassroots Battle against Big Oil," *The Nation*, October 2013, https://www.thenation.com/article/archive/grassroots-battle-against-big-oil.
63. Jim Malewitz, "Curbing Local Control, Abbott Signs 'Denton Fracking Bill,'" *Texas Tribune*, May 2015, https://www.texastribune.org/2015/05/18/abbott-signs-denton-fracking-bill.
64. Interview ##EA-N103-0223.
65. Al Gore, *An Inconvenient Truth: The Crisis of Global Warming*, Revised ed. (Viking Books for Young Readers, 2007).
66. Justin Wm. Moyer, Rebecca Tan, and Dana Hedgpeth, "32 Arrested as 'Climate Rebels' Shut Down Intersections across the District," *The Washington Post*, September 2019, https://www.washingtonpost.com/local/climate-change-protesters-plan-to-flood-downtown-dc-streets-monday-morning/2019/09/20/6b088e94-dbd9-11e9-89d4-37d5ffcac6f4_story.html.
67. "GBI Pushes Back on 'Friendly Fire' Allegations in Shooting at Atlanta Public Safety Training Center Site," Fox 5 Atlanta, February 2023, https://www.fox5atlanta.com/news/atlanta-public-safety-training-cop-city-friendly-fire-allegations-shooting-response.
68. Kaitlyn Radde, "Autopsy Reveals Anti-'Cop City' Activist's Hands Were Raised When Shot and Killed," National Public Radio, March 2023, https://www.npr.org/2023/03/11/1162843992/cop-city-atlanta-activist-autopsy.
69. "'Stop Cop City' Claims Responsibility for Arson to Atlanta Police Car, Chief Says," Fox 5 Atlanta, February 2024, https://www.fox5atlanta.com/news/stop-cop-city-claims-responsibility-for-setting-fire-to-atlanta-police-car.
70. Timothy Pratt, "'Assassinated in Cold Blood': Activist Killed Protesting Georgia's 'Cop City.'" *The Guardian*, January 2023, https://www.theguardian.com/us-news/2023/jan/21/protester-killed-georgia-cop-city-police-shooting.
71. Amna A. Akbar, "The Fight Against Cop City," *Dissent Magazine*, Spring 2023, https://www.dissentmagazine.org/article/the-fight-against-cop-city.
72. Joseph Buddenberg, "Trees Spiked in Atlanta," *Medium*, June 2022, https://jbuddenberg.medium.com/trees-spiked-in-atlanta-905dd917b13e.
73. Odette Yousef, "Rights Groups Are Alarmed over Domestic Terrorist Charges in 'Cop City' Protests," *National Public Radio*, June 2023,

https://www.npr.org/2023/06/28/1184726273/rights-groups-are-alarmed-over-domestic-terrorist-charges-in-cop-city-protests.

74. Ryan Young, Kevin Conlon, and Holly Yan, "61 'Cop City' Protesters Indicted on RICO Charges," CNN, September 2023, https://www.cnn.com/2023/09/06/us/cop-city-protesters-indicted-rico/index.html.

75. R. J. Rico, "Georgia Prosecutors Drop All 15 Counts of Money Laundering against 3 'Cop City' Activists," Associated Press, September 2024, https://apnews.com/article/atlanta-cop-city-charges-dropped-solidarity-fund-360fad48beddfb970b145fc6577cc113.

76. R. J. Rico, "Defendants in Georgia 'Cop City' Case Say They Are in Limbo As Trial Delays Continue," Associated Press, May 2025, https://apnews.com/article/cop-city-rico-charges-61-atlanta-be5ef1ed1951a73870656f61fbbc567b.

77. R. J. Rico, "'Stop Cop City' Attacks Have Caused Costs to Balloon for Atlanta Police Training Center, Officials Say," PBS News, January 2024,. https://www.pbs.org/newshour/politics/stop-cop-city-attacks-have-caused-costs-to-balloon-for-atlanta-police-training-center-officials-say.

78. Interview #EA-N85-0423.

79. Simon Morgan, "Cops and Donuts Go Together More Than You Thought: The Corporations Funding Cop City In Atlanta," *Forbes*, May 2023, https://www.forbes.com/sites/morgansimon/2023/03/14/cops-and-donuts-go-together-more-than-you-thought-the-corporations-funding-cop-city-in-atlanta.

80. Interview #EA-N85FU-0424.

81. "Stop Cop City Goes West: Activists Kick off Tucson Summit," *Atlanta Community Press Collective*, February 2024, https://atlpresscollective.com/2024/02/24/stop-cop-city-goes-west-activists-kick-off-tucson-summit.

82. Interview #EA-N87-0423.

83. David Naguib Pellow, *Total Liberation: What Is Critical Environmental Justice?* (John Wiley & Sons, 2017).

84. Christina Ergas, Laura McKinney, and Shannon Elizabeth Bell, "Intersectionality and the Environment," in *Handbook of Environmental Sociology*, ed. Beth Schaefer Caniglia et al. (Springer International Publishing, 2021), 15–34, https://doi.org/10.1007/978-3-030-77712-8_2.

85. Interview # EA-N92-0523.

86. R. J. Rico, "Muddy Clothes? 'Cop City' Activists Question Police Evidence," Associated Press, March 2023, https://apnews.com/article/cop-city-protest-domestic-terrorism-atlanta-6d114e109d489d316f588f51c7cab0cc.

87. Ariane de Vogue, Tierney Sneed, and Devan Cole, "Supreme Court Issues Report on Dobbs Leak But Says It Hasn't Identified the Leaker," CNN,

January 2023, https://www.cnn.com/2023/01/19/politics/supreme-court-dobbs-report-leak/index.html.
88. Jane's Revenge, "First Communiqué," *Jane's Revenge: The Time Is Now—Stand Up—Take Action*, May 2022, https://janesrevenge.noblogs.org/2022/05/08/first-communique.
89. Tessa Stuart, "Jane's Revenge: Biden's Justice Department Uses Abortion Access Law to Indict Pro-Choice Vandals," *Rolling Stone*, January 2023, https://www.rollingstone.com/politics/politics-news/janes-revenge-biden-prosecution-abortion-1234669486.
90. Jessica Chasmar, "More Than 100 Pro-Life Orgs, Churches Attacked Since Dobbs Leak," *Fox* News, October 2022, https://www.foxnews.com/politics/100-pro-life-orgs-churches-attacked-dobbs-leak.
91. Luke Barr, "Violence by Extremists Could Occur 'for Weeks' in Wake of Supreme Court Decision: DHS," ABC News, June 2022, https://abcnews.go.com/Politics/violence-extremists-occur-weeks-wake-supreme-court-decision/story?id=85664462.
92. Stuart, "Jane's Revenge."
93. "Florida Man Sentenced for Civil Rights Conspiracy Targeting Pregnancy Resource Centers," U.S. Department of Justice Press Release, https://www.justice.gov/opa/pr/florida-man-sentenced-civil-rights-conspiracy-targeting-pregnancy-resource-centers.
94. Interview ##EA-N103-0223.
95. David Propper. "Anti-abortion Buffalo pregnancy center allegedly 'firebombed'." New York Post, June 2022, https://nypost.com/2022/06/07/arson-probed-over-fire-at-buffalo-pro-life-pregnancy-center/.
96. "Israel's Dead: The Names of Those Killed in Hamas Attacks, Massacres and the Israel-Hamas War," *Haaretz*, October 2023, https://archive.ph/20240803235317/https://www.haaretz.com/haaretz-explains/2023-10-19/ty-article-magazine/israels-dead-the-names-of-those-killed-in-hamas-massacres-and-the-israel-hamas-war/0000018b-325c-d450-a3af-7b5cf0210000; and Sam Magdy and Natalie Melzer, "Hamas Says It Will Free 6 Living Hostages and Hand over 4 Bodies, Accelerating Gaza Releases," PBS News, February 2025, https://www.pbs.org/newshour/world/hamas-says-it-will-free-6-living-hostages-and-hand-over-4-bodies-accelerating-gaza-releases.
97. "Reported Impact Snapshot| Gaza Strip (21 August 2024)," United Nations Office for the Coordination of Humanitarian Affairs, August 2024, https://www.ochaopt.org/content/reported-impact-snapshot-gaza-strip-21-august-2024.
98. Wafaa Shurafa and Julia Frankel, "More than 40,000 Palestinians Have Been Killed in Gaza, the Territory's Health Ministry Says," Associated Press, August 2024, https://apnews.com/article/gaza-death-toll-hamas-war-israel-40000-32a79e03c8eb62669412dab23d03219e.
99. Maggie Astor, "Omar Draws Criticism for Suggesting Some Jewish Students Are 'Pro-Genocide'," *The New York Times*, April 2024, https://

www.nytimes.com/2024/04/29/us/politics/ilhan-omar-campus-protests.html.
100. Zoha Qamar, "More Democrats Than Ever Support the Palestinian Cause, and That's Dividing the Party," *FiveThirtyEight*, September 2022, https://fivethirtyeight.com/features/democrats-israeli-palestinian-conflict-divide.
101. Alice Speri, "'A Police State': US Universities Impose Rules to Avoid Repeat of Gaza Protests," *The Guardian*, August 2024, https://www.theguardian.com/us-news/article/2024/aug/17/campus-protest-rules.
102. Nathan Solis, "San Francisco D.A. Brings Charges against Pro-Palestinian Protesters Who Blocked Golden Gate Bridge," *The Los Angeles Times*, August 2024, https://www.latimes.com/california/story/2024-08-13/pro-palestinian-protesters-charged-for-closing-down-golden-gate-bridge.
103. Appalachians against Pipelines, "MVP Protester Locks Himself to Construction Equipment, Highlights Connection between Appalachia and Palestine," *It's Going Down*, May 2024, https://itsgoingdown.org/anti-mvp-lockdown-poor-mtn.
104. Violet Barron, "Pro-Palestine and Climate Justice Movements Converge against Citigroup in New York," *Middle East Eye*, June 2024, https://www.middleeasteye.net/news/war-on-gaza-pro-palestine-climate-justice-movement-converge-citigroup.
105. Interview #EA-N85FU-0424.
106. Interview # EA-N101-0524.
107. Interview #EA-N60FU-0123.
108. Interview #EA-N61FU3-1024.
109. See Manes GREEN RAGE PAGE 81, and Dave Foreman et al., eds., *Earth First!* 2, no. 7 (August 1, 1982). Republished by the Environment & Society Portal, Multimedia Library. http://www.environmentandsociety.org/node/6834.
110. "Extreme Weather and Climate Change," https://science.nasa.gov/climate-change/extreme-weather.
111. Joshua Busby, *States and Nature: The Effects of Climate Change on Security* (Cambridge University Press, 2022).

Chapter 7

1. Kristy Campion, "Defining Ecofascism: Historical Foundations and Contemporary Interpretations in the Extreme Right," *Terrorism and Political Violence* 35, no. 4 (May 19, 2023): 926–44, https://doi.org/10.1080/09546553.2021.1987895. And April Anson, "No One Is a Virus: On American Ecofascism," *Environmental History Now*, September 2023, https://envhistnow.com/2023/09/06/no-one-is-a-virus-on-american-ecofascism.
2. Interview #EA-N73-0223.
3. Khaleda Rahman, "'Great Replacement Theory' Has Inspired 4 Mass Shootings in Recent Years," *Newsweek*, May 2022, https://www.newsweek.

com/great-replacement-theory-inspired-terror-attacks-recent-years-1706953.

4. Dan Amira, "Anders Breivik Plagiarized Ted Kaczynski," *New York Magazine*, July 2011, https://nymag.com/intelligencer/2011/07/anders_breivik_unabomber.html.
5. Alejandro Beutel, "The New Zealand Terrorist's Manifesto: A Look at Some of the Key Narratives, Beliefs and Tropes," *START: National Consortium for the Study of Terrorism and Responses to Terrorism*, April 2019, https://www.start.umd.edu/news/new-zealand-terrorists-manifesto-look-some-key-narratives-beliefs-and-tropes.
6. Daniela Peterka-Benton and Bond Benton, "Online Radicalization Case Study of a Mass Shooting: The Payton Gendron Manifesto," *Journal for Deradicalization*, no. 35 (June 30, 2023): 1–32. And Joyce, Kathryn. "What Is 'Ecofascism'—and What Does It Have to Do with the Buffalo Shooting?," *Salon*, May 2022, https://www.salon.com/2022/05/18/what-is-ecofascism—and-what-does-it-have-to-do-with-the-buffalo-shooting.
7. Payton Gendron, *You Wait for a Signal While Your People Wait for You*, 2022, *Manifesto*.
8. Debbie Elliott, "The Charlottesville Rally 5 Years Later: 'It's What You're Still Trying to Forget,'" National Public Radio, August 2022, https://www.npr.org/2022/08/12/1116942725/the-charlottesville-rally-5-years-later-its-what-youre-still-trying-to-forget.
9. Philip Bump, "What Trump Said with His 'Very Fine People' Comments Vs. What He Meant," *The Washington Post*, June 2024, https://www.washingtonpost.com/politics/2024/06/28/what-trump-said-with-his-very-fine-people-comments-vs-what-he-meant.
10. Chris Cillizza, "How the Ugly, Racist White 'Replacement Theory' Came to Congress," CNN, April 2021, https://www.cnn.com/2021/04/15/politics/scott-perry-white-replacement-theory-tucker-carlson-fox-news/index.html.
11. Jude Joffe-Block and Odette Yousef, "How Trump Is Relying on a Racist Conspiracy Theory to Question Election Results," National Public Radio, September 2024, https://www.npr.org/2024/09/13/g-s1-22583/trump-great-replacement-conspiracy-theory.
12. Miles Klee, "Elon Musk All but Endorses the Great Replacement Conspiracy Theory," *Rolling Stone*, January 2024, https://www.rollingstone.com/culture/culture-news/elon-musk-great-replacement-conspiracy-theory-1234941337.
13. Joel Achenbach, "Two Mass Killings a World Apart Share a Common Theme: 'Ecofascism,'" *The Washington Post*, August 2019, https://www.washingtonpost.com/science/two-mass-murders-a-world-apart-share-a-common-theme-ecofascism/2019/08/18/0079a676-bec4-11e9-b873-63ace636af08_story.html. And Maxine Joselow and Vanessa Montalbano, "Suspect in Buffalo Rampage Cited 'Ecofascism' to Justify Actions," *The*

14. Jake Hanrahan, "Inside the Unabomber's Odd and Furious Online Revival," *Wired*, August 2018, https://www.wired.com/story/unabomber-netflix-tv-series-ted-kaczynski. And Ardian Shajkovci, "Eco-Fascist 'Pine Tree Party' Growing as a Violent Extremism Threat," *Homeland Security Today*, September 2020, https://www.hstoday.us/subject-matter-areas/counterterrorism/eco-fascist-pine-tree-party-growing-as-a-violent-extremism-threat.
15. Joshua Molloy, "Understanding Eco-Fascism: A Thematic Analysis of the Eco-Fascist Subculture on Telegram," *Global Network on Extremism and Technology*, November 2022, https://gnet-research.org/2022/11/02/understanding-eco-fascism-a-thematic-analysis-of-the-eco-fascist-subculture-on-telegram and Brian Hughes, Dave Jones, and Amarnath Amarasingam, "Ecofascism: An Examination of the Far-Right/Ecology Nexus in the Online Space," *Terrorism and Political Violence* 34, no. 5 (July 4, 2022): 997–1023, https://doi.org/10.1080/09546553.2022.2069932.
16. "Terrorgram." Anti-Defamation League. https://extremismterms.adl.org/glossary/terrorgram
17. Hughes, Jones, and Amarasingam, "Ecofascism."
18. Sam Moore and Alex Roberts, *The Rise of Ecofascism: Climate Change and the Far Right*, 1st ed. (Polity, 2022).
19. Staudenmeier, *Ecology Contested*; Campion, "Defining Ecofascism."
20. Ginger Gibson, "Trump Says Immigrants Are 'Poisoning the Blood of Our Country,'" *NBC News*, December 2023, https://www.nbcnews.com/politics/2024-election/trump-says-immigrants-are-poisoning-blood-country-biden-campaign-liken-rcna130141.
21. Joshua Farrell-Molloy and Graham Macklin, "Ted Kaczynski, Anti-Technology Radicalism and Eco-Fascism," June 2022. International Centre for Counter-Terrorism. June 2022, https://www.icct.nl/publication/ted-kaczynski-anti-technology-radicalism-and-eco-fascism.
22. Theodore Kaczynski, "Suggestions for Earth First!ers from FC," Folder 3, Box 82, Kaczynski Papers, University of Michigan Library (Special Collections Library), https://theanarchistlibrary.org/library/suggestions-for-earth-first-ers-from-fc.
23. Theodore John Kaczynski, *Industrial Society and Its Future* (1995).
24. Garrett Hardin, "The Tragedy of the Commons," *Science* 162, no. 3859 (December 13, 1968): 1243–48, https://doi.org/10.1126/science.162.3859.1243.
25. "Garrett Hardin." *Southern Poverty Law Center: Extremism Files.* https://www.splcenter.org/resources/extremist-files/garrett-hardin.
26. Garrett Hardin, "Lifeboat Ethics: The Case against Helping the Poor," *Psychology Today* 8, no. 4 (1974): 38–43.

27. Alex Amend, "First as Tragedy, Then as Fascism," *The Baffler*, September 2019, https://thebaffler.com/latest/first-as-tragedy-then-as-fascism-amend.
28. Pentti Linkola, "A Collection of Essays (1993–2006)," http://ruby.fgcu.edu/courses/twimberley/EnviroPhilo/PenttiEssays.pdf.
29. Graham Macklin, "The Extreme Right, Climate Change and Terrorism." *Terrorism and Political Violence* 34, no. 5 (2022): 969–96.
30. Pentti Linkola, *Can Life Prevail? A Revolutionary Approach to the Environmental Crisis* (Arktos, 2009).
31. Derrick Jensen, *A Language Older Than Words* (Chelsea Green Publishing, 2000), https://www.goodreads.com/book/show/60970.A_Language_Older_Than_Words.
32. Amy Goodman and Derrick Jensen. "Author and Activist Derrick Jensen: The Dominant Culture Is Killing the Planet . . . It's Very Important for Us to Start to Build a Culture of Resistance," *Democracy Now*, November 2010, https://www.democracynow.org/2010/11/26/author_and_activist_derrick_jensen_the. And Roc Morin, "The Anarcho-Primitivist Who Wants Us All to Give Up Technology," *Vice*, June 2014, https://www.vice.com/en/article/john-zerzan-wants-us-to-give-up-all-of-our-technology.
33. Michelle Renée Matisons and Alexander Reid Ross, "Against Deep Green Resistance," *IWW Environmental Unionism Caucus*, July 2015, https://ecology.iww.org/texts/AlexanderReidRoss/AgainstDeepGreenResistance.
34. Jael Holzman, "How a fight over Transgender Rights Derailed Environmentalists in Nevada," *Politico*, February 2022, https://www.politico.com/news/2022/02/06/nevada-transgender-rights-environmentalists-lithium-00001658.
35. Michael Loadenthal, "Feral Fascists and Deep Green Guerrillas: Infrastructural Attack and Accelerationist Terror," *Critical Studies on Terrorism* 15, no. 3 (2022): 169–208 https://doi.org/10.1080/17539153.2022.2031129.
36. Pentti Linkola, *Can Life Prevail?*, 1st ed. (Arktos Media Ltd., 2009).
37. Interview #EA-N78-0223.
38. Interview #AA-N70-0223.
39. Interview #AA-N30-0522.
40. "Black in Oregon: 1840–1870: Later Developments," Oregon Secretary of State, https://sos.oregon.gov/archives/exhibits/black-history/Pages/context/later-developments.aspx.
41. All Things Considered, "People Working on Climate Solutions Are Facing a Big Obstacle: Conspiracy Theories," National Public Radio, October 2023, https://www.npr.org/2023/10/05/1203893268/climate-change-conspiracies-disinformation.
42. Interview #AA-N37-0522.
43. Interview # AA-N37FU-0724.

44. BBC Monitoring, "What Is the Great Reset—and How Did It Get Hijacked by Conspiracy Theories?," BBC, June 2021, https://www.bbc.com/news/blogs-trending-57532368.
45. Joshua Molloy and Eviane Leidig, "The Emerging Raw Food Movement and the 'Great Reset,'" *Global Network on Extremism and Technology*, October 2022, https://gnet-research.org/2022/10/10/the-emerging-raw-food-movement-and-the-great-reset.
46. "Raw Milk," *Food Safety CDC* (Access January 2024), https://www.cdc.gov/food-safety/foods/raw-milk.html.
47. Edward Helmore, "Sold-out Farm Shops, Smuggled Deliveries and Safety Warnings: US Battle over Raw Milk Grows," *The Guardian*, December 2024, https://www.theguardian.com/food/2024/dec/14/raw-milk-us-battle-unpasteurised-safety.
48. Marc Novicoff, "How Raw Milk Went from a Whole Foods Staple to a Conservative Signal," *Politico*, March 2024, https://www.politico.com/news/magazine/2024/03/10/the-alt-right-rebrand-of-raw-milk-00145625.
49. Santul Nerkar, "Raw Milk's Risks Don't Stop Right-Wing Commentators from Defiantly Pushing It," *The New York Times*, May 2024, https://www.nytimes.com/2024/05/24/business/raw-milk-bird-flu-infowars-disinformation.html. Richard Hofstadter, *The Paranoid Style in American Politics* (Knopf Doubleday Publishing Group, 1965); Joseph E. Uscinski and Joseph M. Parent, *American Conspiracy Theories* (Oxford University Press, 2014); Joseph E. Uscinski et al., "American Politics in Two Dimensions: Partisan and Ideological Identities versus Anti-Establishment Orientations," *American Journal of Political Science* 65, no. 4 (2021): 877–95, https://doi.org/10.1111/ajps.12616.
50. Joseph E. Uscinski et al., "Why Do People Believe COVID-19 Conspiracy Theories?," *Harvard Kennedy School Misinformation Review* 1, no. 3 (April 28, 2020), https://doi.org/10.37016/mr-2020-015; J. Eric Oliver and Wendy M. Rahn, "Rise of the Trumpenvolk: Populism in the 2016 Election," *The ANNALS of the American Academy of Political and Social Science* 667, no. 1 (September 1, 2016): 189–206, https://doi.org/10.1177/0002716216662639.
51. Interview # EA-N106-0824.
52. "Glyphosate & Glyphosate Formulations (Research Overview)," National Toxicology Program: U.S. Department of Health and Human Services, June 2016, https://ntp.niehs.nih.gov/whatwestudy/topics/glyphosate. Jan Bellamy. "Monsanto gets injunction against California's mandated cancer warning for glyphosate." *Science Based Medicine*, July 2020. https://sciencebasedmedicine.org/monsanto-gets-injunction-against-californias-mandated-cancer-warning-for-glyphosate/
53. Interview #EA-N109-0924.
54. Linley Sanders, "What US Adults Think of Robert F. Kennedy Jr. and His Views on Vaccines, Fluoride and Raw Milk," Associated Press. January

2025, https://apnews.com/article/rfk-jr-poll-fluoride-vaccinations-milk-abortion-88744534e2371bcfd0cd0b67fd659bd0.
55. Interviews # EA-N110-0924 and #EA-N110FU-1024.
56. "Raw Milk Misconceptions and the Danger of Raw Milk Consumption," U.S. Food and Drug Administration, March 2024, https://www.fda.gov/food/buy-store-serve-safe-food/raw-milk-misconceptions-and-danger-raw-milk-consumption.
57. Chris Moody, "Forget Uber Eats. Modern-day Homesteaders Prefer to Live Off the Land," *The Washington Post*, May 2023, https://www.washingtonpost.com/home/2023/05/10/homesteaders-live-off-land.
58. Interview #EA-N116-1124.
59. Leah Asmelash, "The Truth Behind Those White Streaks Trailing Behind Jets in the Sky," CNN, March 2024, https://www.cnn.com/us/chemtrails-conspiracy-theory-explained-cec.
60. Christina Jewett, "Kennedy's F.D.A. Wish List: Raw Milk, Stem Cells, Heavy Metals," *The New York Times*, November 2024, https://www.nytimes.com/2024/11/12/health/robert-kennedy-jr-fda.html.
61. Erika Lovley, "RFK Jr.: Too Controversial for EPA?," *Politico*, November 2008, https://www.politico.com/story/2008/11/rfk-jr-too-controversial-for-epa-015403.
62. Ann Maher, "Amish and 'Plain People' Vote Turnout Soars, Helps Lift Trump to Victory," *Delaware Valley Journal*, November 2024, https://delawarevalleyjournal.com/amish-and-plain-people-voter-turnout-soars-driven-by-government-raid-and-gop-outreac.
63. Alec Tyson, Cary Funk, and Brian Kennedy, "What the Data Says about Americans' Views of Climate Change," *Pew Research Center* (blog), 2023, https://www.pewresearch.org/short-reads/2023/08/09/what-the-data-says-about-americans-views-of-climate-change.

Chapter 8

1. Chenoweth and Stephan, *Why Civil Resistance Works*; Omar Wasow, "AGENDA SEEDING: How 1960s Black Protests Moved Elites, Public Opinion and Voting," *American Political Science Review* 114, no. 3 (August 2020): 638–59, https://doi.org/10.1017/S000305542000009X.
2. Mia Cathryn Randøy Chamberlain and Ole Jacob Madsen, "Rebels with a Cause: Public Attitudes on Radical Protest Actions—A Review of Empirical Evidence of Radical Flank Effects," *Human Arenas*, March 20, 2025, https://doi.org/10.1007/s42087-025-00485-y; Brent Simpson, Robb Willer, and Matthew Feinberg, "Radical Flanks of Social Movements Can Increase Support for Moderate Factions," *PNAS Nexus* 1, no. 3, (July 2022), pgac110, https://doi.org/10.1093/pnasnexus/pgac110; Haines, *Black Radicals and Civil Rights Mainstream*.
3. To help gain the trust of its members and accurately get survey responses from its activist members, I agreed to omit the name of the environmental direct action group.

4. Malm, *How to Blow Up a Pipeline*.
5. Kim Stanley Robinson, *The Ministry for the Future* (Orbit, 2020).
6. Interview #EA-N51-0622.
7. Markus Ostarek et al., "Radical Climate Protests Linked to Increases in Public Support for Moderate Organizations," *Nature Sustainability* 7, no. 12 (December 2024): 1626–32, https://doi.org/10.1038/s41893-024-01444-1.
8. Interview #EA-N51BM-1024.
9. Pew Research Center, "Public's Positive Economic Ratings Slip; Inflation Still Widely Viewed as Major Problem," Pew Research Center (blog), May 2024, https://www.pewresearch.org/politics/2024/05/23/top-problems-facing-the-u-s.
10. Kate Abnett, "Economy, Migration, War Top Voters' Concerns in EU Election—Survey," Reuters, June 2024, https://www.reuters.com/world/europe/economy-migration-war-top-voters-concerns-eu-election-survey-2024-06-10.
11. Cassady Rosenblum, "Blocking Burning Man and Vandalizing Van Gogh: Climate Activists Are Done Playing Nice," *Rolling Stone*, March 2024, https://www.rollingstone.com/politics/politics-features/climate-movement-rave-revolution-burning-man-1234992798.
12. Damien Gayle, "Just Stop Oil Activists Throw Soup at Van Gogh's Sunflowers after Fellow Protesters Jailed," *The Guardian*, September 2024, https://www.theguardian.com/environment/2024/sep/27/just-stop-oil-activist-phoebe-plummer-jailed-throwing-soup-van-gogh-sunflowers.
13. Spencer S. Hsu, "Activists Sentenced for Red Powder Attacks on U.S. Constitution, Museum," *The Washington Post*, November 2024, https://www.washingtonpost.com/dc-md-va/2024/11/15/national-archives-vandalism-climate-activists-sentenced.
14. Torey Akers, "Protester Charged for Defacing African American Civil War Memorial at US National Gallery of Art," *The Art Newspaper*, February 2024, https://www.theartnewspaper.com/2024/02/09/protest-national-gallery-art-charges-gaudens-memorial.
15. Michelle Lhooq, "Burning Man Attendees Roadblocked By Climate Activists: 'They Have a Privileged Mindset,'" *The Guardian*, August 2023, https://www.theguardian.com/culture/2023/aug/28/burning-man-protest-climate-change-environment.
16. "Declare Emergency! Resolute nonviolent climate action," *Homepage*, https://www.declareemergency.org.
17. Alex Oliveira, "Angry Drivers Rage at Climate Demonstrators Blocking Washington DC Traffic," *New York Post*, August 2023, https://nypost.com/2023/08/29/angry-drivers-rage-at-climate-demonstrators-blocking-washington-dc-traffic.
18. Just Stop Oil, "It's Time for Megalithic Action!—Just Stop Oil Decorate Stonehenge," https://juststopoil.org/2024/06/19/its-time-for-megalithic-action-just-stop-oil-decorate-stonehenge.

244 NOTES

19. Sarah Kerr, "Stonehenge Protest: If You Worry about Damage to British Heritage You Should Listen to Just Stop Oil," *The Conversation*, June 2024, https://theconversation.com/stonehenge-protest-if-you-worry-about-damage-to-british-heritage-you-should-listen-to-just-stop-oil-232934.
20. Tyler Austin Harper, "Maybe Don't Spray-Paint Stonehenge," *The Altantic*, June 2024, https://www.theatlantic.com/ideas/archive/2024/06/stonehenge-spray-paint-climate-protest/678765.
21. Interview #EA-N51N73BM-0624.
22. "Climate Change Crisis: Golf Courses on Borrowed Time As Earth's Weather Patterns Become Wilder," CNN, December 2021, https://www.cnn.com/2021/12/08/golf/climate-change-sustainability-spt-intl-cmd/index.html.
23. Andrew Perez and Tim Dickinson, "The Climate Activists Fighting Off Cane-Wielding Country Club Members." *Rolling Stone*, January 2024. https://www.rollingstone.com/politics/politics-features/climate-defiance-activists-moynihan-bank-america-biden-1234955026.
24. Climate Defiance, "Best Actions" (Accessed April 24, 2025), https://www.climatedefiance.org/best-actions.
25. Interview #EA-N97-0324.
26. Interview #EA-N121BM-1025
27. I'm withholding the action to protect Eli's privacy.
28. Patrick F. Gillham, "Securitizing America: Strategic Incapacitation and the Policing of Protest Since the 11 September 2001 Terrorist Attacks," *Sociology Compass* 5, no. 7 (2011): 636–52, https://doi.org/10.1111/j.1751-9020.2011.00394.x; Evgeny Morozov, *The Net Delusion: The Dark Side of Internet Freedom* (PublicAffairs, 2012); Ilica Mahajan, "Here's How Cops Are Using High-Tech Tools to Monitor Protesters," The Marshall Project, November 12, 2024, https://www.themarshallproject.org/2024/11/12/protest-surveillance-technologies; Rod McCollum and Undark Magazine, "Do Video Doorbells Really Prevent Crime?," *Scientific American*, accessed April 10, 2025, https://www.scientificamerican.com/article/do-video-doorbells-really-prevent-crime.
29. Interview #EA-N47-0622.
30. Interview #EA-N60-0522.
31. Interview # EA-N80FU3-02240924
32. Eamon P. Doherty, *Digital Forensics for Handheld Devices* (CRC Press, 2012).

Chapter 9

1. Interview #EA-N51N73BM-1124,
2. Karen Zraick, "Greenpeace Tries a Novel Tactic in Lawsuit over Dakota Access Pipeline," *The New York Times*, August 2024, https://www.nytimes.com/2024/08/20/climate/greenpeace-dakota-access-lawsuit-slapp.html.

3. Jack Dura, "Greenpeace Must Pay over $660M in Case over Dakota Access Protest Activities, Jury Finds," *Associated Press*, March 2025, https://apnews.com/article/greenpeace-dakota-access-pipeline-lawsuit-verdict-5036944c1d2e7d3d7b704437e8110fbb.
4. Lisa Friedman, "What Trump's Cabinet Picks and Advisers Say about Climate Change," *The New York Times*, December 2024, https://www.nytimes.com/2024/12/04/climate/trump-cabinet-stefanik-zeldin-wright.html.
5. Nate Perez and Rachel Waldholz, "Trump Is Withdrawing from the Paris Agreement (Again), Reversing U.S. Climate Policy," National Public Radio, January 2025, https://www.npr.org/2025/01/21/nx-s1-5266207/trump-paris-agreement-biden-climate-change.
6. Alleen Brown, "Federal Agencies Pushed Extreme View of Cop City Protesters, Records Show," *The Guardian*, December 2023, https://www.theguardian.com/us-news/2023/dec/06/cop-city-atlanta-georgia-environment-protesters-terrorism; and Steffen Seitz, "Conspiracy and Social Movements," *Michigan Law Review* 124 (2025): 1–53.
7. Interview #EA-N68-FU2-0524.
8. Interview #EA-N68FU3-1124.
9. Interview #EA-N61FU3-1124.
10. David Yamane, Jesse DeDeyne, and Alonso Octavio Aravena Méndez, "Who Are the Liberal Gun Owners?," *Sociological Inquiry* 91, no. 2 (2021): 483–98, https://doi.org/10.1111/soin.12406; Rebecca Valek et al., "Political Violence, Racial Violence, and New Gun Ownership: Results from the 2023 National Survey of Gun Policy," *Injury Epidemiology* 11 (September 6, 2024): 48, https://doi.org/10.1186/s40621-024-00527-z; Justin L. Sola and Tara D. Warner, "Firearms, Families, and Financial Distress: Economic Instability and Increased Gun Desire," *Social Science Quarterly* 105, no. 6 (2024): 2017–33, https://doi.org/10.1111/ssqu.13462.
11. Interview #EA-N73FU5-1124,
12. Interview #EA-N101FU-1224.
13. Interview #EA-N73BM-0325.
14. Interview #EA-N115-0225.
15. Interview #EA-N78-0223.
16. Interview #EA-N41-0522.
17. Austyn Gaffney, "As Teenagers, They Protested Trump's Climate Policy. Now What?," *The New York Times*, December 2024, https://www.nytimes.com/2024/12/10/climate/youth-climate-movement-sunrise.html; and Alaa Elassar, Shania Shelton, and Mina Allen, "'Hands Off!' Protesters across US Rally against President Donald Trump and Elon Musk," CNN, April 2025, https://www.cnn.com/2025/04/05/us/hands-off-protests-trump-musk.

18. This refers to political opportunity theory, a prominent strand of social movement theories. See Tarrow, "Social Movements in Contentious Politics"; Doug McAdam, *Political Process and the Development of Black Insurgency, 1930–1970* (University of Chicago Press, 1999); Charles Tilly and Sidney G. Tarrow, *Contentious Politics* (Oxford University Press, 2015).
19. Jeff Mason and Abhirup Roy. "Trump Says Violence Against Tesla Is Domestic Terrorism," March 2025, *Reuters*. https://www.reuters.com/world/us/trump-says-he-will-buy-new-tesla-show-support-musk-2025-03-11.
20. Seiji Yamashita and Tracy J. Wholf, "U.S. Greenpeace Ordered to Pay More Than $660 Million to Fossil Fuel Company over Pipeline Protests," *CBS News*; and Timothy Pratt, "Money-laundering Charges Dropped against Bail Fund in Cop City Protest Case," *The Guardian*, September 2024, https://www.theguardian.com/us-news/2024/sep/19/cop-city-protest-case. This speaks to resource mobilization theory Doug McAdam, John D. McCarthy, and Mayer N. Zald, *Comparative Perspectives on Social Movements: Political Opportunities, Mobilizing Structures, and Cultural Framings* (Cambridge University Press, 1996); John D. McCarthy and Mayer N. Zald, "Resource Mobilization and Social Movements: A Partial Theory," *American Journal of Sociology* 82, no. 6 (May 1977): 1212–41, https://doi.org/10.1086/226464.
21. James M. Jasper, *The Art of Moral Protest: Culture, Biography, and Creativity in Social Movements* (University of Chicago Press, 2008); Wendy Pearlman, "Emotions and the Microfoundations of the Arab Uprisings," *Perspectives on Politics* 11, no. 2 (June 2013): 387–409, https://doi.org/10.1017/S1537592713001072; Scott Atran and Jeremy Ginges, "Devoted Actors and the Moral Foundations of Intractable Intergroup Conflict," in *The Moral Brain: A Multidisciplinary Perspective* (Cambridge, MA: Boston Review, 2015), 69–85, https://doi.org/10.7551/mitpress/9988.001.0001; Philip E. Tetlock, "Thinking the Unthinkable: Sacred Values and Taboo Cognitions," *Trends in Cognitive Sciences* 7, no. 7 (July 1, 2003): 320–24, https://doi.org/10.1016/S1364-6613(03)00135-9.
22. Damien Gayle, "Six Big US Banks Quit Net Zero Alliance before Trump Inauguration," *The Guardian*, January 2025, https://www.theguardian.com/business/2025/jan/08/us-banks-quit-net-zero-alliance-before-trump-inauguration.
23. "Trump's EPA Announces Aggressive Rollback of Environmental Protections," PBS Newshour, March 2025, https://www.pbs.org/newshour/show/trumps-epa-announces-aggressive-rollback-of-environmental-protections; and Dharma Noor, "Outrage as Trump Cites 'Emergency' to Fast-Track Fossil Fuel Projects," *The Guardian*. February 2025, https://www.theguardian.com/us-news/2025/feb/19/trump-fossil-fuel-climate.

24. Madeline Halpert and Mike Wendling, "Who Is Luigi Mangione, CEO Shooting Suspect?," BBC, April 2025, https://www.bbc.com/news/articles/cp9nxee2rod0; and Aaron Katersky, Mark Crudele, Josh Margolin, and Meredith Deliso, "What We Know about Luigi Mangione, Ivy League Grad Charged in CEO's Murder," ABC News, December 2024, https://abcnews.go.com/US/unitedhealthcare-ceo-shooting-suspect/story?id=116460289.
25. Dionee Searcey and Madison Malone Kircher, "Torrent of Hate for Health Insurance Industry Follows C.E.O.'s Killing," *The New York Times*, December 2024, https://www.nytimes.com/2024/12/05/nyregion/social-media-insurance-industry-brian-thompson.html.
26. Interview #EA-N51N61N73BM-1224.
27. Joshua Zeitz, "People Are Cheering on a Shooting. This Theory Could Explain Why," *Politico*, December 2024, https://www.politico.com/news/magazine/2024/12/10/united-healthcare-killer-reaction-theory-00193513.
28. Eric J. Hobsbawm, *Primitive Rebels: Studies in Archaic Forms of Social Movement in the 19th and 20th Centuries* (Manchester University Press, 1959).
29. Alexandra Ulmer, Marisa Taylor, Jeffrey Dastin, and Alexandra Alper, "Exclusive: Musk's DOGE Using AI to Snoop on U.S. Federal Workers, Sources Say," Reuters, April 2025, https://www.reuters.com/technology/artificial-intelligence/musks-doge-using-ai-snoop-us-federal-workers-sources-say-2025-04-08.
30. Michael Liedtke, "Protests against Elon Musk's Purge of US Government Swarm Tesla Showrooms," Associated Press, March 2025, https://apnews.com/article/elon-musk-tesla-doge-protests-a07cb5f20d65d0fb4dcb3547e2b7879c.
31. Pranshu Verma and Trisha Thadani, "Anger at Elon Musk Turns Violent with Molotov Cocktails and Gunfire at Tesla Lots," *The Washington Post*, March 2025, https://www.washingtonpost.com/technology/2025/03/08/elon-musk-tesla-protest-violence-vandalism.
32. Matthew Rehbein, et al., "FBI Launches Task Force Targeting Anti-Tesla 'Domestic Terrorism,'" CNN, March 2025, https://www.cnn.com/2025/03/25/us/fbi-task-force-tesla-attacks-hnk/index.html.
33. "What Is ELF?," ABC News, March 2004, https://abcnews.go.com/US/story?id=96768; and Associated Press, "Convicted Arsonist Finds Wide Support," *The Seattle Times*, June 2005, https://www.seattletimes.com/seattle-news/convicted-arsonist-finds-wide-support.
34. Interview #EA-N101BM-0325.
35. Interview #EA-N22FU2-1124
36. Interview #EA-N61-1022.

Appendix

1. Christian Davenport, *Media Bias, Perspective, and State Repression: The Black Panther Party* (Cambridge University Press, 2009); Nils B. Weidmann, "A Closer Look at Reporting Bias in Conflict Event Data," *American Journal of Political Science* 60, no. 1 (2016): 206–18, https://doi.org/10.1111/ajps.12196.
2. Michael P. Boyle, Douglas M. McLeod, and Cory L. Armstrong, "Adherence to the Protest Paradigm: The Influence of Protest Goals and Tactics on News Coverage in U.S. and International Newspapers," *The International Journal of Press/Politics* 17, no. 2 (April 1, 2012): 127–44, https://doi.org/10.1177/1940161211433837; Francis L. F. Lee, "Triggering the Protest Paradigm: Examining Factors Affecting News Coverage of Protests," *International Journal of Communication* 8, (August 14, 2014): 22.
3. Taeku Lee, *Mobilizing Public Opinion: Black Insurgency and Racial Attitudes in the Civil Rights Era* (University of Chicago Press, 2002); Stephen J. Thackeray et al., "Civil Disobedience Movements Such as School Strike for the Climate Are Raising Public Awareness of the Climate Change Emergency," *Global Change Biology* 26, no. 3 (March 1, 2020): 1042–44, https://doi.org/10.1111/gcb.14978.
4. Layna Mosley, *Interview Research in Political Science.* (Cornell University Press, 2013).

INDEX

For the benefit of digital users, indexed terms that span two pages (e.g., 52–53) may, on occasion, appear on only one of those pages.

Tables and figures are indicated by *t* and *f* following the page number.

A
abortion rights activism, 105, 127–129, 133–134
activism. *See* abortion rights activism; animal liberation movement; climate movement; environmentalism; Indigenous rights activism; Palestinian activism; pathways into activism; pipeline activism; racial equality activism; radical environmentalism; social justice activism
Adam (anarcho-primitivist activist), 60–63, 70–71, 169–170
ALF. *See* Animal Liberation Front (ALF)
AFL/ELF. *See* "Family, The"
Alicia (climate justice activist), 130–132, 172–173, 183–184
anarchism. *See also* green anarchism
  deep ecology and, 17, 40–41
  ecofascism and, 143
  flag colors associated with, 41
  pathways into activism and, 50–51, 100–101
  property destruction and, 115
  punk support for, 51, 55–56, 61, 62
  scene of, 33, 68, 79, 93–94, 164
  shift from previous approaches to, 39–41, 59
  total liberation development of, 50–51
  WTO protests in Seattle and, 79
anarcho-primitivism, 62–63, 67, 139–140, 158–159
Animal Enterprise Protection Act (1992), 49–50, 96–97
Animal Enterprise Terrorism Act (2006), 49–50, 53, 96–97
Animal Liberation (Singer), 46–47
Animal Liberation Front (ALF). *See also* "Family, The"; Operation Backfire (2004–2006)
  actions carried out under banner of, 47
  community support and, 78
  direct action emphasized by, 46

Animal Liberation Front (ALF) (*Continued*)
  ecoterrorism attributed to, 84–85
  ELF's overlap with, 74–75
  FBI estimation of acts of, 88–89
  founding of, 46
  goals of, 46
  post-9/11 context of, 84–85, 94
  property destruction and, 43
  punk and, 51, 56
  repression against, 78–81, 85, 88–89, 94–95
  sources for direct actions of, 13–14
  veganism required for claiming an action under, 46
animal liberation movement, vegan straight edge. *See also* Animal Liberation Front (ALF); Stop Huntingdon Animal Cruelty (SHAC); vegan straight edge
  arson and, 45–46
  civil disobedience and, 56–57
  direct action and, 47–48
  emergence of, 45
  overview of, 58–59
  pathways into activism and, 43, 45, 76, 96, 100–101
  punk's relation to, 51, 58–59
  radical environmentalism and, 50, 53, 56–58
  repression and, 49–50, 97
  sabotage and, 45–46, 58
  speciesism and, 46–48
  tactics of, 50, 57–58
  total liberation development of, 50–51
Antifa (movement), 82, 105, 133, 168, 171, 179
anti-globalization movement, 75, 122–123, 133, 157, 164
antisemitism, 8, 129–130, 136–138, 143–144
anti-vax movement, 144–148, 153
arson
  animal liberation movement and, 45–46
  climate movement and, 155
  ELF's use of, 5–6, 13, 20, 71–73, 90
  green anarchism and, 68
  pipeline activism and, 93–94
  radical environmentalism and, 5–6, 10, 16–17, 156–157
  repression and, 90–91, 95, 98–99, 107
  as a tactic, 76–77, 81, 98–99, 154, 156–157
  trends in use of, 16–17, 16*f*, 73, 91, 92, 98, 156–157

B
Bands of Mercy, 45–46, 74
Bari, Judi
  car bombing against, 4, 36, 39–40
  criticism of, 36, 38, 67
  disciples of, 4, 35–36
  Earth First! led by, 4
  influence of, 25, 38, 40
  on Kaczynski's influence on environmentalism, 67
  labor organizing efforts of, 4, 35–36
  reconsideration of tactics by Earth First! and, 38
  visionary qualities attributed to, 35
Bernard (Earth First! activist)
  on activists arming themselves, 170
  challenge of interviewing, 102
  description of, 102–103
  grief at collapse of the movement of, 103–104
  on Luigi Mangione's positive effects for the movement, 181
  as metaphor for radical environmentalism, 104, 186
  pathway into activism of, 102–103
  on sacred experience of nature, 103

on social issues taking precedence
   over environment, 133–134
 Trump's reelection and, 170
 upbringing of, 102–103
Biden, Joe, 107, 113–114, 116–117,
   144–145, 158–159, 167–169
Black Lives Matter (BLM), 1–2,
   14–15, 82, 104–105, 120–121,
   126, 132–133
Blake (activist and ELF
   publicizer), 81–83, 94–95
Bookchin, Murray. *See also* social
   ecology
 activist identity and, 32–33
 criticism of, 31
 Foreman's rift with, 30–32
 influence of, 31, 40
 Institute for Social Ecology founded
   by, 31
 political views of, 30–31, 40
 upbringing of, 30–31
Brandon (anti-repression
   organizer), 122–125, 130
Brett (activist), 55–56, 84–85
Buffalo shooting (2022), 136–138,
   143–144

C
Cameron (veteran turned activist)
 on capacity of ELF/AFL for intense
   actions, 78
 description of, 1–2
 ecofascism as overblown
   for, 135–136
 on Luigi Mangione reactions, 182
 on military experience, 2
 pathway into activism of, 2
 on permissibility of having
   children, 3–4
 on Trump as destroying
   environmental movement, 166
 Trump's reelection and, 166–172
Carlson, Tucker, 137–138, 144–145

Chana (animal rights and
   environmental activist), 3–5
Christchurch, NZ mosque shooting
   (2019), 136–138, 143–144
civil disobedience
 animal liberation movement
   and, 56–57
 challenge of obtaining information
   on, 13–14
 climate change and, 5, 83, 105–106,
   117–119
 forms of, 17
 green anarchism and, 68
 moral high ground attained
   through, 118–119
 NGO support for, 105–108, 167,
   179–180
 Palestinian activism and, 155
 pipeline activism and, 106–107,
   110–112
 property destruction eschewed in
   favor of, 154
 public opinion on, 155
 radical environmentalism and,
   11–13, 17–18, 108–109,
   156–157, 177–180, 185
 as radical today, 155
 as a tactic, 12–13, 17–18, 35–36,
   45–46, 107, 108–109, 155
 trends in use of, 16–17, 16f,
   108–109
Civil Rights Movement, 83, 175–176
Clean Air Act (1963), 20–21
Clean Water Act (1972), 20–21
climate change
 civil disobedience and, 5, 83,
   105–106, 117–119
 denial about, 113, 143–144, 167,
   174
 doom about, 6–7, 174
 extreme weather increased by, 7
 fossil fuel industry and, 106, 113,
   115, 118–119, 132, 158, 167,
   177–178

climate change (*Continued*)
   net-zero emissions initiatives and, 178
   permanent destruction from, 98
   pipeline activism prompted by, 112–113
   policy problem as slow-burning wildfire on, 167–168
   political rescramble on, 152–153
   public opinion on, 7, 158
   racially unequal impact of, 158–159
   radical environmentalism and, 5, 7–8, 18, 19, 177, 180, 182–183, 185
   radical tactics prompted by, 5, 20–21, 118, 154–157, 174
   UN guidelines for averting catastrophe of, 6–7
Climate Defiance, 161–162
climate justice movement, 11, 20–21, 118, 119–120, 125, 130, 132–133, 174–175, 179–180
climate movement
   arson and, 155
   global climate movement, 158
   NGOs and, 105–106, 118–119, 167, 168–169, 175, 178
   pathways into activism and, 119–120
   publicly-disruptive tactics in, 160–164
   repression and, 164
   sabotage and, 112–113, 118
   tactics of, 116–117, 157–160
   uncertainty of path forward on, 103–104, 164
   Youth Climate Movement, 104, 116–118
conservation movement, 9–10, 14–15, 23, 32–33, 36–37, 42, 44, 136–137
conservative movement, 9, 40, 145–146
conspiracy theories, 8–9, 136, 143–145, 151–152
COVID-19 pandemic, 4–5, 144–147, 149–153

D
Dakota Access Pipeline protests (2017)
   goal of, 109–110
   Greenpeace lawsuit resulting from, 166–167
   monkeywrenching in, 110
   pathways into activism through, 118
   responsibility claimed for sabotage against, 110
   sabotage during, 110, 112
   tactics of, 104–105, 109
Dan (anti-pipeline activist), 112–116
deep ecology
   activist identity and, 32–33
   anarchism and, 17, 40–41
   definition of, 17
   ecofascism's relation to, 142–144
   green anarchism and, 69
   immigration and, 28
   Kaczynski and, 65–66, 68–70
   population question and, 28, 64–65
   slur of ecofascist against supporters of, 31
   social ecology's rift with, 31–33, 42
   wilderness as intrinsically valuable in, 30
Democrats (US), 7, 116–117, 137–138, 153, 170–171, 178
direct action. *See also* arson; monkeywrenching; property destruction; radical tactics; sabotage
   animal liberation movement and, 47–48
   categories of, 13, 16, 119
   challenge of obtaining information on, 13–14

construction of database of, 187–188
database of, 187–189
definition of, 13
embrace of, 11–12
methodological approach to research on, 13–16
normalized counts of, 189
peaceful protest contrasted with, 13
as a philosophy, 13
punk's support for, 51–53
radical environmentalism united by use of, 11–13
trends in, 15–17, 15f, 16f, 188t, 189
unethical direct action, 53
views on, 13, 46, 49–50, 52–53, 56–57, 76, 132
Dobbs v. Jackson Women's Health Organization (2022), 127

E
Earth Day, 5, 10
Earth First!. *See also* Bari, Judi; Bernard (Earth First! activist); *Earth First! Journal*; Foreman, Dave; Isaac (Earth First! core member); Mark (Earth First! core member)
anarchist development of, 22, 32, 39–41, 59
appeal of, 25, 33–34, 40
challenges to ecocentric focus of, 19–20
changes in approach of, 22, 29, 32–35, 39–41, 59
civil disobedience used by, 10–11, 19–20, 37–38
conservation movement's influence on, 23
crossroads faced by, 39–40
decentralized structure of, 24–25
deep ecology and, 40–41
ecocentrism as founding principle of, 17, 24–26, 29
ELF and, 56
emergence of, 5
founding of, 23
Glenn Canyon Dam banner drop of, 23
goal of, 11
influence of, 5, 11, 29
leadership of, 4, 25
media appearance of, 34
monkeywrenching as defining issue in early days of, 24–26, 29
outlaw image of, 25–26, 29
overview of, 5, 10–11, 22–26, 41–42
pathways into activism and, 23–24, 32
philosophical basis of, 33–34
population question and, 26–28
public opinion and, 37–38
radical environmentalism's relation to, 4–6, 10–11, 17, 23, 25–27
reconsideration of radical tactics in, 37–38
as reflecting the networks and subcultures that formed it, 42
sabotage used by, 5–6, 10–11, 23, 24–25
social ecology implemented in, 39–40
takeaways on, 41–42
tree-sits of, 37–38, 62
tree spiking associated with, 24, 37
wilderness initially emphasized by, 22–23, 26, 29, 39–41
Earth First! Journal
communiqués published in, 24–25
content of, 31
ELF debate in, 83
Kaczynski-link claim response of, 66
pagan calendar in, 33
quasi-religious nature of, 33
violence incitement and, 65–66

Earth Liberation Front (ELF). *See also* "Family, The"; Operation Backfire (2004–2006)
  ALF's overlap with, 74–75
  anarchists in, 93–94
  arson and bombing use by, 5–6, 13, 20, 45, 71–73, 90
  calling cards of, 73, 80–81
  challenge of estimating attacks of, 73
  communiqués of, 71, 80–81
  community support and, 78
  criticism of, 6.81–84
  decentralized structure of, 17–18, 72
  documentary on rise and fall of, 6, 62, 87
  Earth First! as inspiration for, 5, 17–18, 44, 56
  ecoterrorism attributed to, 20, 84–85, 88–89
  emergence of, 15–16, 20, 63, 66–67, 71
  era of, 17–18, 21
  escalation of tactics by, 20, 71–72, 77
  Eugene, OR activist scene and, 62–63, 72, 85
  FBI estimation of acts of, 88–89
  first direct action of, 71
  forest defense campaigns of activists of, 72
  green anarchist ideology of, 72
  informants used against, 91–93, 101, 173–174
  Kaczynski's relation to emergence of, 63, 66–67
  legacy of, 83
  naming of, 72
  notable attacks carried out by, 73
  overview of, 61–63, 85
  pathways into, 72, 74–75
  post-9/11 context of, 84–85, 94
  principles of, 72–73
  property destruction and, 72
  punk and, 56
  radical environmentalism's relation to, 5–6, 17–18, 20, 56–57
  repression against, 20, 78–82, 84–85
  sabotage used by, 6, 72, 76–77
  spokespeople for, 73–74
  tactics of, 20, 71–72, 77, 81–82, 95
  Vail Ski Resort arson by supporters of, 71
  WTO protests in Seattle and, 75
ecocentrism
  criticism of, 19–20
  Earth First! founded upon, 17, 24–26, 29
  resistance and, 11
  total liberation development of, 50–51
Ecodefense (Foreman and Haywood), 30, 76
ecofascism
  accelerationism and, 138
  anarchism and, 143
  conspiracy theories and, 136–137, 143–144
  deep ecology's relation to, 142–144
  definition of, 135
  emergence of, 138
  environmental concerns not true motivation of, 135–137, 139, 143–144
  features of, 135
  green nationalism and, 136–137
  historical precedents of, 136
  immigration and, 135–136, 140–143
  Kaczynski's influence on, 70, 138, 139–140
  label of, 135
  Linkola as main inspiration for, 141
  manifestos of supporters of, 136–137, 143–144

online activism as defining feature of, 138–140
as overblown, 135–136
overview of, 135–137
population question as motivating, 8–9, 26–27, 31, 135–137, 140–141
radical environmentalism and, 139, 153
wilderness and, 143–144
ecology, deep. *See* deep ecology
ecoterrorism
chilling effect of label of, 84–85
congressional hearing on, 88–89
criticism of concept of, 89
definition of, 5, 88–89
as greatest domestic terrorist threat, 5–6, 85, 88–90
label of, 5–6, 85, 88–90
repression and, 88–89, 100
Ehrlich, Paul, 9–10, 26
ELF. *See* Earth Liberation Front (ELF)
ELF/AFL. *See* "Family, The"
Eli (young activist), 162–164
El Paso shooting (2019), 136–137, 143–144
Energy Transfer Partners, 109, 166–167, 176
environmentalism. *See also* radical environmentalism
birth of modern form of, 5
early major works in, 8–11
first killing of an activist by law enforcement in, 121
grievances and frustrations with, 23–24
legislation surrounding, 20–21
mainstream approaches to, 8, 11–12, 23, 25, 32, 41–42
New Left and, 10
origins of, 8–11
pollution and, 10
population question and, 8–10
racist and far-right ideas and, 8–9

rise of, 8
sabotage and, 10
social issues and, 10
tactics of, 8, 10
White nationalism and, 8
environmental justice, 124–125
Environmental Protection Agency (EPA), 152, 176, 180
Eugene, OR
anarchist scene in, 62–63, 74–75, 79, 100, 164
arsons near, 71–72
green anarchism centered in, 67–68, 71–72
law enforcement view of activism in, 78–80
punk scene in, 61–62
radical environmentalism centered in, 11, 61, 62–63, 78, 80, 85, 95, 164, 185
repression as marking end of activist scene in, 62, 78–79, 95, 100
tree-sit in, 62
Whiteaker neighborhood of, 61
Extinction Rebellion, 18, 117–118, 160–161

F
Faith (climate justice activist), 119–120, 128–129
"Family, The," 74–75, 79, 80, 88, 90–95
far right. *See* ecofascism
FBI
civil rights violations of activists by, 36
ecoterrorism as number one domestic terror threat for, 5–6, 18, 88–89
"The Family" targeted by, 85
informants used by, 89, 101
Joint Terrorism Task Force led by, 63–64, 88, 90–91

FBI (*Continued*)
    radical animal rights movement targeted by, 97
    Unabomber investigation of, 63–65, 139–140
Ferguson, Jacob, 61, 90–95, 97
Foreman, Dave
    activist identity of, 30
    appeal of, 29–30, 33
    Bookchin's rift with, 30–32
    cowboy counterculture image cultivated by, 25
    criticism of, 29–30, 39
    on deep ecological value of wilderness, 30
    Earth First! founding membership of, 23, 30
    ecofascism and, 139
    on Ethiopian famine, 30
    exit from Earth First! of, 32, 39–40
    leftist direction of Earth First! criticized by, 39
    monkeywrenching defended by, 30
    pathway into activism of, 23–24
    population question emphasized by, 27–28, 30
    quasi-religious dimensions of the movement and, 33
fossil fuel industry, 106, 113, 115, 118–119, 132, 158, 167, 177–178
Friends of the Earth, 24, 26

G
Gary (animal liberation activist), 31, 47–48, 54–55, 58
Gaza war (2023-2025), 129–130, 169–170
George Floyd protests (2020), 82, 105, 120–121, 126, 132, 174–175
global warming. *See* climate change
Grace (climate activist), 86–88, 101
Grant (Earth First! activist), 40–41, 54–55
Grant, Madison
    American conservative movement co-founded by, 9
    environmental movement role of, 9
    influence of, 8–9, 70, 139
    racial views of, 8–9, 70, 136, 139
Great Replacement Theory, 8–9, 136–138, 143–144
Green, Jackson, 158–159, 166–167
green anarchism
    arson and, 68
    civil disobedience and, 68
    deep ecology and, 69
    definition of, 50–51
    development of, 50–51, 66–68
    ELF's embrace of, 17–18
    intellectual vanguard of, 141–142
    Kaczynski influenced by, 66–69, 85
    leftist nature of, 69
    property destruction and, 55
    sabotage and, 66–68
    scene of, 66–68, 71–72, 74, 93–94, 104
    shift toward, 42
    social ecology as basis of, 42
    social justice approach of, 68
    total liberation and, 11, 42, 74, 104–105
Green Anarchy (magazine), 67–68, 80
Green New Deal, 116–117, 164
Greenpeace, 48, 112, 166–169, 171, 176, 178
Green Scare
    activist experience during, 93–95, 98–100
    animal liberation movement and, 100–101
    beginning of, 88
    congressional hearing on ecoterrorism and, 88–89
    criticism of terminology of, 99
    definition of, 6
    direct action and, 15–16
    Eugene activist scene ended by, 100
    informant use during, 93–94, 179

optimism following period of, 106
pathway into activism impacted
    by, 100–101
property destruction and, 98–99
radical environment movement
    crippled by, 6, 14, 15–16, 88,
    94–96, 98–100, 165, 179
sabotage and, 14
subsequent activism
    following, 108–110, 132–133

H
Hamas, 129–130
Hansen, James, 106–107
hardcore (commitment to activism), 44, 50, 92–93, 164. *See also* punk; vegan straight edge
Hardin, Garrett, 140–143
Helen (off-grid homesteader), 149–152
Hitler, Adolf, 8–9, 30–31
Hoffman, Abbie, 10, 161
homestead movement, 145–146, 148, 149–152
How to Blow up a Pipeline (Malm), 83, 118–119, 156–157

I
identity of activists, 14–15, 30, 32–33, 36, 55–56, 60–63, 76, 110–111
If a Tree Falls (documentary), 6, 62, 87
immigration
    anti-immigration groups, 27–29
    deep ecology and, 28
    ecofascism and, 135–136, 140–143
    population question and, 9–10, 27–28
    racial views of, 26–29, 135, 139
    reduction attempts for, 28–29
    Tanton network and, 28–29, 140–141
Inconvenient Truth, An
    (documentary), 119–120

Indigenous rights activism, 18, 20, 104–105, 109–110
Industrial Society and Its Manifesto
    (Kaczynski), 64, 68–69
Inflation Reduction Act of 2022
    (US), 116–117
informants, 89, 91–95, 101, 173–174
Institute for Social Ecology, 31
International Workers of the World
    (IWW), 35–36, 38
Isaac (Earth First! core member)
    on Earth First!'s change in
        approach, 34–35
    friendship with other founding
        members of, 24
    on monkeywrenching
        support, 24–25
    pathway into activism of, 23–24
    on population question, 26–27
    upbringing of, 23–24
Israeli-Palestinian conflict, 12, 87, 129–130, 169. *See also* Gaza war (2023-2025); Palestinian activism

J
Jack (law enforcement officer), 78–80, 91–92
January 6th insurrection
    (2021), 128–129
Jesse (activist and ELF publicizer)
    arrests of, 56–57
    on difficulty of standing up to state
        repression, 95
    on direct action, 56–57
    on effectiveness of ELF's tactics, 82, 95
    ELF spokesperson role of, 82
    on interconnection between activist
        movements, 133
    Malm's mention as frustrating
        to, 84
    on Operation Backfire, 95
    pathway into activism of, 56–57

Jesse (activist and ELF publicizer) (*Continued*)
   on radical environmentalism's persistence, 82
   on surveillance state, 165
Jim (conservation activist), 33–34, 142, 143, 174–175
justice. *See* climate justice movement; environmental justice; social ecology; social justice activism
Just Stop Oil, 18, 157–158, 160

K
Kaczynski, Theodore "Ted"
   anarchism and, 66–67
   background of, 65
   criticism of, 69–70
   deep ecology and, 65–66, 68–70
   on Earth First!'s change of approach, 68–69
   Earth First!'s influence on, 66, 70, 139–140
   ecofascism influenced by, 70, 138, 139–140
   ELF influenced by, 63, 66–67
   far right influenced by, 70
   FBI investigation of, 63–65
   green anarchism influenced by, 66–69, 85
   human experimentation on, 65
   imprisonment of, 65
   influences on, 64–65, 67–68, 70
   leftists critiqued by, 68–69, 139–140
   letters mailed to media outlets by, 64
   manifesto of, 64–65, 68–69
   on McVeigh, 69
   mental illness attributed to, 65
   on pathway into radical action, 67–68
   popular view of, 65
   prison experiences of, 69
   radical environmentalism's relation to, 35, 65–70
   student agreement with, 5–6
   suicide of, 65
   Unabomber attacks of, 15–16, 35, 63–64
   victims of, 63
   wilderness and, 65–67
   worldview of, 64–65
Ken (activist and *Earth First! Journal* editor), 25–28, 33
Kennedy, Robert F., Jr., 106–107, 148, 149, 151–152
Kevin (Earth First! activist), 35–37
Keystone XL pipeline protest (2011), 106–107, 119
Koehler, Bart, 22–26

L
Lee, Ronnie, 45–46, 51
leftist activism. *See* anarchism; racial equality activism; social ecology; social justice activism
lifeboat ethics, 140–143
"Lifeboat Ethics" (Hardin), 140–141
Linkola, Pentti, 141–143
Luann (activist), 124–126
Luke (activist), 52–53, 96–98

M
Machin, Joe, 113–114, 161
Malm, Andreas, 83–84, 115, 156–157
Mangione, Luigi, 180–182
Man Swarm (Foreman), 27–28
Mark (Earth First! core member)
   activist identity of, 36
   Bari criticized by, 36, 38
   civil disobedience and, 37–38
   climate NGOs criticized by, 175
   Earth First! core membership of, 36–37
   Earth First!'s leftist-anarchist development criticized by, 41
   on ELF, 93

on goals of sabotage, 37
monkeywrenching views of, 37
pathway into activism of, 36–37
on pessimism of climate
  activists, 175–176
political views of, 36–37
public opinion polls conducted
  by, 37–38
radical tactics as alienating and, 38
on Redwood Summer
  successes, 38–39
sabotage views of, 37
tactics reconsideration by Earth
  First! and, 37–38
tree spiking discussed by, 37–38
upbringing of, 36–37
on violence use, 41, 175–176
Max (activist and antifascist
  academic), 68, 70, 143–146
McKibben, Bill, 104–108, 154
McVeigh, Timothy, 69–70, 81
methodology
  approach to radical
    environmentalism, 12–17
  construction of database of eco
    direct actions, 187–188
  database of eco direct
    actions, 187–189
  demographics and procedures for
    surveys and interviews, 191–196
  email invitation to interview
    subjects, 193
  in-depth qualitative
    interviews, 189–191
  interview structure and
    questions, 14–15
  normalized counts of eco direct
    actions, 189
  US population surveys, 191–196
  yearly eco direct actions, 188*t*
militia movement, 6, 40, 146
Molly (raw milk enthusiast), 147–149
Monkey Wrench Gang, The
  (Abbey), 22–23, 49, 70

monkeywrenching
  classic book on, 76
  definition of, 22–23
  as a philosophy, 24
  pipeline activism and, 110
  as a tactic, 24–26, 30, 33–37, 110
  trends in use of, 17, 108–109
  wilderness and, 33
Mountain Valley Pipeline protests
  (2024), 113–115, 130
movements. *See* animal liberation
  movement; climate move-
  ment; conservation movement;
  environmentalism; radical
  environmentalism; radical
  movements; social movements
musical bands, 45, 51–52, 57
Musk, Elon, 137–138, 183

N
Nathan (direct action activist)
  activist identity and, 76
  arson used by, 76–77
  on being primed for direct
    action, 76
  challenge of interviewing, 75–76
  ELF tactics and, 77
  on Ferguson's police
    informing, 93–94
  on lack of extreme tactics in face of
    climate threat, 129
  Malm's mention as frustrating
    to, 84
  on Operation Backfire, 93–94
  pathway into activism of, 76
  on personal toll of clandestine
    activism, 77
  upbringing of, 76
  on use of arson and sabotage, 76–77
nature. *See* deep ecology; wilderness
Nazism, 54–55, 67, 69–70, 115,
  137–139, 211 n.25
New Day Bakery, 60–61

NGOs. *See* non-governmental organizations (NGOs)
Nicole (movement lawyer and activist)
  double lives of activists and, 77–78
  on "The Family," 92–93
  legal advising by, 87
  Operation Backfire's impact and, 92–93
  pathway into activism of, 77–78, 87
  security measures taken by, 86–87
  on shock at Ferguson becoming an informant, 92–93
9/11. *See* September 11th attacks (2001)
non-governmental organizations (NGOs). *See also* Greenpeace
  activism model based around, 105–106
  chilling effect on, 167
  civil disobedience supported by, 105–108, 167, 179–180
  climate NGOs, 105–106, 118–119, 167, 168–169, 175, 178
  fossil fuel industry and, 118–119
  incremental change approach of, 11–12
  mainstream environmental NGOs, 107–108, 119
  non-radical tactics favored by, 107–108
  property destruction and, 107–108, 164
  radical environmentalism and, 11–12, 164, 168–169, 178, 182–183
  radical tactics rejected by mainstream, 107–108, 164, 175
  repression and, 168–169, 176, 177, 179, 180
  sabotage and, 108–109, 178
  social justice NGOs, 172–173
  terrorism and, 168–169
nonviolent tactics, 24–25, 41, 45–46, 48, 68, 81, 98–99, 118–119, 154–155. *See also* civil disobedience

O
Oakridge U.S. Forest Ranger station arson (1996), 71, 78–79
Obama, Barack, 106–107, 109, 152
Occupy Wall Street, 120, 122–123, 133
October 7th, 2023 Hamas attack on Israel, 129–130
Oklahoma City Bombing (1995), 69
Operation Backfire (2004–2006). *See also* Earth Liberation Front (ELF)
  arrests and sentences in, 90–91
  arson as prompting, 90
  context for, 90
  creation of, 90–91
  decrease in radical tactics resulting from, 91
  definition of, 88
  "The Family" targeted by, 88, 90–93
  informants used in, 90–93
  larger activist scene diminished by, 93–94
  overview of, 88
  radical environmentalism impacted by, 91, 93–95, 98, 100, 179
  sabotage impacted by, 91
  Stop Cop City movement contrasted with, 123
overpopulation. *See* population question

P
Pacific Northwest. *See also* Eugene, OR
  anarchist scene in, 13, 55, 75, 100
  animal liberation movement in, 55
  coalescence of movements in, 55–56

ecofascist dream of building state in, 143
ELF cells in, 72, 88
end of activist scene in, 91, 95–96, 100
green anarchist scene in, 66–68, 71–72, 74, 93–94, 104
Kaczynski's reception in, 66–68
new activist campaigns in, 104–105
punk scene in, 52, 54–55
radical environmental science in, 3, 33, 68, 103, 104
repression in, 20, 91, 95–96, 100
total liberation in, 74
vegan hardcore scene in, 45
vibe of, 55–56
WTO protests in, 75
Paez Terán, Manuel Esteban ("Tortuguita"), 120–121
Palestinian activism, 130–132, 155
Parker (forest defender), 125–127
Passing of the Great Race, The (Grant), 8–9, 136
pathways into activism
  activist identity and, 14–15, 33
  anarchism and, 50–51, 100–101
  animal liberation movement and, 43, 45, 76, 96, 100–101
  anti-pression organizing and, 122–123
  classroom visit on, 43–44, 56
  climate movement and, 119–120
  definition of, 14–15
  Earth First! and, 23–24, 32
  Greenpeace and, 48
  pipeline activism and, 111–112, 114–116, 121
  punk and, 44, 52–54, 100–101
  radical environmentalism and, 11, 14–15, 20, 32
  recruitment networks in, 19–20
  sabotage and, 20
  Sierra Club and, 11, 23–24, 76, 161
  tactics impacted by variation in, 20

vegan straight edge and, 45, 52
People for the Ethical Treatment of Animals (PETA), 3–4, 47
Persian Gulf War (1990-1991), 56, 80–81
pipeline activism. *See also* Dakota Access Pipeline protests (2017); Standing Rock pipeline protest (2016-2017)
  activist identity and, 110–111
  arson and, 93–94
  civil disobedience and, 106–107, 110–112
  climate change as prompting, 112–113
  Indigenous rights movement and, 115–116
  Keystone XL pipeline protest and, 106–107, 119
  monkeywrenching and, 110
  pathways into activism and, 111–112, 114–116, 121
  previous activism contrasted with, 110–111
  property destruction and, 109–110
  repression as holding back, 115–116
  sabotage and, 110–113
  tactics of, 111–113, 115
  Valve Turners and, 104
  wilderness and, 107
political violence, 2, 12, 18, 170, 181, 184–185
Population Bomb, The (Ehrlich), 9–10, 26
population question
  conspiracy theories and, 8–9
  control and reduction of the population in, 30–31
  deep ecology and, 28, 64–65
  definition of, 9–10
  ecofascism motivated by, 8–9, 26–27, 31, 135–137, 140–141

population question (*Continued*)
  environmentalism and, 8–10
  immigration and, 9–10, 27–28
  radical environmentalism and, 5, 8–11
  reproduction's permissibility and, 2–5
  stigma surrounding concerns about, 26–27
  zero population growth (ZPG) movement, 9–10, 28–29, 44, 136–137
property destruction
  anarchism and, 115
  civil disobedience preferred over, 154
  effectiveness of, 154
  green anarchism and, 55
  NGOs and, 107–108, 164
  pipeline activism and, 109–110
  radical environmentalism and, 5–6, 16, 17–20, 154–157
  repression and, 115, 123
  taboo surrounding, 105–106
  as a tactic, 55, 82–83, 98–99, 126, 162, 164
  terrorism label against, 6, 84, 88–89, 183
  trends in use of, 16, 105, 107, 154
protests. *See* Dakota Access Pipeline protests (2017); George Floyd protests (2020); Keystone XL pipeline protest (2011); Mountain Valley Pipeline protests (2024); Standing Rock pipeline protest (2016-2017); Stop Cop City protest (2021); World Trade Organization (WTO) protests (1999)
punk. *See also* vegan straight edge
  anarchism supported in, 51, 55–56, 61, 62
  animal liberation movement's relation to, 51, 58–59
  decrease in influence of, 57
  development of, 51
  direct action supported in, 51–53
  far-right supporters of, 54–55
  neo-Nazi skinhead clashes with supporters of, 54–55
  pathways into activism and, 44, 52–54, 100–101
  radical environmentalism and, 11, 14–15, 19–20, 45
  sabotage and, 58
  scene of, 44, 51–57, 60, 100–101
  straight edge subculture of, 42, 51–52, 164
  US arrival of, 51–52
  zines and, 51–52

R
racial equality activism, 10–11, 19–20, 105, 108–109, 124–125
radical environmentalism. *See also* anarchism; Animal Liberation Front (ALF); arson; climate movement; deep ecology; Earth First!; Earth Liberation Front (ELF); ecocentrism; ecofascism; ecoterrorism; methodology; non-governmental organizations (NGOs); pathways into activism; pipeline activism; population question; property destruction; punk; radical tactics; repression; sabotage; social ecology; terrorism; vegan straight edge; wilderness
  aims of activists in, 5
  challenges of researching, 12–14
  contemporary political context of, 3
  decentralized structure of, 11, 13
  definition of, 11–12
  demobilization and deescalation future scenario for, 179–180

development of, 8–11, 17–20, 42, 82
direct action as uniting feature of, 11–13
escalation and radicalization future scenario for, 180–182
Eugene, OR as center of, 11, 61, 62–63, 78, 80, 85, 95, 164, 185
frustrations with mainstream environmentalism giving rise to, 11–12
fusion of movements and causes informing, 121
future scenarios for, 177–185
incremental change rejected in, 11–12
Kaczynski's relation to, 35, 65–70
limitations of data on, 17
main features of, 11–12
media coverage of, 12–13
motivation for current volume on, 5–8
networks and subcultures reflected in, 42
ordinary activism contrasted with, 13
overview of, 1–8, 19–21, 184–186
pro-democracy fusion future scenario for, 182–184
pseudonym use in research on, 1–2
research questions of current volume on, 6, 18–21
resistance as necessary in, 11
self-defense ethos of, 5
shared ethos as basis of, 41–42
status quo future scenario for, 177–178
structure of current volume on, 21
suspicion toward outsiders in, 12–13
tactics of, 5–7, 11–12
tensions and, 8–11
timeframe for research of current volume on, 17–18
violence and, 5–6
radical movements, 11, 19, 42, 174–175
radical tactics. *See also* arson; direct action; monkeywrenching; property destruction; sabotage
climate change as prompting, 5–6, 20–21, 118, 154–157, 174
debates about use of, 37–38, 81–83, 154–158, 160
decreases in, 6–7, 16–17, 38, 155–157
diversity of, 115
effectiveness of, 5–7, 11–12, 19, 154–158, 162, 174
future of, 14–15, 174–176, 185
NGOs as rejecting, 107–108, 164, 175
prevalence of extreme forms of, 45
public opinion on, 38, 155–156, 156f
reconsideration of, 37–38
repression as preventing more, 115
trends in, 15–17, 15f, 16f, 38, 155–157, 188t, 189
raw milk movement, 144–149, 151–153
Redwood Summer (1990), 4, 38–39
repression. *See also* ecoterrorism; Green Scare; informants; Jack (law enforcement officer); Operation Backfire (2004–2006); Rick (law enforcement officer); terrorism
animal liberation movement and, 49–50, 97
arson and, 90–91, 95, 98–99, 107
climate movement and, 164
difficulty of standing up to, 95
ecoterrorism and, 88–89, 100
increased legal penalties in, 100
legislation surrounding, 49–50, 53, 96–97

repression (*Continued*)
  necessity defenses in court cases and, 110–113
  NGOs and, 168–169, 176, 177, 179, 180
  pipeline activism held back by, 115–116
  property destruction and, 115, 123
  radical environmentalism impacted by, 62, 78–79, 95, 98, 100, 107, 123–124
  radical tactics prevented by, 115
  RICO charges, 121–124
  security measures taken by activists to avoid, 87–88
  September 11th attacks and, 94–95
  social media and, 164
  surveillance in, 18–21, 84, 164–165, 173–174, 179
  terrorism and, 91, 94–95, 97, 110, 125, 168, 179
Republicans (US), 3, 10, 119, 127, 137–138, 145, 153
Reznicek, Jessica, 110–112
Richard (academic and activist), 28–29, 142–143
Rick (law enforcement officer), 80, 92
RICO charges, 121–124
right-wing extremism. *See* ecofascism
Roadless Area Review and Evaluation (RARE II), 23
Road to Revolution, The (Kaczynski), 68–69
Robert (animal liberation activist)
  advice for young activists of, 165
  classroom visit of, 43–44, 99
  direct actions list of, 13–14
  on Green Scare, 99–100
  hardcore ethos of, 44
  pathway into activism of, 44–45, 52
  prison sentence of, 43
  on punk's decreased influence, 57
  on regret he didn't do more, 44
  on use of direct action list, 13–14
  vegan hardcore punk scene and, 52
  zines and, 52
Rodgers, Bill, 74–75, 90–91
Roe v. Wade (1973), 105, 127–129
Rosebraugh, Craig, 73–74, 89, 101
Roselle, Mike, 22–23, 25, 39, 59

S

sabotage. *See also* monkeywrenching
  animal liberation movement and, 45–46, 58
  challenge of researching, 12–14
  climate movement and, 112–113, 118
  early uses of, 10
  green anarchism and, 66–68
  guidebook for, 30
  media coverage of, 12–13
  NGOs and, 108–109, 178
  open question on, 21
  Operation Backfire's impact on, 91
  pathways into activism and, 20
  pipeline activism and, 110–113
  punk and, 58
  radical environmentalism and, 5, 11–13, 16–18, 154–157
  research on effectiveness of, 154–157
  as a tactic, 11–12, 37, 42, 105
  trends in use of, 16–18, 16f, 20, 91, 92, 108–109, 156–157
Sea Shepherd Conservation Society, 48–50
Seattle, WA WTO protests, 75, 79, 80
"Second Thoughts of an Eco Warrior" (Foreman), 32
September 11th attacks (2001)
  Global War on Terrorism following, 84, 95
  repression following, 94–95
  surveillance state following, 84, 164
  terrorism label following, 5–6, 18, 20, 78, 97

SHAC. *See* Stop Huntingdon Animal Cruelty (SHAC)
Sierra Club, 11, 23–24, 76, 106–107, 161
Silent Spring (Carson), 10, 31
social ecology
   acceptance of, 39–40, 42
   activist identity and, 32–33
   deep ecology's rift with, 31–33, 42
   definition of, 31
   development of, 31
   Earth First!'s implementation of, 39–40
   green anarchism based on, 42
   Institute for Social Ecology, 31
   total liberation and, 42, 133
social justice activism, 18, 32, 34, 68, 108–109, 116–117, 124–125, 132–134, 172–173
social media, 107, 147–148, 150–151, 158–159, 161, 164
social movements, 18–19, 82–83, 100, 176–177
Soros, George, 144–146, 179
Southern Poverty Law Center (SPLC), 29
Standing Rock pipeline protest (2016-2017)
   activists as "water protectors" in, 109–110
   arrests during, 109
   context of, 109
   Indigenous-led nature of, 92, 104–105
   media coverage of, 104, 109
   military-like operation of, 111–112
   radical environmentalism trends exemplified by, 109–110
   tactics in, 111–112
statue protests, 137–138, 158–159
Staudenmaier, Peter, 211 n.25
Stephen (ALF activist), 53–54, 98–99
Stop Cop City protest (2021)
   forest defenders and, 121–122, 125, 126
   goals of, 104, 121
   green anarchism and, 104–105
   influences on, 121
   media attention on, 125
   pathways into, 122–126
   prison abolition movement and, 104–105
   repression against, 121–124, 179
   sabotage use by, 126–127
   shift in activism signaled by, 121
   tactics of, 104–105, 126–127
   total liberation and, 104–105
Stop Huntingdon Animal Cruelty (SHAC)
   ALF roots of, 50
   criticism of, 49–50
   direct action encouraged by, 49–50
   formation of, 49–50
   goal of, 49–50
   leaderless structure of, 96
   online activism and, 53
   repression against activists of, 96–97
   SHAC 7, 49–50, 54, 91
   tactics of, 49–50
   website reporting direct actions of, 49–50
straight edge. *See* punk; vegan straight edge
Sue (raw milk farmer), 146–148
Sunrise Movement, 116–120, 131–132, 178
surveillance, 18–21, 84, 164–165, 173–174, 179

T
tactics. *See* civil disobedience; nonviolent tactics; radical tactics
Tanton network, 28–29, 140–141
Ted (animal rights and environmental activist), 49, 57–58

terrorism. *See also* ecoterrorism
   "The Family" charged with enhancements based on, 90–91
   domestic terror charges, 5–6, 18, 20, 78, 121–123
   ecoterrorism as number one domestic terror threat, 5–6, 18, 88–89
   Global War on Terrorism, 84, 95
   labeling of radical tactics as, 5–6, 18, 20, 78, 84–85, 88–90, 97, 183
   NGOs and, 168–169
   property destruction labeled as, 6, 84, 88–89, 183
   repression and, 91, 94–95, 97, 110, 125, 168, 179
   September 11th attacks leading to focus on, 5–6, 18, 20, 78, 97
   tactics shift due to focus on, 94
350.org, 104, 106–109, 119, 161
Thunberg, Greta, 58, 104, 116, 120, 174–175
Tim (direct action organizer)
   on direct action as a philosophy, 13
   on Luigi Mangione reactions, 181
   NGO-activism and, 168–169
   on Obama's disappointing presidency, 106
   pathway into activism of, 157
   on spray-painting tactic, 160
   training of activists by, 109–110
   Trump's reelection and, 168–169
timber industry, 23–24, 35–40, 63, 66, 177
total liberation, 11, 17–18, 42, 50–51, 57, 74, 104–105, 121, 133
"Tragedy of the Commons, The" (Hardin), 140
tree spiking, 24, 37–38, 104–105, 121
Trump, Donald
   activists arming themselves upon reelection of, 170
   Amish support for, 152–153
   Charlottesville, VA far right march comments of, 137–138
   climate change policies of, 167–168, 176
   as destroying future for environmental movement, 166
   executive orders targeting climate activism of, 167
   Great Replacement Theory echoed by, 137–138
   immigration and, 27–28, 139, 172
   Nazi talking points on immigration echoed by, 139
   people of color supporters of, 172
   pipeline activism and, 107, 109
   radical environmentalism impacted by, 20–21, 166, 170–174, 176, 177–180, 182–184, 186
   reelection of, 166–167
   repression under, 167–168, 171, 173–174, 179
   RJK Jr. nominated by, 152

U

Unabomber attacks, 15–16, 35, 63–64. *See also* Kaczynski, Theodore "Ted"
UN Climate Action Summit, 116
U.S. Forest Rangers, 23–24, 40
U.S. Forest Service, 23–24, 40, 72, 167

V

vaccine skepticism, 144–148, 153
Vail Ski Resort arson (1997), 71, 73, 74
Valve Turners, 18, 104, 110–113
vegan straight edge. *See also* animal liberation movement
   activist identity and, 55–56
   alienation caused by, 57–58
   criticism of, 57–58
   decrease in influence of, 57
   definition of, 43–44
   development of, 43–44, 51–52

naming of, 51–52
pathways into activism and, 45, 52
radical environmentalism influenced by, 54, 57
as reaction, 51–52
zines in, 51–52
violence. *See* political violence; radical tactics; repression
Violet (anti-pipeline activist), 111–116

W

Warner Creek forest defense campaign (1995–1996), 72, 74–75, 79
Watson, Paul Joseph, 48–49
Weather Underground, 83, 165
White Genocide, 136–137, 143–144
White nationalism, 8–10, 29, 143–144
wilderness
    biocentrism and, 33
    conservationist approach to, 9, 32
    Earth First!'s initial focus on, 22–23, 26, 29, 39–41
    ecofascism and, 143–144
    existential threat to, 11–12
    intrinsic value of, 24–25, 33
    mainstream environmentalism and, 8, 23, 25, 32, 41–42
    monkeywrenching and, 33
    pipeline activism and, 107
    radical environmentalism and, 5, 11–12, 41
    shift away from emphasis on, 32, 34, 39–41, 107, 108–109, 118, 133–134
    social justice activism contrasted with, 34, 124–125
Wolke, Howie, 23, 30
World Economic Forum (WEF), 144–145
World Trade Center bombing (1993), 69
World Trade Organization (WTO) protests (1999), 75, 79, 80

Y

Yellow Finch Tree-sit (2018-2021), 114–115
Youth Climate Movement, 104, 116–118

Z

zero population growth (ZPG) movement, 9–10, 28–29, 44, 136–137
Zerzan, John, 67–68
zines, 43–45, 51–52, 54, 55–56, 68, 76–77